2012

Biography of a Time Traveler

The Journey of José Arguelles

By

Stephanie South

NEW PAGE BOOKS
A division of The Career Press, Inc.
Franklin Lakes, NJ

2012: BIOGRAPHY OF A TIME TRAVELER
EDITED BY JODI BRANDON
TYPESET BY EILEEN MUNSON
Cover design by Lucia Rossman/Digi Dog Design
Original cover concept by Kelly Harding
Printed in the U.S.A.

To order this title, please call toll-free 1-800-CAREER-1 (NJ and Canada: 201-848-0310) to order using VISA or MasterCard, or for further information on books from Career Press.

The Career Press, Inc., 3 Tice Road, PO Box 687,
Franklin Lakes, NJ 07417
www.careerpress.com
www.newpagebooks.com

Library of Congress Cataloging-in-Publication Data

2012 : biography of a time traveler : the journey of Jose Argüelles / by Stephanie South.
    p. cm.
Includes index.
ISBN 978-1-60163-065-0
    1. Argüelles, José, 1939– 2. Prophets—United States—Biography. 3. Prophecies (Occultism) 4. Mayas—Prophecies. I. Title.

BF1815.A74S68 2009
130.92—dc22

                                                2008054800

Dedicated

to

Valum Votan

May the highest dream prevail for all!

Acknowledgments

First and foremost infinite thanks to José Arguelles for his endless patience and graciousness throughout this process, and without whose magnificent soul this story wouldn't be.

Deep thanks to Jacob Wyatt and Kelly Harding—the Rhythmic Twins—for their tireless dedication, support, and magical assistance throughout this process.

Thanks to Sarah Aschenbach for her skilled editing and helping make the text sparkle. Also thanks to Ginny Nichols and Elizabeth Whitney, who were of great assistance during the earlier stages of this text.

Gratitude to Lady Lois Hunt of Mulgan for her intuition in connecting the dream, and to Jared Rosen, who connected the dream at the next level.

Special thanks and appreciation to Bill Gladstone for all of his assistance and for following the synchronicities that led to the publishing of this book. Also thanks to Adam Schwartz, Michael and Laurie Pye, Kirsten Dalley, and Jodi Brandon at New Page Books for their enthusiasm to get this book out swiftly.

Many thanks to Stef and Mike in Holland for their selfless dedication throughout this process and assistance on many dimensions.

Deep appreciation to Ron South for his belief, love, and support from the beginning. Also thanks to Ed Higbee for his care and assistance on many levels during the final stages of this process.

Special thanks to Lloydine-Bolon Ik, Alice and Jess Eastman, and Hirohide Yanase.

Also thanks to Pedro Hernandez Peppers, Mertxze Zuza, July de Portilla, Flaviah, Stefano Narduzzi, Forrest O´Farrell (Planetary Sun), Vandir Casagrande, Carlos Garcia, Anibal Luporini, Claudia Gomez, Vasumi, Claire, Hermione Olsen and Ben, Eden and Bob Sky (Ben 4 & Ben 5), Jaron (White Wizard), Nate, Tracie, Jordyn, Jacob, Tyler, JoAnn Gaynor McEachran, Rodrigo Urrea, Chantal, Veronique in France, Kim Kindersley, and all the beautiful whale dreamers—and last, but not least, thanks to the Creator and all the invisible spirit guides.

Contents

Foreword
Rainbow Bridge-Builder

I first encountered José Arguelles's work when a friend of mine gave me *The Mayan Factor* as a birthday present. I read through it quickly and found it entertaining, but I couldn't take it seriously at that point. Although I had already absorbed the psychedelic philosopher Terence McKenna's ideas about the potential for a rapid shift into a new realization of time, space, and consciousness in 2012, the prospect of a "Galactic Mayan" civilization that space-time-tripped to earth to encode a knowledge system and engineer a transformation of human consciousness seemed fantastically implausible. A few years later, I was sent a copy of *Time and the Technosphere* by José's publisher, some months after 9/11.

Reading *Time and the Technosphere*, I couldn't escape the suspicion that José was on to something—that he had found an angle of approach, melding numerical puzzles and prophetic hints, which revealed a hidden teleology, opening new avenues into the future. Studying his work was in itself psychedelic, as it challenged my most basic conceptions about the nature of reality. I returned to *The Mayan Factor*, and this time I was able to enter more deeply into his way of thought. One morning in my local café, I read his proposition that the "Galactic Maya" were returning to Earth, now, as us, as we attain their level of psychic awareness and synchronic consciousness. As I considered this idea, I had the sensation of an alien intelligence and ancient sentience awakening within me.

Later, I was fortunate enough to have the opportunity to spend several days with José and Stephanie at their home in Oregon. According to

José's Dreamspell calendar, I was his perfect "helping partner," and, as we drove around pine forests and snow-capped mountains in his old truck, the three of us felt a real sense of familiarity. Some of the things that José told me during that visit stayed with me permanently, deeply influencing my approach to life. At one point, José was telling me how humanity would begin to voluntarily take down the post-industrial "technosphere" as we approached 2012, returning the planet to a pristine garden, preferring to live in small groups, and engaging in telepathic ceremonies. I argued that this seemed impossible—that we were headed for wars and ecocide, not a return to the garden.

"My job as a visionary is to envision the best possible outcome for humanity," he explained. "If I don't do it, who will?" This seemed shockingly sensible to me. Most people, most of the time, allow their conception of what is possible to be determined by the mass culture that surrounds them. My psychedelic experiences had revealed that our social constructs were temporary artifices, and they could be reimagined and reinvented as soon as enough of us decided to take the matter into our own hands. I realized that this could only happen if courageous individuals demanded what seemed impossible in the context of their time.

I decided that the job description of visionary suited my particular talents. I would also dedicate myself to envisioning the "best possible outcome for humanity," and bringing it into realization. Another thing that I learned from José was the necessity to have complete dedication to the task at hand. Many people may have a great idea or artistic vision, but, when they encounter resistance or ridicule, they will abandon their ideal in order to take a safer path. José's life story reveals a different stance, where one learns to accept and almost enjoy the gigantic obstacles encountered along the path as a series of spiritual challenges. By dealing with these challenges, you sharpen your own faculties and increase your capacities. As Nietzsche put it, "The deed creates the doer—almost as an afterthought."

Another element of José's thought that impacted my own worldview is the primacy he gives to art and design—much like William Blake, who realized that "the imagination is not a State: it is the Human existence in itself." Our imagination, it seems, does not simply create things that are not there, but interacts with the invisible fields of the archetypes residing in what Arguelles calls the "noosphere," the thought-envelope that surrounds the Earth. As individuals, as shamans and visionaries, we mediate between these dimensions of shimmering potentiality and our material world. Blake wrote:

> If the Spectator could Enter into these images in his imagination approaching them on the Fiery Chariot of his Contemplative Thought, if he could enter into Noah's Rainbow or into his bosom, or could make a Friend & Companion of one of these Images of wonder, which always intreats him to leave mortal things (as he must know), then he would arise from his grave, then would he meet the Lord of the Air & then would he be happy.

In the biographical narrative presented here, we learn that José had the direct experience of entering into the imaginal plane, making a "friend and companion" out of Pakal Votan, ancient wizard-king of Palenque. Any doubts that I might have felt about this visitation were erased when I had my own introduction to the god-form or archetype of Quetzalcoatl, who spoke through me, transmitting prophecy, while I was in the Brazilian Amazon. The basic thrust of my transmission was similar to the Telektonon prophecy channeled by José, foreseeing the year 2012 as the threshold for a massive alteration in our psychic and physical existence.

Reality appears to be an art form, where the myth-making capacity of the human imagination is ultimately more powerful than any technology or technique. José compacted this notion into an elegant formula in which "time is art." At the same time, each one of us appears to be both a unique expression of this galactic-scaled conceptual performance piece, and, potentially, an artist in our own right, able to revise the script when we discover our inspiration.

As I write this, it is hard to escape the presentiment that 2012 is coming right on schedule. This week, the U.S. government is seeking to force a $700 billion bailout of our destroyed financial system down the throats of a public that is already suffering beneath a mountain of debt. The United States continues to take in $2 billion per day to help fuel a $1 trillion military budget, as the martial adventures of our global Empire continue in Afghanistan, in Iraq, and across the world. At a time when resources such as fuel and water are becoming increasingly scarce as climate change accelerates, it seems we are moving toward a rapid crescendo that will force a transformation of our planetary culture.

One way to look at the control culture of Empire—with its predatory wars, destructive technologies, and mechanisms of indoctrination—is as a kind of virus or infection of our planet by an alien mindset. The autoimmune system-response to the virus of Empire includes the global reactivation of Earth-honoring shamanic practices and the awakening of the human imagination. As his life story reveals, José has been a noble warrior in this cause, fighting for a transformative vision of human possibility and a worldview that builds a rainbow bridge between the psychocosmos explored by indigenous shamans and the scientific rationalism of the modern world. Although time (and not too much of it) will tell, I suspect that José will be honored as one of the most important thinkers in human history, providing a model for conscious evolution into a psychic, synchronic, and harmonic way of being.

Daniel Pinchbeck
New York, NY
Electric Moon 14
Yellow Resonant Star
October 3, 2008

Introduction

2012: Biography of a Time Traveler is a universal story.

This is the story of the transformation of a man who held to his vision all of his life. From the time he was 14, he was moved, guided, and led by this vision. This is no ordinary vision. It is the vision of the closing of the cycle of history—2012—and the opening of the new cycle. As this story shows, to hold such a vision, to nurture it, and to let it speak its truth is in itself a prophetic and mythic assignment.

2012: Biography of a Time Traveler is the story of a visionary for our time. Because this is such an all-encompassing message, it seemed the story should be told in as simple a manner as possible. By presenting José´s life as a story, I felt I could more directly engage the reader to understand, in a personal way, the meaning of the message.

This is neither a traditional biography nor an academic one. Rather, it reveals the psychomythic transformation of one human who realizes himself as the universal human, and brings forth a simple message for humankind: Return to the cycles of nature before it's too late! In single-minded pursuit of delivering this message, José traveled the world several times over. As a consequence, the richness of his life experience is astonishingly varied and unique.

2012: Biography of a Time Traveler serves as a cosmic alarm clock reminding us of the Greater Dream laid out in signs and synchronicities, if we have the courage to listen. This story also shows that perseverance and pursuit of truth are not humanly controlled, but divinely guided. Such inspired pursuits naturally cause one to seek pathways outside of the social norm. The life of José Arguelles is the story of an iconoclastic visionary. Despite all odds, it was necessary for him to break some rules. How else could genuinely new information and a renewed vision of reality come into being?

2012: Biography of a Time Traveler was born in a dream. Prior to meeting José, I had a vivid dream where I saw him walking along a vacant street in a large sprawling city, strangely empty—the world had stopped—and he was demonstrating to me time travel. Several dreams followed in which José appeared demonstrating time travel and telepathy often in remote locations. I then met him in 1998 at the 28th annual Whole Earth Festival in Davis, California. This is where I first heard his message: The human species is living in artificial time!

It was through following my dreams and a string of synchronicities that this book came to be. This is only the first half of the original text. This story is based on questions and answers and conversations, as well as on reading his works inclusive of books, papers, personal letters, articles, documents, and so forth. Throughout this process, my highest interest was to let his life story speak for itself. I was not interested in getting other accounts or points of view, as the world is full of opinions of every kind. I wanted the story to be told in as raw and real a way as possible so that it might show another way of being for those who are receptive.

This is a spiritual adventure of prophetic proportions and something that touches on the life of every human being on this planet today. Two thousand twelve is only a few years away; it is the end of the Mayan Great Cycle—and the beginning of a new evolutionary era. What will happen? That is the question on many people's minds. I hope this book will shed light on the answers.

PART I

From
Distant Tulan
to
Planet Earth

Chapter 1
Creative Genesis

*We are Maya. We arose out of the very illusion of
ourselves. Because we are the primal masters of time
and illusion, we are the fearless ones who take on
incarnation after incarnation in order to settle and
tame all planets. For to tame is to harmonize, and so
we are the masters of harmony as well.*

—José Arguelles, *The Arcturus Probe*

The galactic time traveler carefully considered the circumstances
of his incarnation in order to maximize all of the experiences he
needed to fully embody the universal human at the closing of
the cycle and the opening of the new, beginning in 2012.

He descended into the world of the mechanical clock at 6:20 p.m.
on January 24, 1939, in St. Mary's Hospital in Rochester, Minnesota, a
Catholic hospital operated by the Order of the Nuns of St. Mary's. For
his earthly duties, he was given the name Joseph Anthony Arguelles
(Joe). Later, he would be known as José. Little did his parents know
that the name on the birth certificate and the baby born were two entirely different phenomena.

Ten mechanical minutes later, at 6:30 p.m., his identical twin brother,
Ivan Wallace Arguelles, was born. He would be Joe's trusted companion for the first 20 years of his life. In many shamanic/indigenous traditions, the twin is a sacred sign of a gifted being. Often one or both
twins would be trained to perform shamanic functions. In the *Popol
Vuh*, the sacred text of the Quiché Maya, the originators and culture
heroes are twins, Hunahpu and Xbalanque. The Mexican prophet
Quetzalcoatl was also such a twin.

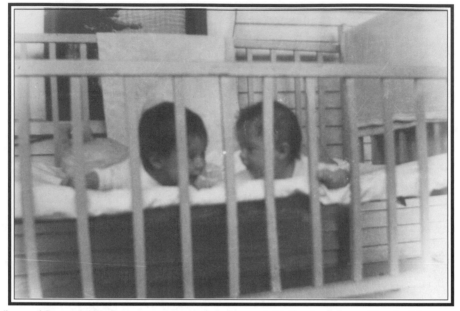

Joe and Ivan, 1939. Image courtesy of and copyright the José Arguelles Archive.

Not coincidentally, Joe and Ivan were born to Enrique and Ethel Arguelles on their 11th wedding anniversary; it was also Ethel's 30th birthday.

Enrique Sabino Arguelles was born in Guadalajara, Mexico, on November 12, 1904, the first of seven children born to Sabino and Maria Gomez Marquez: Enrique, Aurora, Antonio, Manuel and Carmen (twins), Lucia, and Julio. Well before World War I, Sabino Arguelles, a merchant, emigrated from the city of Gijon, Asturias, in Northern Spain to Guadalajara, Mexico, where he worked as a plumber and eventually owned a plumbing and hardware business. His proudest career achievement was building the original sewer system in Mazatlan. Enrique's mother, Maria Gomez Marquez, was a mysterious person who descended from the Indian tribes in northwest Mexico and died before seeing her twin grandchildren.

During the Mexican Revolution, Sabino moved his family back to Spain for a few years and enrolled Enrique in Jesuit Seminary School. Enrique eagerly signed up for extra art classes and continued his artistic activities throughout his life. Endowed with an innate musical ability, Enrique taught himself to play the piano at a young age. With a flair for adventure, Enrique claimed that he once ran away from Jesuit Seminary School and lived among a band of gypsies.

A few years later, his family returned to Mexico, and, under the strong influence of his parents, Enrique began medical school at the University of Mexico. This didn't last long, and he soon dropped out. He realized his true spirit was more akin to that of a romantic bohemian artist; besides, he couldn't stand the sight of blood.

With a few of his friends, he formed a band that played in local establishments and also provided musical accompaniment for silent moving pictures. In later years, he often bragged of this achievement. Though Enrique never earned a college degree, he continued with his creative ventures and eventually became famous in Minnesota for his mural paintings in restaurant bars and hotels.

Enrique worked many jobs in order to provide for his family. When Joe and Ivan were born, he was working as a high-ranking lieutenant in the Mexico City Police Force. The most momentous experience for Officer Enrique occurred in 1940, when, as he often told it, he "saw Trotsky's brains."

In 1922, after the death of Lenin (the leader of the 1917 Russian Revolution), two main figures emerged in Russia: Joseph Stalin and Leon Trotsky. By the 1930s, Stalin dominated in a totalitarian manner and Trotsky, who believed in permanent revolution, was driven into exile. Mexico eventually became his asylum. Enrique, an avid, self-styled Communist, was proud that Mexico opened its doors to Trotsky. On August 20, 1940, after Stalin's people found Trotsky and assassinated him with a pick ax, Enrique claimed to have been the first officer on the scene. "I saw Trotsky's brains! They were three times as big as anyone else's! That's how smart he was!"

Ethel Pearl Arguelles was born in Eyota, Minnesota, on January 24, 1909, the second of three children born to northern German immigrants Martin and Laura Meyer. She had an older brother, Wallace, and a younger brother, Vernon.

Martin Meyer was a small-town insurance salesman from Potsdam, Minnesota. Laura Meyer (formally Laura Hein) came from Eyota, Minnesota, and was fond of domestic life, spending much time gardening, baking, and canning fruits and vegetables.

After graduating high school in the summer of 1927, Ethel enrolled at Rochester Junior College, where she began her study of Spanish. A few months into her studies, Ethel boarded a train for Mexico City with her Spanish class to study and attend classes at the University of

Ethel and Enrique Arguelles, 1929. Image courtesy of and copyright the José Arguelles Archive.

Mexico for a few weeks. The first week there, Ethel attended a dance held by the Mexican student body, where she met Enrique Arguelles. She was immediately taken by his passionate fervor for life and art. The following Monday after Spanish class at the University, Ethel found Enrique waiting outside the classroom. She never went back to another class.

Ethel often told how Enrique "courted and wooed" her, taking her to many beautiful sites by day, then out dancing almost every night. Enrique even hired a mariachi band to serenade Ethel beneath the window of the room where she was staying. Soon, her allotted time in Mexico was up. With funds running low, Ethel reluctantly returned to Rochester, but only long enough to earn enough money to go back. This did not take long, and she soon moved to Mexico City and started working at the American Embassy while continuing to see Enrique.

Two years later, on January 24, 1929, her 20th birthday, Ethel married Enrique in Mexico City. At the time, she was working at the First National Bank while Enrique was eking out a living with his art and music. By 1931, Ethel became pregnant with their first child.

Well into her pregnancy, Ethel took a weeklong train ride alone from Mexico to her parents' home in Rochester, Minnesota, where she gave birth to Laurita Ethel Arguelles on September 16, 1931. She and Laurita repeated the trip to Rochester eight years later when Ethel gave birth to twin boys.

Ethel kept Joe and Ivan at their grandparents' home in Minnesota for the first six months of their life, before returning to Mexico City. When Joe later asked his mother why he and his brother were not born in Mexico, she told him that she wanted them to be born in America, "just in case they might want to become the president of the United States."

The first five years of Joe's life were idyllic. The family lived in Mexico City at 48 Tula Street (Calle Tula), in a residential apartment building not far from the famous Chapultepec Park. The one-block-long Tula Street was named after the great city of the Toltecs, the capital of Quetzalcoatl's cultural empire in the present state of Hidalgo. Tula is also known as Tollan, the mythic name of the original home of the Maya, somewhere among the stars.

Although they didn't speak until the age of 3, Joe and Ivan developed their own secret twin language, known only to themselves. When they did begin speaking, they both spoke perfect English and Spanish without confusion. In their early years, Joe and Ivan were each other's best amusement. On one occasion, they had a wild time finger-painting in their crib like expressionist artists, using the closest available medium—their excrement—smearing it with delirious joy in great swabs above their crib. This did not amuse their mother, who unhappily discovered them in the midst of their artistic frenzy and quickly put an end to their experiment.

The rich cultural ambience of Mexico City, coupled with the vibrational quality of the Mexican people, made a deep impression in Joe's being, instilling in him an insatiable curiosity about the mysteries of that land. Although his mother had dropped out of junior college and his father had never earned a college degree, they were cultured and artistic people with strong feelings about the power of the common people.

At this time, almost everyone in Latin America had a maid, and the Arguelles family was no exception. Joe was fond of their maid, Chavela, who often took him and his brother to Chapultepec Park (a big city park in Mexico City) where they strolled down the long sidewalks, eating pistachio ice cream cones under clear blue skies.

The Arguelles family lived a number of floors up in a spacious apartment complex, which felt warm and mysterious to Joe. Every day in the center of the apartment courtyard, a little old grandmother sat from morning until night, patiently flattening one corn tortilla after another with her hands. Joe watched in amazement as she skillfully placed each tortilla on a flat piece of tin and then cooked it over a fire. A fresh tortilla was served to anyone who passed by; to Joe there was nothing better than a tortilla hot off the tin.

After quitting his job at the police force, Enrique readily accepted another job as an aide for the ex-president of Mexico, Lázaro Cárdenas. Cárdenas served his term from 1934 to 1940, and was famous for nationalizing the oil industry and kicking Standard Oil out of Mexico. (In the 1930s, Mexico leaned toward Socialism and even Marxism.) Enrique became Cárdenas's right-hand man, which required frequent travel to the Northwest Territories of Mexico. During the war, meetings were held at Catalina Island, where Enrique functioned as an interpreter. Proud of the fact that he was so close to the former president, whom he considered an exemplary man, Enrique often told his family, "Cárdenas's heart is with the poor people and the Indians."

One of Joe's fondest childhood memories was attending the birthday party for Cárdenas's son, Cuauhtemoc, in Mexico City. There was a great air of festive celebration, with large colorful piñatas, delightful food, music, and swirls of happy people expressing joy, wonder, amusement, and amazement. Cuahetemoc's name was taken from the last Aztec emperor and means "fallen eagle." He would become prominent in the 1990s as a radical independent challenger to the PRI, the Mexican ruling party that his father helped establish. Though Cuahetamoc failed in his bid to become president of Mexico, he eventually became the mayor of Mexico City.

Ivan, Laurita, and Joe, Mexico, 1941. Image courtesy of and copyright the José Arguelles Archive.

Joe's mother often accompanied his father on long trips, leaving him and Ivan with Chavela and their sister Laurita, who provided nurturance and security for her brothers at this time. Though he loved his sister and Chavela dearly, Joe always eagerly awaited his parents' return. Oftentimes, his mother surprised them with small gifts and delicious brown sugar and cactus candy from their travels. Joe particularly craved the attention of his mother, whom he perceived to be a noble, aristocratic being, loving and caring; he associated her with Bambi, and he loved her nose.

On the weekends, the Arguelles family often visited Grandpa Sabino at his large mysterious home in Mexico City. Grandpa Sabino and his new wife, whom the twins called "Aunt Pache," had an import/export business and were quite wealthy. Visiting Grandpa Sabino filled Joe's heart with indescribable tranquility. He especially liked his grandfather's pet parrot, who responded to a knock at the door by saying, "*Nadie esta en la casa* (Nobody's home)."

It was at Grandpa Sabino's house that Joe first pondered the meaning of death. In 1942, his Uncle Vernie, a pilot for the U.S. Air Force during early World War II, died in a plane crash. His mother tearfully read the telegram to the family, reporting that her youngest brother had been in a plane crash somewhere in northern Africa; everyone on board had died. Stricken with grief, Ethel told Laurita to take the twins away to Grandpa Sabino's house. Three-year-old Joe sat on the steps of his grandfather's house with his brother and sister, trying to figure out what it meant that Uncle Vernie was dead. Where did Uncle Vernie go? What does it mean to be dead? Pondering these questions, Joe was suddenly gripped by a strong sensation that gave way to an overwhelmingly lucid sense of deep penetrating space.

The war also came home to Joe through the German family who lived next door in their apartment complex on Calle Tula. Every one whispered around this family, who, as Joe later determined, still had allegiances to Hitler's Germany. To Joe, they seemed like regular, normal people; they had a daughter named Lieschen and a wonderful daschund wiener dog he loved to pet. He wondered what the purpose of war was and why it had to change the way people felt about each other.

In the summer of 1943, the Arguelles family made a trip back to Rochester, Minnesota, to visit Ethel's parents. It was here that Joe had two pivotal experiences that stirred a memory or knowing in the core of his being. The two experiences occurred one day when his family paid a visit to his country cousin's house in southern Minnesota. On the drive over, Joe and Ivan were told that they would see their first cow; there were no cows where they lived in Mexico City.

When Joe saw the beast, he was awestruck. He stared, for what seemed like eternity, into its eyes until he was no longer a child and the cow was no longer a cow. A mystical rapport occurred between boy and cow, transcending them both beyond all boundaries and definitions. In an instant, Joe realized the arbitrary nature of names. He saw that without the name "cow," the creature might have more meaning to people.

Joe and Ivan, Minnesota, 1944.
Image courtesy of and copyright
the José Arguelles Archive.

Later on that same day, Joe approached his cousin, who was mowing the lawn. He was baffled by how the grass could seemingly fly out of the wheels of the lawn mower. Determined to solve the mystery of the flying grass, Joe came from behind his cousin, and with his right hand, thrust his middle finger into the seemingly invisible part of the lawn mower. He immediately found that the invisible part was filled with sharp blades, which sliced the tip of his finger, leaving it hanging by only a thin piece of skin. Joe screamed for his mother, who came quickly and wrapped a white handkerchief around his finger. The handkerchief rapidly turned crimson. He was whisked to St. Mary's Hospital in Rochester, where he had been born four years earlier, and the next morning he was released with his finger sewn back on.

These two incidents left indelible impressions on young Joe: The first was a boundary-dissolving, awakened memory of the intrinsic connection of all life, regardless of species; and the second was of searing pain, which taught him the hazards of experimenting in the material plane without sufficient knowledge.

Chapter 2
The United States

We used to wonder where war lived,
what it was that made it so vile. And now
we realize that we know where it
lives…inside ourselves.

—Albert Camus

Joe was 5 years old when his family moved into a cockroach-infested house in Mexicali, on the U.S. border. The move was determined by Enrique's job with Cardenas, who was spending increasing time working in Baja California, especially Ensenada. The color and vibrancy Joe had experienced in Mexico City had been replaced with the bleak, dust-ridden Mexicali and its infernally hot climate. For Joe, the highlight of this time was crossing over to Calexico, a town on the California side of the border, where his mother bought him and his siblings root beer popsicles.

Joe and his family again packed their belongings and headed for Los Angeles in late 1944 when Enrique got a job as a foreman at Fisher Foundries, a sandblasting plant there. They stayed at the downtown Hotel Baltimore while searching for a permanent home. After several dreary days at the hotel, they found a new three-bedroom house at 11870 Lucille Street in Culver City, a suburban subdivision not far from Venice Beach and near the Howard Hughes airport and MGM Studios. The house was a warm welcome after their days in Mexicali; Joe and Ivan were thrilled with their new room and bunk beds.

Despite increased physical comforts, Joe and Ivan soon became aware of problems in their family, mainly due to their father's drinking. One day, while on a family drive through downtown Los Angeles, Enrique got angry with Joe and Ivan and said they were carrying on "like Heckyl and Jeckyl," the talking cartoon magpies. Enraged at his sons' incessant chattering, Enrique pulled over and threw the twins out onto the sidewalk of a busy street and drove off. The boys were terrified. Fortunately, Enrique came back a few moments later to pick them up. Still, this incident filled Joe with a deep feeling of abandonment and confusion.

Scenes like this became recurring events in the Arguelles household, particularly on Sundays, when Enrique would be hung over and in a foul mood. Ethel would sit silently in her chair with tears in her eyes, too frightened to say anything.

The Arguelles family, Culver City, California, 1945. Image courtesy of and copyright the José Arguelles Archive.

During this time, Ethel began taking her children to church. When Joe first saw the Spanish mission style Lutheran church with its red tile roof, a feeling of dread arose in him. Intuitively, he understood that it represented repression of primary intuitive experience and plunder of native lands. He found the entire experience stifling and claustrophobic. It was the last place he wanted to be. But seeing his mother's sincerity, he felt sympathy for her, and so he went dutifully and quietly to church and Sunday school.

While living in Culver City, three memorable historic events occurred: The first was when President Franklin Roosevelt died on April 12, 1945. Ethel was quite liberal and an ardent supporter of Roosevelt. When she heard the news of his death over the radio, she became hysterical and ran next door to the neighbor's house, forgetting that the neighbor was a staunch Republican and happy with the news!

The second event had even more impact on Joe, and that was the bombing of Hiroshima. Joe first heard the news when his daily radio program was interrupted to announce that a big bomb had been dropped on a Japanese city. The radio announcer said the bomb looked like a big fireball and that no one had seen anything like it. They didn't know how many people had been killed. The announcement stopped Joe in his tracks. What was this about? He had a vague feeling that it was something he was meant to hear so he could remember something else, but what was it he was supposed to remember? He tried to visualize the bombing and became terrified. The contemplation of Hiroshima and Nagasaki brought him to a heightened state of awareness, making him acutely conscious of the devastating effects of war. The horror of this reality seized him with an inexpressible longing for harmony and peace.

The radio announcer said the bombing would soon end the war. What did this mean? Fear of war was commonplace, and there were still brownouts at night. When the sirens went off, everyone was ordered to turn out their lights in case airplanes came swooping in to drop bombs. Joe was just learning to read; one of the first words he learned was *war*, which screamed out from the headlines of all the newspapers.

The third memorable event of 1945 was V-J Day (Victory over Japan Day) on September 2nd. The streets were filled with the sound of car horns and victorious shouts because the Japanese had surrendered. Earlier, on V-E Day (Victory in Europe Day); May 8, 1945), people had been honking their horns, but the atmosphere was not nearly as celebratory as it was on V-J day, because finally the war was really over. Even Joe's father was gleefully honking his horn when he came home from work. This mood of festivity left Joe feeling empty and confused; if so many people had been killed, why was everyone so happy?

In the fall of 1945, Joe and Ivan started first grade at Playa Del Rey School in Culver City, where they were students in Ms. Reichert's class, while Laurita entered high school at Venice High School. Every day, Joe and Ivan walked to and from school through the lima bean fields. Returning home from school, Joe and Ivan raced to the radio to listen to their favorite programs: *Superman* and *Green Lantern*. They found radio a great medium to further stimulate their imaginations. Joe sometimes wondered if the voices he heard were actually coming from little people inside the radio. He loved the sound effects, especially on the show *Inner Sanctum*, with a creaking door that sounded so real it sent shivers up his spine. He also liked listening to a popular program called *The Shadow*, which began with a haunting line spoken in a low voice: "Only the shadow knows what evil lurks in the hearts of men."

He loved everything about the radio, even the commercials, particularly the Franco-American spaghetti ads where he could hear soldiers eating spaghetti in the trenches. Every time Joe ate spaghetti, he felt like a soldier in a trench. The media influence was profound on young Joe, who often thought about and repeated what he heard, making lines from his favorite radio shows and commercial jingles part of his referential reality.

Joe and Ivan often visited a classmate who lived among the lima bean fields. They especially liked his cute pet rabbits. One day, their friend invited them to dinner, and Joe began to eat what he thought was a chicken thigh. It tasted funny, not at all like chicken. Then he found out the shocking truth: He was eating one of the cute pet rabbits! He immediately became sick to his stomach and had to go home.

Chapter 3
Strange Programs

Much unhappiness has come into the world because of bewilderment and things left unsaid.

—Fyodor Dostoevsky

Early in 1946, Joe's life as he knew it dissolved when his mother was diagnosed with tuberculosis. On Christmas Day in 1945, after he had unwrapped a model aircraft carrier, wooden toys, and little airplanes, he was told that the family would be moving to his grandparents' house in Rochester, Minnesota, because the Los Angeles pollution was not good for his mother's deteriorating health. Though his mother blamed her illness partially on the smog, Joe knew better. He often saw her hunched over, chain-smoking cigarettes and coughing.

Immediately after his seventh birthday, Joe found himself boarding a train to Minnesota with his family and a few belongings. The ride seemed to take forever. Gazing out the window on a cold, starry night, Joe saw snow as he had never seen it before. He also saw a lone coyote in the blue moonlight and reflected that the solitary creature must feel just as he did.

When he arrived at his grandparents' house, he immediately noticed a painting on the wall of a single coyote in the snow. A shiver ran through Joe's body. This proved to be an omen of the next two years. That same evening, his grandmother took him and his brother aside and said, "I hope you don't grow up to be a dirty Mexican like your father." The next day, Ethel was taken to the tuberculosis sanitarium in Canon Falls, Minnesota, about 50 miles north of Rochester, where she stayed for almost two years.

At that time, Rochester was a relatively small, bitterly cold, white-dominated town famous for the world-renowned Mayo Clinic. Joe's grandparents' large home also served as a boarding house, but when their grandchildren arrived they were forced to give up two of the rooms, one for Laurita and a tiny bedroom on the second floor for Joe and Ivan. Enrique, who was now working as a cook at St. Mary's Hospital, was given the largely unfinished attic. He made the best of it and created a cozy alcove, with a little bed and a worktable with a window view.

Although there was a bathroom on the second floor where the boys slept, their grandparents made them walk to the basement to use the bathroom. One night, a sleepy Joe accidentally urinated on the toilet seat and was met the next day by his grim-looking grandfather, who said in an angry German accent, "I'll rub your nose in da pisch!" Joe had been uprooted from his idyllic, semi-tropical lifestyle with his family and felt alienated in his new environment.

Grandmother Laura demanded the twins remain as quiet as possible. She didn't like them hanging around in the living room. Joe found the living room musty and old, yet it was also soft and mysterious, with its intriguing books behind glass-doored bookshelves. Most notable was a large German Bible next to a ceramic skull with a movable jaw. The boys were made to do everything absolutely correctly around their grandmother, and so learned how to be silent. On the surface, this appeared to be a stark time, but inwardly Joe learned to think for himself and realized that ultimately he was responsible for his own happiness.

When the weather warmed up, Joe and Ivan stayed in the attic with their father, who put up a twin bed for them to sleep in just off the alcove. The boys liked being close to their father and out of their grandparents' sight.

In February 1946, Joe and Ivan entered first grade at Lincoln Elementary School in Rochester. They were immediately given various IQ tests, and, because of their genius-level scores, they were skipped from the first grade into the third grade. At first, they protested to being moved two grades ahead, because they were physically small for their age, and being in a class with big third-graders seemed scary. A compromise was made, and Joe and Ivan were placed in the second-grade classroom taught by Ms. Taylor.

Being the only Mexican-American students in a white-dominated school, they encountered much prejudice from the other children. On their first day of school, a few of their classmates told Joe and Ivan they were Indians, not Americans, and on one occasion Joe got his tooth knocked out playing football on the playground. The twins often spoke Spanish to each other for comfort, but that was soon put to a halt when the class bully, "Bo" Bostrum, took Joe and Ivan aside, grabbed them by their throats, and said, "We don't ever want to hear you talking that Indian language 'round here again! Do you understand?" The menacing threat was effective, and the boys stopped speaking Spanish altogether, so that what had been naturally learned was eventually nearly forgotten.

One day, Joe and Ivan were walking through town, looking at toys in a store window, when a woman approached them and, thinking they were cute twins, bought them each a cap gun. When they returned home, Grandmother Laura saw the cap guns and immediately accused the boys of stealing. After giving them a scolding, she tore the guns out of their hands and forcefully threw them down on the coffee table, shattering the glass top, much to her own surprise. Joe and Ivan secretly thought their grandmother's behavior was amusing, and it was all they could do to keep themselves from laughing. However, this programming of mistrust left a deep wound in Joe that would manifest a few years later as a stage of thievery.

Simultaneously, another program was installed in Joe. This program told him he was brilliant—a genius. These two programs did not complement one another and served to set a deep tone of confusion in Joe's still-forming psyche. On top of that, he was horribly sensitive and didn't know how to deal with it.

Laurita, who both Joe and Ivan had once felt so comforted by, started high school and entered into a wild, rebellious phase. She had many friends, and boys at school liked her; she was the exotic girl from Mexico, which was rare in Minnesota. Joe realized his sister was moving into a whole other world and saw her less and less.

While in the tuberculosis sanitarium, Ethel underwent an operation; the tuberculosis had damaged one of her lungs, and she had part of it removed, along with two ribs. At home, Enrique's drinking was becoming increasingly problematic. On their first Christmas in Minnesota, Enrique came home drunk and lost his keys in the snow. Joe was saddened to see his father in a confused state, fumbling for his keys on the ground. With his mother far away, his sister becoming more removed, and his father growing alienated from them, Joe and Ivan were forced to rely on their strict grandmother for love and guidance.

Chapter 4
The Discovery of Art

Generally the artist was left to himself
while society neglectfully rushed along
its uncreative way.

—José Arguelles, *The*
Transformative Vision

Once a month, Joe was taken to the tuberculosis sanitarium to visit his mother for only a few moments at a time. Entering the cold, sterile sanitarium deep in the country was like having an eerie dream filled with spooky forms, especially when the Sun was shining. His mother would appear behind a glass wall, tired and sickly, and wearing a floral housedress buttoned to the throat. Her appearance always shocked Joe; she seemed so far away, so distant, a ghostly apparition of the caring, nurturing mother he had once known. He deeply wished to connect with her, but had no idea what to say.

Around this time, Joe often observed his father painting and drawing, and, because he wasn't sure how to communicate with his mother in words, he thought he could learn to create pictures for her. One day, much to his father's delight, 7-year-old Joe asked him for a drawing lesson. Enrique happily gave Joe a few instructions on perspective drawing and showed him how to draw shadows and make objects appear closer or farther away. Joe was amazed at what good effects Enrique produced, just by drawing shadows. He viewed his father as a master at *chiaroscuro* (light/dark).

Determinedly, Joe practiced drawing mountains, cacti, and trees until he got the hang of it. Soon he was drawing animals, especially deer and moose, set in the forest with orange sunsets and orange clouds reflected in a lake. Colors had a tremendously sensual quality that he could almost taste. Each color transported him to a different, faraway world. He made most of his drawings and paintings for his mother, and added a handwritten "get well" message at the bottom.

Enrique greatly encouraged Joe's efforts at drawing, gently pointing out techniques for better effects. Finding he had artistic talent, and exercising it, filled Joe with a new sense of power. Soon, he was drawing all the time. He could access an indescribable sense of fulfillment by creating an image pleasing to other people and to himself. He felt he had discovered the magic formula that elevated him out of an otherwise depressing and lonely life circumstance. This artistic seed would later flower in many surprising ways.

In the springtime, Joe liked to help his grandmother in the garden; he especially loved to turn over the soil. He also started visiting his grandfather out in his shop in the garage, where he had a stone wheel for sharpening knives and often made apricot brandy and dandelion wine. Every Sunday after church, the family gathered for a formal meal, and Joe and Ivan were each given a thimbleful of dandelion wine.

On one occasion, Grandpa Martin took Joe and Ivan fishing for sunfish. Joe was horrified when he realized there was a hook in the fish's mouth; after he saw his grandfather gutting the fish, he resolved never to go fishing again. Berry picking suited him much better, and he often went with his grandfather in the summertime. Despite the mosquitoes, these were enjoyable times. They took the fresh berries back to his grandmother, who made delicious pies, jams, and jellies.

Each week, Grandmother Laura brought Joe and Ivan to Sunday school at Trinity Lutheran Church. The twins dreaded Sunday school. The redeeming feature was the little library in the Sunday school room. It had a few good books, particularly *Second Book of Marvels—The Orient* by Richard Halliburton. This travel book, with its photos of exotic places in the desert, including Mecca, sparked Joe's sense of adventure. He was also intrigued by the Bible story of Joseph with his coat of many colors. Somehow he could identify with the story of Joseph, who was abandoned by his brothers and thrown into a well. In the story, the king recognizes Joseph as an interpreter of dreams. Because of this, the king says he can have whatever he wants, and Joseph becomes the accountant of the royal stores. Joe wondered if something like this would also happen to him; after all, his name was also Joseph.

Following Sunday school class, Joe and Ivan were made to sit through church, where they would stare into the creased red necks of farmers while Minister Eifert, a stern, Germanic, fundamentalist Lutheran, spewed long, boring, fear-based sermons. The only thing inspiring about church, to Joe, was the exhilarating and triumphant-sounding processional and recessional music played by organist Mr. Zeielske, who sometimes played Bach. Overall, the weekly church experience did not breed curiosity or inspiration, and Joe could never figure out why people felt so obligated to attend.

Every year, like clockwork, Joe and Ivan's Sunday school class was made to rehearse for the big Christmas program, which was orchestrated to tell the story of the birth of Jesus. It seemed to Joe that most of the children had no idea what they were enacting and just shouted out their lines without knowing what they meant.

After returning home from the Sunday school performance, on the first Christmas Eve at his grandparents' house, Joe found that beneath the decorated tree were many colorfully wrapped presents of all sizes. When they had left for the performance, the tree was empty.

"Looks like Santa came down the chimney while we were at church!" Grandpa Meyer said. Joe found this comment incredulous. Santa was supposed to come down a fireplace, but there was no fireplace in the house! The house did have a chimney, but it led to the furnace in the basement. Joe decided to examine this area thoroughly. He would determine for himself whether his grandfather's claim was true. The chimney by the stairs leading to the basement, he found, contained only a small, round metal plate, no larger than a pie pan, which opened into the chimney. No Santa could get through that small hole. Joe decided Santa was a hoax.

Third grade proved more inspiring for Joe than second. He had an encouraging new teacher, Ms. Madden. He was now enthusiastically drawing and coloring almost every day. He also gained much creative inspiration from the public library across from the Mayo Clinic, where he and his brother spent hours poring through books. He especially liked books about faraway places, fantasies, and fairytales with stories about castles. He also loved his grandparents' big, beautiful book containing the collected writings of Joseph Conrad, including "Heart of Darkness," Joe's favorite. Conrad's stories, many of which were about the sea, sailing, and navigation and had relatively exotic themes—like people finding themselves in strange times and places with strange people—especially appealed to Joe. He knew he was one of those people.

Chapter 5
Mother's Release

*Life is the farce which everyone
has to perform.*

—Arthur Rimbaud

*904 Seventh Avenue SW. Image courtesy of and copyright the José Arguelles
Archive.*

In the early autumn of 1948, after two years of confinement, Joe's
mother was released from the tuberculosis sanitarium. Enrique and
Ethel bought a house in the southwest quarter of Rochester at the
foot of what was called "Pill Hill," where many doctors at the Mayo

Clinic lived. It was a great relief for the entire family to move into their own home at 904 Seventh Avenue Southwest. It had a big backyard, and a public swimming pool and park were within walking distance. Just 10 blocks from their house was the public library, where Joe and Ivan spent many long Saturday mornings; they were both voracious readers.

Joe and Ivan were thrilled to move into their new bedroom. Their father painted it bright blue with a mural of the South Pacific Islands. This new home felt dreamy, yet comforting and familiar to Joe. He loved to explore the alleys and trees in the neighborhood, and often went on long hikes with his brother and their dog, Duke, in the nearby country, along the Zumbro River. Oftentimes, down by the river, both Joe and Ivan felt they could hear Indians chanting.

Joe and Ivan began fourth grade at Edison Elementary School, two blocks from their home. Laurita was in her junior year, so she was able to remain at the same school. Making friends at Edison Elementary was much easier for Joe and Ivan than it had been at Lincoln; their classmates seemed more open-minded and less prejudiced. Although many of the classes were boring, the teachers were warm and friendly. To alleviate classroom tedium, Joe developed an inner technique: Quietly he whispered to himself the name Clark Kent, over and over until all the sounds ran together. This exercise seemed to make the whole classroom disappear.

In fifth grade, Joe began having fainting spells at school, particularly when there was a large congregation of children in a small space. He wasn't sure whether they were actually fainting spells, but he would get nauseous and dizzy, and it was a good opportunity to be ushered into the nurse's office where he could lie down and be away from it all. After one too many fainting spells, the nurse wondered what the problem might be. The doctor told him he was slightly nearsighted and would have to wear glasses. Ivan already wore glasses, but Joe had never thought he would have to. He had mixed feelings about the glasses and wore them on and off until he reached his fifties, when he decided he no longer needed them.

At the encouragement of his mother, Joe took an afternoon job delivering newspapers for the *St. Paul Pioneer Press and Dispatch*. He worked for a year on this route before transferring to an early-morning route for the *Minneapolis Star Tribune*, where his brother also worked. In the wintertime Rochester got bitterly cold, and Joe awakened each morning before dawn, bundle up in a jacket and scarf, and dutifully load the newspapers onto his sled. His dog, Duke, ran alongside as Joe pulled the sled and tossed newspapers from door to door. One of Joe's favorite radio programs at the time was *Sergeant Preston of the Yukon*, which featured his dog, King. Sergeant Preston was with the Royal Canadian Mounted Police, and his turf was the Yukon Territory. The show started with Sergeant Preston shouting, "Onward, King. Onward, you huskies!" followed by romantic music pressing forward into the unknown. This was a great inspiration to Joe, who was certain his dog, Duke, was like Sergeant Preston's dog, King, and the snowy streets were the Yukon.

Mrs. Condon's boarding house was his last stop of the day. She and her guests seemed delighted when Joe showed up with the newspaper in the morning. They gave him coffee and fresh, homemade donuts. He especially loved the jelly-filled bismarcks. Having a paper route gave Joe a sense of independence and accomplishment he hadn't known before. He continued the job into ninth grade.

On Seventh Avenue, his father's artistic/musical side finally had freedom of expression, much to the delight of Joe and Ivan, who thought their father's taste in music was excellent. Enrique often played his collection of classic 78 phonograph records that included Beethoven's *Pastoral Symphony* and Handel's *Organ Concerti*. Joe and Ivan loved to entertain their parents by dancing to Boccherini's minuet in G. During this time, Joe developed a habit of composing symphonies in his head. He'd hear the woodwinds followed by the strings; these built into mighty crescendos capped by the thumping of the tympanums before easing off into a quiet, almost lullaby melody, played by an oboe. To this day, he still hears those symphonies in his head, especially when he walks in nature.

Both Enrique and Ethel encouraged their children to cultivate the arts, as they both shared a deep love for art and music. Some of their happiest times were when they collaborated in some form of music or art. Ethel loved to write poetry, and both she and Enrique were fine piano players, each in their unique way. Ethel loved to play 19th-century romantic compositions like waltzes of Johann Strauss and sometimes even Chopin. Enrique also played the piano, but his playing was more sporadic and improvisational. On many occasions, Joe and Ivan awoke in the middle of the night to the sound of their father passionately striking the piano keys downstairs. Joe was profoundly struck by how sensitive and poignant the musical vibrations sounded—haunting and melancholy.

On other less-inspiring occasions, Joe and Ivan awoke abruptly to blasts of mariachi music, sambas, or tangos from their father's phonograph in his basement room. Enrique arrived home in the middle of the night from his job as a bartender at the Continental Room, sometimes with a crowd of people from the bar. No one wanted to confront Enrique in the middle of this scene, and nothing was ever said about it the next day. This created a layer of falseness in the family unit that served to alienate Joe.

In fifth grade, Joe and Ivan frequently attended movies on the weekends. One of their favorites was *The Third Man*, a Graham Greene thriller starring Orson Welles. This movie, which takes place in Vienna after World War II, impressed Joe more than any other because of its artistic flare and theme of good and evil. Joe's favorite scene was when Harry Lime (Orson Welles) says: "In Italy in a brief period of fifty years under the bloody rule of the Borgias and the Medici, you have Leonardo, Raphael, and Michelangelo! In Switzerland, you have one thousand years of democracy, and what do you get? The cuckoo clock!" Joe and Ivan enthusiastically recommended the movie to their parents, who, upon seeing it, were amazed at what great taste their twins had—and at such a young age!

Each week, Joe and Ivan eagerly awaited the Sunday newspaper. It always contained an aerial photo of different small towns in Minnesota, accompanied by a story about the history of the town. After studying the aerial photos, Joe and Ivan spent hours drawing maps of the city on cut and flattened-out brown paper grocery bags. Soon, they were creating detailed maps of imaginary cities, including railroads, factories, mountains, bays, wealthy neighborhoods, and slums. They were thrilled to discover Hudson Map Company in Minneapolis and used their weekly allowance money to buy different American city maps.

When Joe and Ivan were in sixth grade, their sister Laurita got married to her boyfriend, David Kinsley, whom she had met only a few months earlier at the Valencia Ballroom Dance Hall in Rochester. Dave was a farm worker from Stewartville, a small town about 10 miles south of Rochester. Dave eventually became a tree trimmer and was affectionately known by the family as "Digger Dave." Joe saw Digger Dave as a big, cuddly, grizzly bear; he was slightly gruff, but always well meaning, and had a warm sense of humor.

On October 28, 1949, Laurita and Dave had a simple wedding ceremony. One of Laurita's friends sang the Lord's Prayer. It took on new meaning for Joe, as he had never heard it presented so passionately. Though Joe was sad to see Laurita leave home, she seemed happy with her new husband. He felt his sister was destined for a happy life, though what it might be like, he couldn't even imagine.

After Laurita moved in with her new husband, Ivan moved into her old rose-colored room, and Joe happily stayed in the room painted with the South Sea Islands. This room inspired in him nostalgia for some lost world in a faraway time.

In sixth grade Joe entered the annual school spelling bee, which was broadcast live on the radio. Joe was the first participant asked to spell a word. That word was *money*. Joe rapidly blurted out "m-o-n-y" and was immediately disqualified from the contest, much to his chagrin and the annoyance of his team members.

At this time, Joe began playing the bass horn or sousaphone, a larger version of a tuba that wraps around the body. Playing this instrument taught Joe how to synchronize rhythm with the rest of the band and opened the doorway into the realm of music. Joe played the sousaphone until age 17, after which he didn't play music again until he was 27, when he found the instrument of his passion: the bamboo flute. (He outgrew being a member of the high school band and instead pursued painting.)

Junior High School proved challenging for Joe, and life seemed confusing. Being at a new school with a new socialization process, he wasn't sure how to fit in. Many of his classmates played sports. Joe and Ivan desperately wanted a basketball hoop so they could practice. When they made this request to their father, he refused; he was an artist with a great dislike for American sports and everything they represented. As a result, Joe and Ivan were considered relatively wimpy according to junior high and high school social standards.

In seventh and eighth grades, all male students were required to take shop class. The seventh-grade shop teacher, Mr. Poppenburg, was a sports fanatic who favored boys who were demonstrably athletic. No matter how hard he tried, Joe didn't do well in Mr. Poppenburg's class. The final assignment was to build a wooden birdhouse. Joe did his best, but received a C- for his efforts. In frustration, Joe, Ivan, and their classmate, Duncan Masson, took their unworthy birdhouses to a vacant lot on the other side of the block where they lived and burned them.

In 1951, Grandpa Meyer died. This came as a shock to the whole family. Joe and Ivan were excused from school to attend the funeral, which was held at the Lutheran church. Approaching the open casket, Joe peered at Grandpa Meyer, who, despite appearing a bit waxy, looked like he was peacefully sleeping. During the funeral service, Joe was touched to see Grandma Meyer sitting next to the coffin, brushing flies away from Grandpa's face. After the funeral, everyone proceeded to the cemetery, where the hole was already dug, and watched the coffin lowered into the grave. This left Joe feeling empty and with a deep inner questioning about the meaning of life and death.

Around this time, Joe's paper route took him to Hillside Apartments, where he began stealing milk money left for the milkman. At first, he took just the occasional dollar, but soon he became greedy and took more, until one day in eighth grade he got a call telling him to report to a Mr. Dison at the city juvenile delinquent center.

Trembling, Joe reported to Mr. Dison's office. Mr. Dison told him it was clear that the only person who could possibly be taking money from the milk bottles was him. Mr. Dison threatened Joe that he was going to call his parents that afternoon.

After the meeting, Joe ran all the way home; he knew neither of his parents was home that afternoon. He waited and waited for the call from Mr. Dison, but it never came. That was the end of his paper route.

In eighth grade, Joe and Ivan tested at genius levels on their IQ tests. Joe went with Ivan and their mother to the school office, where they had been called in to hear their test scores. Their mother was informed that a score of 140 indicates genius level, and that Ivan scored 144 and Joe scored 148. Walking back from the meeting with the counselor, Joe had a happy sensation that at least something in him was being affirmed by this strange school system that he was attending. This knowledge affected him at a profound level, and, between eighth and ninth grades, he felt, for the first time, deeply serious. He felt serious about his painting and pursuing his interests in art, and he felt serious about comprehending all the books he read. In general, he felt serious about putting his life on some type of course that would justify his being called a "genius."

Chapter 6
Teotihuacán

Pyramid of the Sun, Teotihuacán. Photo courtesy of Jacob Wyatt.

The event that shaped Joe's destiny occurred in Chiapas, Mexico, on June 15, 1952. Joe was 13 when archaeologist Alberto Ruz discovered the extraordinary tomb of Pacal Votan, a ruler of ancient Palenque.

In 1949, Ruz noticed a curious stone in the floor of the pyramid at the top of the Temple of the Inscriptions in Palenque. When he lifted the stone, he saw massive amounts of rubble and one other thing: an enigmatic tube that appeared to be made out of ceramic tiles. Later, Ruz said he never would have thought to remove the rubble if not for that tube. He started digging out the stairway that ran from the floor of the temple at the top of the pyramid, down to the tomb into the sarcophagus below.

As he dug out the rubble, Ruz noticed that the tube ran all the way down into the tomb itself. It took him three years of digging to reach the huge door of the tomb. The door had been sealed since 692 AD. Ruz said that, when he opened that door, he thought he could feel the thoughts and breath of the last people who closed it, more than a thousand years before, escaping. If it had not been for the tube, the tomb of Pacal Votan would not have been discovered. What was that tube? Ruz referred to it as a *psychoduct* and said it functioned as an oracle through which Pacal Votan (whose body was buried in the tomb) could speak from the Earth to the temple above.

In the same year as the discovery of the tomb, Carl Jung published his famous essay on synchronicity, a year later James Watson and Francis Crick cracked the DNA code, and shortly after American scientist James Van Allen discovered the Earth's two radiation belts.

At this time, Joe was taking catechism classes and was confirmed as a full member of the Missouri Synod Lutheran Church. This meant he could now officially take Holy Communion.

Although both Joe and Ivan also showed a proficiency in art, their father showed obvious favoritism toward Joe in this area, not giving Ivan much encouragement. This was disheartening to Joe; Ivan was the closest human being on Earth to him. He knew how bad his brother felt, and he didn't enjoy being favored at his expense. By the time they were in the eighth grade, Ivan made a decision to forego artistic efforts in drawing or painting and instead focused his energy on studying languages and writing poetry. As a result, he became proficient in many languages, and ended up becoming a university librarian and an award-winning poet.

In ninth grade, Joe's artistic abilities began to flower, with the encouragement of his art teacher, Mr. Anderson. One of Joe's most memorable paintings of this time was a charcoal mural recollecting his first airplane ride to Minneapolis with his mother and brother.

In the summer of 1953, after Joe's first two seven-year cycles were complete, his father became nostalgic for his native land and decided to take the twins to Mexico. This trip marked the pinnacle year of Joe's life, awakening the programming and pattern of his life mission.

At 14, Joe embodied an amazing set of paradoxes fed by an insatiable intellectual curiosity. He devoured an enormous number of books in a wide range of topics from fiction (lots of John Steinbeck) to philosophy, as well as many types of art and history books. By the time his father took him to Mexico, he already possessed a well-formed artistic sensibility and a sound knowledge base. His father had an interesting library, but most of the books were in Spanish, which Joe didn't read well at the time, but he liked flipping through the books on Mexican art and Mexican folk art. He also enjoyed reading books about artistic educational experiments in Mexico.

In July 1953, Joe, Enrique, and Ivan packed their bags into the 1949 dark blue Chevy Sedan they'd inherited from Grandpa Meyer. Exhilaration filled the air as the three of them set off on the road for the long drive from Minnesota to Mexico City. Never before had Joe and Ivan been on such an adventure with their father.

The drive south was leisurely, and Enrique was on his best behavior. Following the route of the old Pan-American Highway, Enrique excitedly told the twins one tale after another regarding the ancient culture of Mexico and their ancestors. The twins listened enthusiastically and eagerly looked forward to finally seeing all of the relatives they had heard about but could scarcely remember, having left Mexico City when they were only 5 years old.

But for Joe, there was a special excitement: He was going to see with his own eyes the pyramids of Teotihuacán; that was all he could think about. In poring over the books in his father's library, he had some glimmering awareness of the greatness of the pyramids of ancient Mexico, especially those of Teotihuacán. Built and occupied between BC 300 and 600 AD, this mysterious Toltec city was abandoned around 750 AD. What had happened?

It was a wonderful drive, and Joe loved staying in obscure motels in strange little towns like Tamazunchale, which all the tourists pronounced "Thomas and Charlie."

After six days of driving, they reached Mexico. The first stop was Monterrey, where they stayed with Aunt Aurora, who had married into the wealthy De la Borde silver mining family. Then they drove to Mexico City to visit Uncle Julio, Enrique's youngest brother.

Upon arriving at Uncle Julio's, they were greeted by Aunt Lupe, cousins Maria, Eugenia, and Christina, and, of course, Uncle Julio. Joe found Uncle Julio a comical, cultured character and an avid pyramid enthusiast. Like Enrique, Julio also worked as a bartender at Club Jena, one of the more sophisticated spots in Central Mexico City. Uncle Julio's small but comfortable house in Colonia Del Valle was bursting with warm, colorful paintings. Julio and Enrique also shared a love for Russian Communist music, especially the famous Russian/Soviet composer, Dmitri Shostakovich. This was the first time Joe and Ivan were introduced to Shostakovich's *Fifth Symphony*; they found it electrifying.

Uncle Julio made sure that the twins were taken to all of the cultural monuments in Mexico City; still, all Joe could think about was when he was going to see the pyramids in Teotihuacán. Finally, it happened.

Not many people were visiting when they first arrived at Teotihuacán—just a few students and a few tourists. Uncle Julio was in a lively mood, talking animatedly about the wonders of ancient Mexico and how fantastic the minds of the builders must have been to conceive a city so grand and dramatic, so epic in scale. The first stop was at the Citadel of Quetzalcoatl, where both Joe and Ivan were enamored with the Tlaloc and Quetzalcoatl heads adorning the pyramid. As they walked up the "Avenue of the Dead" toward the Pyramid of the Moon, Uncle Julio was still talking excitedly.

Listening to Uncle Julio, Joe peered to his right. There it was! The magnificent Pyramid of the Sun! So grand, so monumental, the Pyramid shimmered in full sunlight like a fantastic dream. Joe suddenly bolted ahead, racing at top speed toward the Pyramid, where he eagerly climbed the steps of the immense earthen structure. He wanted to be the first to reach the top. Breathless, he found himself virtually alone on the great platform atop the Pyramid of the Sun. Something shifted inside him. Everything took on a crystalline clarity, unusually sharp in focus; the fine details of faces and clothes on the people all the way down to the end of the Avenue of the Dead were suddenly clear. A deep knowing stirred within him. He fell silent.

> *Teotihuacán—place where the seekers of the One Creator*
> *God listen in silence to the songs of creation.*

Joe looked around. Sky, brilliant and blue. Mountains everywhere, echoing the forms of the pyramids.

*Teotihuacán—place where the Toltec warriors receive the
light of a distant star.*

He saw the great stretch of the Avenue of the Dead, with the Pyramid
of the Moon up to the right. And down below were the humans of the
present era.

Teotihuacán—place where the people receive their godly powers.

A few college students in white-sleeved shirts and a sprinkling of
tourists all talked to each other as if oblivious to where they were.

*Teotihuacán—place where the jaguars dance with the
flowers of wisdom.*

Peddlers—puny little beings of the modern world—were hawking
ceramic whistles.

Teotihuacán—place of the teachers of the geometry of time.

Where were the great masters who had designed and built this
city with such profound perfection and geometry? As Joe gazed
around, this question penetrated his being.

*Teotihuacán—place where the sun of knowledge burns in the
heart causing the flowers to become song and the song to grow
roots.*

Everything fell away.

*Teotihuacán—place where the earthly self disappears in the
light of the morning star.*

A shining white light, emanating from within, bathed everything
in a soft glow.

Teotihuacán—place of the acquiring of a true face.

And then the earthly world disappeared.

All that remained inside Joe was a feeling, a presentiment, a thirst,
a willingness, a vision, and a vow to find the knowledge of the masters
who built and designed Teotihuacán and bring it back to this modern
world where maybe—just maybe—it would make everything cosmic
once again.

Little did Joe know at the time, but the central thread of what he
was pursuing would lead him to decode a prophetic tradition of the
ancient Maya that leads directly to the present time. His particular mission would not uncover anything, however. What needed to be uncovered was already uncovered: the tomb of Pacal Votan. His mission

would be to decode what had already come to light. Also, little did he know that, 49 years later, he would be honored for his mission in a powerful ceremony conducted by nine indigenous elders atop the very same pyramid.

Joe and Ivan, Pyramid of Quetzalcoatl, Teotihuacán, 1953. Image courtesy of and copyright the José Arguelles Archive.

From this point on, Joe's path was guided by the vision reawakened in him at this time. Before he could realize the vision, however, he would pass through numerous gateways—each one offering a different facet of an archetypal embodiment to be played out.

On the drive back home from Mexico City, Joe had a dream that he got back to Minnesota and went to his friend Walt McDonald's house. Walt lived two blocks up the street from Joe on Seventh Avenue. In his dream, Joe knocked on the door, and Walt's father opened it. Dressed in shorts and with shaving cream on his face, he told Joe that Walt wasn't home.

When Joe returned to Minnesota he went to his friend Walt's house and knocked on the door. Walt's father opened it, dressed in shorts and with shaving cream on his face. He told Joe Walt wasn't home. This precognitive dream was the tip of the iceberg of what was to come. He felt strange, ancient, supernatural forces stirring within. The initiation had occurred. The awakening had begun, although a long road lay ahead.

Chapter 7
Mayan Remembering

*In order to escape rapidly mounting calendric chaos,
the Mayan priests devised a simple numerical
system which even today stands as one of the
brilliant achievements of the human mind.*

—Sylvanus Morley, The Ancient Maya

By the fall of his 10th-grade year, Joe started to think of himself as an artist. He begged his art teacher, Mr. Rudkin, to let him use the art studio to paint after school. Although Mr. Rudkin was not inspired like Mr. Anderson, he saw that Joe was sincere, and so he gave him permission to stay in the art studio as long as he wanted after school. With no one around, Joe was free to follow his oil paints and brushes into the far reaches of his imagination. He created landscape oil paintings, imaginal scenes from Steinbeck's books, and pictures of imaginary blonde women. He was also fond of painting desolate scenes, as well as many stark and anguished self-portraits.

He painted at the high school art studio until around 5 p.m. and then headed over to the Rochester Public Library, where he had a job shelving books until 9 p.m. The librarian's name was Trudy Munson. She was fond of Joe and often pointed out books for him to read. He loved his library job; it gave him the opportunity to explore and discover new realities and ways of thinking. He also spent much time in the Kellogg Reading Room, poring over their many encyclopedias and rare books.

Being introspective and inquisitive, Joe searched for the meaning of his existence through Greek and Medieval existentialist philosophy, history, and biographies of artists. By the time he graduated from high school, he had quite a collection of books about famous artists; his

Joe in the Kellogg Reading Room, 1954.
Image courtesy of and copyright the José Arguelles Archive.

favorites were Van Gogh and Rembrandt. He often studied paintings of famous artists, etching them into his mind. Always he was thinking, "What is life about? What does it all mean?"

His continuous questioning brought about a deep listless longing, but for what, he didn't know. He had a recurring, haunting feeling that somehow, something important had passed, only he couldn't remember what it was. Something mysterious, yet familiar. Was it something from the past? Or was it something from the future? What happened? He thought perhaps something happened in the past that would never return…unless…there was a new future.

Then it fell into his hands. As he was filing books at the public library, Joe noticed a book called *The Ancient Maya*, by Sylvanus Griswold Morley. He opened it to a chapter on astronomy and mathematics, and read about the "dot-bar notation" system. A light went on in his head as he read how the ancient Maya counted by factors of 20 (vigesimal), rather than 10 (decimal). He immediately taught himself the Mayan dot-bar notation system, which he often practiced during his boring physics class. While playing with these numbers, he wondered what it meant that there were "countless cycles within cycles."

He also gleaned from Morley's book that the basis of the Mayan calendar was a 260-day cycle. Upon learning this, Joe immediately perceived that the Mayan mathematical system was contained by this 260-day cycle. This knowledge was the key that opened his mind to the consideration of a larger order of reality coexisting with his own. Discovering this book was like finding a treasure map, long hidden, that led him to an endlessly fascinating contemplation. As he studied it, he also read P.D. Ouspensky's *Tertium Organum*, with its description of the fourth dimension and parallel universes, and inner doors began to open.

In his 10th-grade English class, Joe was asked to give a speech about what he would do when he grew up. He proclaimed that he wanted to be a doctor of philosophy. He knew that philosophy literally meant "love of wisdom," so he explained to his class that he would like to be one who cures people through the love of wisdom. Ms. Husby, his English teacher, was surprised by his unusual speech; his classmates thought he was strange.

In the classroom, Joe was generally shy and introverted, and, though he had an interest in girls, he had a hard time making connections. Ivan didn't have this problem. From ninth grade through his senior year, Ivan had a single girlfriend: Mary Lou Willard, who would later be the subject of his award-winning poetry book, *Looking for Mary Lou*.

Joe spent many days, particularly Sundays, alone by the Zumbro River, brooding over various topics, such as art, history, philosophy, and the nature of God, always with a fascination for the civilization of ancient Mexico. In the 1950s, there wasn't much known on the civilization of the Maya, but Joe read everything he could get his hands on, including books about the Aztec and Inca civilizations. By the time he graduated from high school, he had a deep understanding of the general characteristics and history of ancient civilizations of the New World.

Joe and Ivan spent most evenings in Joe's little room listening to rhythm and blues from the Nashville 50,000-watt AM radio station WLAC. This was a powerful bonding time for the twins. They began to recognize some important artists: Muddy Waters, Bo Diddley, Chuck Berry, Little Walter, B.B. King, John Lee Hooker, as well as lesser-known artists like Slim Harpo, Jimmy Reed, and Otis Rush. They found the music raw, powerful, and highly stimulating. Most of the artists were making records on the Chess Records and Checker Records labels in Chicago, and soon Joe and Ivan had built up a large collection of more than 200 vintage 45 RPMs. This was an incubation period in musical history, leading up to the birth of rock and roll.

During the end of their 10th-grade year, the high school counselor called Joe and Ivan to his office and encouraged them to sign up for the early entrance program at the University of Chicago. Neither Joe nor Ivan felt ready for college yet. They were already a year ahead in their school placement, as well as being twins and Mexican-Americans. They felt going to college early would only increase their sense of alienation.

During summertime, Joe often went on camping trips with his friends. Instead of sleeping, he sat outside, contemplating the vastness of the nighttime sky. When his friends got up and asked him what he was doing, all he could ever tell them was, "The stars, it's the stars."

In the summer of 1954, between 10th and 11th grades, Joe and Ivan started to drink in an effort to "harden" their personalities. Up until now their classmates considered them wimpy intellectuals. Early in their junior year, their parents took a vacation to the North Woods, leaving Joe and Ivan in charge of the house for a week. They threw a big party and got people at the pool halls to buy them plenty of beer. The twins soon became notorious in high school for their drinking, and by their senior years they were outrageous.

Joe had read many books by John Steinbeck and James T. Farrell, which gave him the idea to hang out with down-and-out people at pool halls. On the weekends, he and Ivan got people from the pool halls to buy them two half pints of J.W. Dant whiskey. Their father, who was still working as a bartender at the Continental Room in the Carlton Hotel, was also drunk much of the time. Even though he loved his father, Joe's sympathies were with his mother. Still in a somewhat weakened state from her years of tuberculosis, she complained a lot, but did nothing to improve her situation. During the days she took long naps, and she still smoked cigarettes.

Enrique fixed up the basement for himself, creating an artistic nook where he could read, contemplate, drink, and ultimately get away from it all. Being a Mexican Communist with strong opinions in a predominantly white, Christian-dominated town, Enrique often struggled with maintaining his identity. Often when he came home drunk, he looked at Joe, beat his chest, and said in his broken English, "I'm Communist! Do you think something is wrong with that, Yo-seph?" Joe assured him nothing was wrong with that.

In the middle of their senior year, both Joe and Ivan were removed from the honor society because of their reputation for drinking. Nonetheless, they continued to excel in their studies. In his senior year, Joe took a journalism class with a teacher named Ms. Whidman, who encouraged his creativity. The high point of his journalism class was the special Easter issue of 1956. Joe wrote the main feature story about Christ's crucifixion in a style that combined an existentialist viewpoint with the flavor and quality of a John Steinbeck novel. He also contributed a black-and-white ink drawing of Christ on the cross.

On the weekends, Joe and Ivan liked to hang out at various dance halls, including the Valencia Ballroom and the Playmor Ballroom. These were rough, rowdy places that blared country music. (Rock and roll was yet to break onto the scene.) Joe and Ivan often woke up with black eyes and bloody noses.

One night before taking Communion at church, Joe and Ivan drank heavily at the dance hall. They were hung over and, when they got up to drink the Communion wine, Ivan took one sip and passed out at the altar. No one seemed to pay attention as Joe dragged Ivan from the altar back to the pew where they'd been sitting.

Soon a dance hall called "In the Moo'd" opened. It was a milk bar. Joe and Ivan would show up drunk with half pints of whiskey hidden in the inner pocket of their leather jackets. They met many interesting characters and got booze from an older man nicknamed "Sheriff." On weekends, Joe and Ivan would get Sheriff into a friend's car, give him money, and drive him to a small town to buy them alcohol. Joe and Ivan would crack up as Sheriff tried to remember what he was supposed to get.

"So you want me to get you six two-packs of smedmons walka?" Sheriff would ask. "No," the twins would say, laughing. "Two six-packs and a bottle of Smirnov Vodka."

In the summer between their junior and senior years, Joe and Ivan, along with their friend Tom Lake, took a train ride to Chicago, where they stayed at the YMCA in the downtown district. Joe liked the creative feeling and the gritty texture of the city. He couldn't wait until his next visit. That summer, he worked as a pressure cooker at Libby's Pea and Corn packing plant, where he met David Johnson, who would be a reoccurring character in his life.

At this point, Joe didn't know what he would do after high-school graduation. His vision from Teotihuacán was strong within him, though he didn't see a way to apply his pursuit of the knowledge of ancient Mexico within his cultural conditions. He wanted to learn more about Mayan mathematics and the calendar, but the options seemed limited.

He considered becoming an archaeologist, but it was a narrow discipline. His family didn't motivate him to go to college, so he thought he might hitchhike to California and get a job as a migrant worker.

In March 1956, a representative from Valparaiso, the German Lutheran College outside of Chicago, knocked on his door. He told Joe his grades were good and that he'd like to offer him a scholarship. Joe asked the college representative what was good about the school. "Well," replied the representative, "we have a great basketball team and many of our graduates become good insurance sales representatives." Although this response was less than inspiring, Joe figured it couldn't be that bad; it was near Chicago, and he would be in close proximity to the Art Institute, which contained many of the paintings he'd seen only in books.

Joe and Ivan, Rochester, 1956. Image courtesy of and copyright the José Arguelles Archive.

PART II

From Existential Lutheran to Shipwrecked Sailor

Chapter 8
Shifting Identities

*The courage to be is the courage
to accept oneself, in spite of being
unacceptable.*

—Paul Tillich

When he arrived at Valparaiso University in the fall of 1956, Joe's feelings were twofold: He felt the exhilaration of new life opportunities but also a slight apprehension, knowing the size of his dream was much greater than the confines of a small Lutheran college in northern Indiana. Nonetheless, he accepted the path that had opened.

Joe was assigned two roommates. One was secretive and sensitive; the other was bold and ambitious, his sights set on becoming an insurance salesman. Though his dormmates were nice enough, Joe perceived the limitations of consciousness that prevailed in the conventional, middle-class Lutheran belief system in the school community.

Joe's theology teacher, Mr. Bepler, a self-proclaimed Protestant existentialist, provided the high point of his otherwise dismal year at Valparaiso. Mr. Bepler encouraged Joe to seek self-knowledge and to consider what it meant to be a Christian with regard to the existential viewpoint of being human. Joe appreciated Mr. Bepler's thought-provoking questions, such as *How can you know God from within, without any church structures?*

Through long discussions, Mr. Bepler affirmed that Joe should be free to choose his own spiritual path. He presented him with the book *The Courage to Be* by theologian Paul Tillich. Tillich wrote that "...conflicts between the old, which tries to maintain itself, often with new means, and the new, which deprives the old of its intrinsic power, produce anxiety in all directions." Joe was relieved to hear this.

On weekends, Joe often ventured to Chicago alone, visiting museums by day and walking around the University of Chicago campus at night. Growing up in white-dominated Rochester, he was excited to see so many black people in the Chicago neighborhoods. He felt from them a fascinating new energy, creative and alive in ways he'd yet to experience. At night, he frequented the 24-hour B & G Coffee Shop, lingering over their "bottomless cup of coffee" and contemplating his next steps.

He enjoyed his newfound independence, but he had little in common with his college classmates and was lonely. It was also the first time he had ever been away from Ivan, who was attending the University of Minnesota in Minneapolis. During this year apart, they kept a lively correspondence and decided they were not ready to be apart. They agreed to apply to the University of Chicago for the next school year so they could be together again.

They were both accepted for midyear entrance in February 1958. Joe was also accepted to the Chicago Art Institute, but decided he would get a better education at the University of Chicago; besides, his brother would be there.

When he got to the University of Chicago, he finally followed the advice of his high-school friends, who, when he graduated, told him he shouldn't call himself *Joe* anymore, but rather *José*, as it was "much more artistic-sounding" and thus more fitting to his character.

José entered the University of Chicago in the winter of 1957–58, a time near the end of the Eisenhower era and in the middle of the Cold War. A sense of political radicalism not known in many other parts of the country pervaded the Chicago campus, making it a forerunner among college campuses at the time. The only other exception was San Francisco's North Beach. The beatnik generation was being birthed, and there was a fresh vibrancy, a new and tangible cultural horizon.

Though Chicago was an elitist school, the general sentiment of the undergraduates was nonconformist and highly socialistic, even tending toward anarchy. The students were typically serious, deep thinkers. Many of them listened to Woody Guthrie's philosophical folk rock as well as Big Bill Broonzy's acoustic, urban blues. Likewise, the professors were passionate. They were committed to high academic values and esteemed the humanities as a respectable liberal arts curriculum. José was pleased to find the University promoted comparative study of philosophy and religion, along with art and music.

The University of Chicago felt fresh, stimulating, and intellectually challenging, compared to José's former experience at Valparaiso. Finally, he felt he'd entered into the right scene and environment; he was now free to explore and discover himself. Here, he was no longer Joe—the small-town boy from Minnesota—but José—the radical bohemian coming into his own.

The big news in Chicago at that time was the phenomenal urban renewal program on the Southside ghetto in the Hyde Park neighborhood. On the streets, it was known as the "urban removal" program. José and Ivan lived in many of these rundown apartment buildings before they were torn down. Rent was next to nothing, and José loved the artistic freedom afforded by living in such temporary dwellings. He was free to fling paint on the ceiling, color the walls, and, in general, transform his living space into an experimental art canvas whenever he so desired—and with no negative consequences!

Scholarships and part-time jobs paid the rent. José got a job filing x-rays at the University of Chicago Medical Center. His main coworkers were two gay African-American lab technicians whose names were Alfred and Larry, but who insisted on being called *Alfreda* and *Laurabell*. They invited him to all their parties, where he met a vast array of wild, creative characters. At one party, they introduced 19-year-old José to a young black prostitute named Connie Youngblood, who initiated him in sex. He and Connie became friends, and she often took him to various rhythm and blues jazz clubs on the south side of town.

To José, there was nothing like the raw, dynamic emotion of the blues; its soulful rhythms stirred a deep inner exhilaration. Muddy Waters was his favorite, and Ivan's as well. After a night of partying, José and Ivan looked up Muddy Waters in the phone book, knowing his birth name was McKinley Morganfield. Much to their surprise, his number was listed. It was 3 a.m. when they called his home to ask if he would be playing in their area any time soon. A sleepy-but-polite Muddy Waters answered. José told him that he and his brother were from Minnesota and had collected all of his records since the mid-1950s. "Minnesota!" exclaimed Muddy Waters in his Mississippi drawl. "Why, that must be 10,000 miles from here!"

For the twins, speaking to Muddy Waters was a colossal, even mythic, event, and they told anyone who would listen about their conversation. Two weeks later, José and Ivan showed up to see Muddy Waters play at the smoky, dimly lit club on 78th Street, where Little Walter accompanied him on blues harp. The power of Muddy Waters's voice, and the artistic timing and integrity of his guitar, as well as the imaginative blues harp accompaniment of Little Walter, created an unprecedented musical experience for José and Ivan.

Having consumed just enough alcohol to remove all inhibitions, José couldn't resist hopping onstage, Ivan just behind him, to fulfill his dream of singing alongside his favorite blues artist. Muddy Waters was kind and tolerant as José enthusiastically joined in for a soulful rendition of "I'm a Man"; after all, there weren't many white boys passionately attending black rhythm and blues shows.

On another occasion, José and Ivan went to see John Lee Hooker play at a nightclub on Hyde Park Boulevard. They eagerly arrived at 10 p.m. to experience one of their favorite blues musicians. To their great delight, they were virtually the only ones in the audience, so, for the better part of the night, it was as if the Mississippi bluesman performed solely for the twins. After the show, they were able to converse with Hooker, asking him many questions. José asked Hooker where he learned to play his unique guitar style. Hooker told the twins that his father had inherited some African traditions, and he cut inner tubes of tires into strips, tied them to tree branches, and then strummed them. José and Ivan were grateful to learn the source of John Lee Hooker's famous dynamic strumming technique.

Each week, José looked forward to the new issue of *Muhammad Speaks*, a weekly newspaper with a radical point of view, written and published by the Honorable Elijah Muhammad, founder of the Nation of Islam. José found the newspaper possessed a mysterious dignity and authority that seemed almost alien, even compared to a white Socialist point of view. Getting the Muslim perspective on world events became important to José, who felt magnetically drawn to the ingenuity he felt from Muhammad and his followers. Little did he know that 34 years later he would be sitting in Elijah Muhammad's dining room chair in Mexico.

In the middle of the "urban removal" debris, José and Ivan were introduced to the Cellar Boheme, a key club that operated without a license. To get in, you had to know the right people. The entrance was through a largely hidden door on an angular lean-to where a little shelter covered the stairs leading to an underground basement. The large basement primarily featured musical and poetical performances by African-American literary artists. José and Ivan found the Cellar Boheme a lively place with vibrant characters, many of whom they befriended, namely Paul Butterfield, the white blues harmonica player and forerunner of white blues singing in the 1960s. Along with rhythm and blues, José was turned on to contemporary jazz, especially be-boppers Charlie Parker and Miles Davis.

In 1958, a strange atmosphere pervaded America. The Soviet Union launched *Sputnik*, the first satellite to orbit Earth. What was once passed off as science fiction had become a reality, and José wondered just how far the modern world would go with its technological infatuation.

As an artist, José wanted to outwardly project his inner feelings, and, as a result, his wardrobe consisted of nothing but black socks, black sneakers, black Levis, black turtleneck sweaters, a black overcoat, and dark sunglasses. He felt himself to be an outsider, standing outside the being of the external world. His "outsider" image was completed by an attitude of romanticism that bordered on self-pity. His motto was the William Blake quote "The road to the palace of wisdom is paved with excess." At an intuitive level, he knew he must enter another state of mind if he was going to unite with his whole being.

On the other side of José's "outsider" persona was a serious and disciplined student who was well aware that he was obtaining a broad cultural education. He identified with visionary painters, such as Vincent Van Gogh and Jackson Pollack, and absorbed as much existential literature of the post–World War II period as possible. Among his favorites were French existentialist philosophers and writers Jean-Paul Sartre and Albert Camus. These influences caused him to further seek and pursue esoteric ways.

Late in the fall of 1958, José met Ginger Plant, a fiery redheaded freshman with strong opinions about everything. She was José's first real girlfriend, though their union didn't last long. They considered themselves a hip, artsy couple; they frequented North Side jazz clubs in Chicago. Ginger came from a Jewish family in Great Neck, New York, a wealthy suburb along the North Shore of Long Island.

In early spring of 1959, Ginger took José on his first trip to New York City and introduced him to all the "happening" clubs and bars, including the Cedar Bar in the Greenwich Village area, where all the expressionist artists hung out. He was in awe of the artistic and uninhibited lifestyle he encountered; it was much different from what he had known growing up. He was further impressed that Ginger's family owned a summer home in the Hamptons, the Southside of Long Island where many artists lived, most notably Jackson Pollack.

However, Ginger had her own difficulties, and her parents didn't take kindly to their daughter's new boyfriend. After the school year ended, Ginger returned home to her parents. Feeling Ginger slipping away, José caught a train to New York with the intention of proposing marriage. Traveling alone to New York, he made his way to her family's summer home in the Hamptons and knocked at the door. Her parents answered, and they made it clear to him that there was no way Ginger was going to see him, let alone have a relationship with him. Ginger's father handed him five 100-dollar bills and told him never to call again. José was crushed. Sadly, he took the money and never saw Ginger again.

Chapter 9
Beatnik Years

*I saw the best minds of my generation destroyed
by madness, starving hysterical naked, dragging
themselves through the negro streets at dawn
looking for an angry fix, angelheaded hipsters
burning for the ancient heavenly connection to
the starry dynamo in the machinery of night.*

—Allen Ginsberg, "Howl"

College wasn't the same without Ginger, and, because she had been his first serious girlfriend, he couldn't shake the feeling that he had missed a wonderful opportunity. On top of this, he rarely saw his brother anymore. Ivan had fallen in love with a Jewish girl named Claire Birnbaum, and, much to José's surprise, they got married. Their marriage lasted scarcely a year.

For José, 1959 was a dismal year and seemed to reflect the overall mental environment of the late 1950s. He grew wilder. Beginning his senior year in college, he experienced bouts of depression, cutting his wrists with razor blades, and smashing his hands through glass windows. A nervous breakdown ensued, and he spent time in the psychiatric ward at the University of Chicago.

Upon release, he took peyote for the first time and wandered alone through the Chicago Art Institute, feeling as if he was in an underwater aquarium. New inspiration soon came in the form of the beatnik movement. It was a refreshing contrast to the shutdown mind of the 1950s, characterized by the obsessive witch-hunt of McCarthyism, negative psychological effects of the Cold War, and intensive continued testing of atomic weapons.

The inspiring poetry of Jack Kerouac and Allen Ginsberg came just in time, giving José a fresh outlook on life and setting him on a bohemian course. For him, the main attraction of this alternative, beatnik counterculture was the rejection of middle-class American values, and an embrace of exotic jazz, art, and literature, culminating in the vision of a radically new worldview.

He got a job on campus at *The Chicago Review*, a university literary journal that published some of the "beat" poetry. This didn't last long, as the journal was shut down and censored by certain conservative university professors, who found the bohemian vision "objectionable" at best. The deciding professors, however, did allow the *The Chicago Review* to sponsor a lecture by Alan Watts in late 1959.

José had great respect for the mind of Alan Watts, but he didn't connect with the way Buddhism was presented in his lecture. José felt the audience might have colored his perceptions. Many there were high on peyote and mushrooms, which made the overall atmosphere a curious mix of Zen Buddhism and offbeat socialism. This event highlighted the flavor of the times, which was an equal mix of exploration and ferment.

Art was everything to José. He loved nothing more than to surrender his whole being and soul to the creation of passionate works. Through experimental painting and studying the lives of great artists and their various forms of expression, José, once again, became acutely aware of the gulf between the knowledge of the ancients and that of modern artists. In this contemplation, the realization dawned that the content of *what* is known is one thing, but *how* it is known is a whole other matter. He saw that *how* people go about doing things produces results intrinsically tied to the process and intention. José knew the *how* of the knowledge that built places like Teotihuacán was different from the *how* in the creations of the modern world. From his studies and contemplation, he understood the reason for this predicament lay in individualistic egos that were taking art increasingly further from its true root and source.

In his last year as an undergraduate student, José took an advanced painting class. He often painted abstract expressionist pictures with fellow artist Pete Butterfield (Paul's older brother). José's chief inspirations were Franz Klein, Jackson Pollack, and Willem de Kooning. One day, Pete introduced a canvas with simple, smooth, flat matte colors painted perfectly inside quasi-geometrical zones. Looking at the painting, José felt empty inside. There was no spontaneous expression, no genuine feeling—just a flat, abstract jigsaw puzzle.

"Wow, what happened to you, man?" José asked Pete.

"Nothin'," Pete replied proudly. "This is the latest style; haven't you heard? It's called *hard edge*." José was dimly aware of "hard edge" from flipping through art journals, but he was stunned by the notion that art was merely a matter of changing style.

If art is just a game of style, José thought, then I want nothing to do with it. To him, painting was passion, and he had been painting his guts out. He thought a true artist was more like a creative channel of a higher reality, not an inventor of cheap tricks or clever mannerisms. The experience left him wondering how to reconcile art with life. It was 1960, and for the next six years José produced little as a painter except an occasional morose self-portrait and a lot of absent-minded doodling. He knew that, before he could ever paint again, he would have to rethink the meaning of being an artist. Two years later, this burning dilemma drove him to devote himself entirely to graduate study of art history. He wanted to understand the rebellion of modern artists whose work was becoming increasingly obscure, and why they were neglecting to create beauty and reflect cosmic wholeness.

However, before this was to occur, José would first be expelled from academia. When José, who was in the top 15 percent of his class, was named to the Dean's honor list and was only one quarter away from graduation in the spring of 1960, he was expelled from college for allegedly acting as the ringleader of a marijuana-smoking gang of students who allegedly were out to corrupt the undergraduate females. He was prohibited from setting foot in Hyde Park south of 55th Street. He felt the punishment was extreme.

Expulsion stopped him in his tracks; he was disheartened and had no idea how to break the news to his parents. He was living alone on the other side of 55th Street, working at a picture-framing gallery run by a young Jewish couple, the Altmans. Soon after being expelled, he had an accident at work. He was picking up a piece of glass to put inside a frame when the glass slipped from his hand. As he reached out with his left hand to catch it before it shattered, the corner of the glass pierced his right hand, cutting through his tendon sheathe and causing him partial loss of mobility. The Altmans rushed him to the emergency room, where a doctor sewed up and bandaged the incision. The nervous couple was apologetic to José. They had no insurance and hoped he would not sue them. He assured them everything would be fine. Relieved, the Altmans gave him a modest severance pay.

José decided there was nothing left to do but hitchhike to San Francisco and fulfill his *On the Road* beatnik dream. He spent the weekend before his departure with his friends, who had also been expelled, watching the Republican convention on television as Barry Goldwater was nominated to run against John F. Kennedy.

On Monday morning, carrying nothing but a small backpack, José went to Highway 66 in the outskirts of Chicago and put out his thumb. Within moments, a young man named Bill from Buffalo, New York, stopped to pick him up. Bill had no money and was trying to make it to Venice Beach, California. José had money *and* amphetamines, but no driver's license. It was a perfect match for a beatnik adventure. As it turned out, the young man was running away from home and had stolen the vehicle from his uncle's used car lot.

The first night, they got as far as Kansas, where they stopped and slept in an open field. The next morning José said, "Listen, Bill. I've got some amphetamines. Have you ever tried these?"

Bill had not. José told him that they would get to California faster if they took the amphetamines. So, on Tuesday morning, José and Bill ingested a handful of amphetamines and drove through Oklahoma and Texas, and into New Mexico, where they stopped and camped out under the brilliant stars.

The next morning, with cash running low and the gas tank nearly empty, José and Bill picked up a hitchhiker, used his money to fill up the gas tank, and kept driving to Los Angeles. As they were driving across the Mojave Desert, they noticed that one of the front tires was developing a bubble and the inner tube was beginning to visibly protrude. Ignoring the tire, they kept driving and somehow made it safely to Venice Beach. José stayed in Venice for a few days with Bill and his brother, and then continued hitchhiking to San Francisco.

Arriving in San Francisco in the summer of 1960 with a bandaged hand and no money did not deter José from enjoying three glorious weeks on the streets of San Francisco. He soaked in the vibrations of the bohemian community of North Beach, with its artistic coffee houses and galleries; Vesuvio's Bar and Grill and the City Lights Bookstore were key gathering places. At night, he slept at a beatnik crash pad referred to him by an old friend. He panhandled in Chinatown on Sundays to earn money for food. In those three weeks, he felt a new freedom—a liberation of his spirit that he'd never known before. Knowing this time was just an interlude on his path of destiny made the experience all the more sweet and significant.

But, before he knew it, the sweetness was replaced by a dull anxiety. José returned to Minnesota and spent a few dreary weeks with his parents, explaining his college expulsion and determining his next step. While at his parents' home, he came to a deep inner resolve to somehow return to college and finish his undergraduate studies. With focused determination, he pursued and was soon granted permission to take courses at the University of Chicago's downtown center, where he became a fiercely dedicated student majoring in humanities and German and Russian literature.

He rented an apartment on the Near North Side and took a job at Marshall Field department store. Though he still wasn't legally allowed in Hyde Park, he often ventured to 51st Street on the north edge to visit a group of friends who lived in a large apartment. One of the friends was Elena Gustaites, a Lithuanian dancer who had spent the end of the war in refugee camps in Germany. Acutely artistic, with a background as a ballerina, Elena was fond of avant-garde film and literature. She often engaged José in passionate discourses regarding art, society, and culture. Though José considered her more of a buddy and was not interested in being bound to a "serious" relationship, she was enamored of him and persistent. Soon they became lovers. By wintertime, they learned the shocking news that Elena was pregnant. Neither of them felt anywhere near ready to have a baby, and after careful consideration they agreed the only thing to do was get an abortion.

In 1960, abortions were illegal in most states, including Illinois, and were almost unheard of. They managed to track down an abortionist in a suburb of Detroit, Michigan, and shortly after Christmas took a bus ride to Detroit. While Elena was undergoing the procedure, José waited nervously in the motel room, feeling as though he was living a painful chapter right out of a Dostoevsky novel. This experience forged a heavy emotional bond between José and Elena. They soon moved into a small house together on Menomenee Street, in a slightly rundown, artist-friendly neighborhood in Chicago's Old Town.

Chapter 10
Midnight Mystic

I often think the night is more alive and
more richly colored than the day.

—Vincent Van Gogh

The summer after earning his BA from the University of Chicago in 1961, José received notice to report to his draft board for a mandatory physical exam prior to induction into the U.S. Army. There was no way he was going to allow himself to be conscripted into the military forces. The only way out was to receive a 4-F rating, meaning he would have to be utterly rejected.

Still shaken from the abortion experience with Elena and from dealing with the reverberations of his college expulsion, José's internal resources were drained. He needed structure and stability in his life, so he made a pact with Elena: If he managed to get classified as a 4-F, they would marry.

The night before the physical exam, José and his friend Clyde Flowers, a jazz musician from the University of Chicago, came up with a plan sure to make the army officials see just what objectionable characters they were. From the time he was a boy and experienced the devastating news and images of Hiroshima and Nagasaki, José resolved that war and military action were simply not humane ways to resolve issues. For this reason, he and Clyde agreed to stay up all night, drinking beer and eating beans from a can. The next morning, having had no sleep and suffering from a bad hangover and the beans going through their systems, José and Clyde reported for the physical exam. José looked and smelled horrible and also answered positively to all the key questions: Yes, he was a homosexual. Yes, he had had homosexual experiences. Yes, he used drugs.

At the end of the exam, he was called into an office to meet with a psychiatrist, who told him he had severe psychiatric problems and was therefore going to be classified as 4-F. The psychiatrist highly recommended he begin therapy, immediately. Though José knew the therapy prescription was probably accurate at that time, he was happy that his objective to maintain a credo of nonviolence and nonmilitary action was fulfilled.

On November 11th (11/11) of that year, 22-year-old José married 21-year-old Elena in a traditional wedding at Bond Chapel, a small gothic church at the University of Chicago. José took a job as a telephone clerk at Kroch's and Brentano's, a bookstore not far from their house. José liked being in the company of books, but the work was unsatisfying. His only hope of survival, he decided, was to enroll in graduate school. Ultimately, he viewed graduate school as an institutional game, but it was a game he felt he had to play in order to acquire the necessary discipline and worldly credibility to go where he had to go and do what he had to do—even though he had no idea what that might be. By then he was certain he would never travel the route of the modern painter. He was more interested in studying artistic and cultural values so he might unravel the dilemma of modern art. Once he found that out, he was certain he would know what to do.

In the fall of 1962, he was admitted into the Master's degree program in art history at the University of Chicago, one of the elite graduate schools in the country. José and Elena moved back to the Hyde Park area and took up residence in a modest three-room apartment. Elena dropped out of college and took a full-time job as a secretary in the department of history at the University of Chicago in order to financially support José through graduate school. Because of his undergraduate performance, many professors were wary of him, but he quickly proved he was a dedicated student. In his spare time, he pursued his interest in ancient Mexico. Because no classes were offered on the subject, he independently applied his knowledge of other cultures to his analysis and understanding of the history of ancient Mexico.

Late at night, José studied the writings of many mystics, including Jacob Boehme. His favorite classes were those with mystical undercurrents exploring the nature of perception and form, such as medieval art history and aesthetics. He loved the neo-Platonist philosophers, particularly the work of Plotinus, and the medieval mystics Meister Eckhart, St. Theresa, and St. John of the Cross. He also discovered

Perennial Philosophy by Aldous Huxley, which he considered a brilliant, unitive summation of Eastern and Western mysticism. The principle of unitive thought was of utmost importance to him, and he sought out works that spoke of this unity.

Because of this view, José was able to develop a highly critical perception of the history of art, particularly the history of modern art. He was acutely aware that, as the emphasis on individualism increases, the quality of the sacred decreases. At this point he was not yet familiar with the terms *esoteric* or *hermetic*; it was all just mysticism to him. It was only after he went to Paris in 1965 and experienced LSD for the first time that the hermetic doors swung open. His LSD experiences would give him what he felt was a direct experiential confirmation of truths perceived by the mystics.

Although he appreciated Elena's support, José wasn't content living a routine, conventional existence. For a while, the marriage had provided the stability they both seemed to need; however, as José's visionary horizons began to soar, he soon felt he was drowning in bleak, passionless oblivion. A wild fire was growing in him. He thought maybe he didn't fit the husband mold. One night, after a prolonged period of sobriety, he went out for a night of drinking and got beaten up by a gang of boys.

After this experience, José sought help from therapist Gerald Vogel, who invited him to be a subject in his dream laboratory experiment. Therefore, on certain nights of the week at precisely 11 p.m., José reported to the dream lab. He would lie down on a bed and an assistant would attach 17 electrodes onto his head. Then the lights would go out, and he would fall asleep. Whenever he had a dream, a voice sounded from a speaker wall next to his bed: "Mr. Arguelles. Mr. Arguelles. Could you please tell us what you were just dreaming?" He would roll over to face the speaker wall and report his dream, which was recorded as research data for Dr. Vogel.

For José, the dream lab opened a secret window into the realm of mystery. It provided a refreshing contrast to the somewhat drab, ordinary life of a hardworking graduate student and husband. In one episode, he dreamed that he was walking down the beach in Greece in the 19th century talking about the impact of industrialism on the artist—but he soon realized that this was not a dream at all, but a vivid past life recollection. When the voice called on him to report his dream, he heard it but he could not speak. He felt he was on a very long journey spiraling through time, and it seemed to take him forever to finally return to the dream bed and report the so-called dream. At that moment, José remembered the precognitive dream he had experienced when he was 14 after returning from Teotihuacán. Somehow, he knew, the two experiences were linked. And somehow, these paranormal time-traveling dream episodes had something to do with what he had read in *Perennial Philosophy* and the search for the One. Suddenly, he realized that everything was connected to his Great Search.

The mystical interests connected with José's experience at Teotihuacán found their way into his studies. He realized he had a deeper motive than to simply earn an MA or PhD in art history. The experience at Teotihuacán and the experience in the painting studio were connected, as were discoveries he was making of 18th- and 19th-century European art. Although he really loved studying the art of India, China, and Japan because it represented something whole and sacred, he knew he had to focus on modern European Romantic art in order to understand his deeper existential dilemma.

In this process, his mentor and guardian, Joshua Taylor, guided him. Taylor, a professor of modern art, was a veritable father figure to José and championed his cause against the other, more conservative, professors. Without Taylor's help and guidance, José would not have been admitted into graduate school.

Taylor, a studious bachelor with a vacation house in Taxco, Mexico, made a name for himself as an expert on the Italian "Futurist" movement and later went on to become the curator of the art division of the Smithsonian Institution. Sensitive to José's interests, Taylor guided him in the direction of Romanticism, as much for its theory as for the actual works of art it produced. José came to understand that the Romantic artists were dealing with the loss of the sacred view in their own world of early-19th-century industrial Europe.

As he read about Romantic artists and their theories, José identified with their cause. For his master's thesis, he wrote a paper on the little-known English visionary painter Samuel Palmer. During the 1820s, while Palmer was a disciple of William Blake, he produced a small body of unique and luminous landscapes. José probed the nature and meaning of Palmer's eccentric vision, exposing an attempt to capture the cosmic style of earlier medieval art. However, José found a pattern in Palmer's life that was repeated by other modern artists: a great flash of inspiration in youth, but an inability to sustain the vision. José considered Palmer's later work ordinary and bourgeois; he had produced comfortable landscapes that the upper-middle-class patrons of urban London appreciated. Seeing this common pattern of self-sabotage among artists made a deep impression on José. Wondering if *he* would be able to sustain his own vision, he resolved not to succumb to the pressures of society to conform.

In June 1963, José received his master's degree in art history and was awarded a full-tuition scholarship for his first year of study in the PhD program. Around this time, he and Elena traveled to New York City for Ivan's wedding to Marilla Calhoun Elder, an artistically inclined Southern woman Ivan had met at the University of Chicago. The somewhat bohemian wedding took place on the Upper West Side of Manhattan Island in New York City. During the wedding, it became apparent to José how far apart he and his brother had grown. Whereas his own lifestyle was formal and academic, Ivan's was comparatively anarchic, with much the same flavor of his beatnik years. Ivan was still in search of himself. Ultimately, he launched a career as a librarian and poet.

Chapter 11
Peace and Dharma

*I have a dream that one day every valley shall be
exalted, every hill and mountain shall be made
low, the rough places will be made straight and
the glory of the Lord shall be revealed and all
flesh shall see it together.*

—Martin Luther King, Jr.

D uring the summer of 1963, the civil rights movement became
very active both in the South and in northern cities like Chicago.
José became interested in the Student National Coordinating
Council (SNCC), a radical, student-oriented organization at the university, as well as Martin Luther King's Southern Christian Leadership
Conference (SCLC).

Many of José's closest friends were black students and artists—all of
whom made him acutely aware of the gross injustice African Americans
had suffered over the previous 300 years in the white-dominant
American society. He heard stories of lynchings in the South and saw
firsthand the notoriously bad living conditions in the ghettoes of the
Westside and Southside of Chicago. Deeply stirred, José participated
in marches through segregated neighborhoods, where people were resisting the right of blacks to buy property. He also tutored black inner-city high school children in the subjects of history, art, and culture.

The big buzz in all civil rights activities that summer was the March
on Washington, organized by Martin Luther King, Jr. After educating
himself about the event, José decided he had to be there. Before he
knew it, he was on a chartered train from Chicago to Washington,
D.C., with many other activists.

Arriving in Washington on the morning of August 28, 1963, José felt surges of positive energy as he entered the great masses gathered for the cause of social justice and world peace. The feeling of solidarity between more than 200,000 black and white people held an inexplicable power that penetrated his core. This well-organized march took them from central Washington to the Mall and ended in front of the Lincoln Memorial.

Upon reaching their destination, the mood grew celebratory and festive. Unforgettable performances by artists such as Joan Baez and Bob Dylan, who sang "Blowin' in the Wind," dominated the main stage of the Lincoln Memorial. But, of course, the most memorable moment was the electrifying "I Have a Dream" speech, powerfully delivered by none other than Martin Luther King, Jr. Once the rally was over, the crowd spontaneously broke into an inspired rendition of "We Shall Overcome" before peacefully dispersing. For José, Martin Luther King, Jr. was a genuine hero and example. He knew the courage and vision he possessed were true virtues to be emulated. He thought it fortunate and rare for a person to have a real cause to devote and dedicate one's life to.

On November 22, 1963, José was absorbed in his graduate studies in the basement coffee shop at Swift Hall at the university when the news rang out that John F. Kennedy had been assassinated. Everything stopped. The world came to a standstill. Waves of shock rippled through the air. José went to his friend's house to watch the news on television and then joined the rest of the nation for deep reflection and mourning. The impact of John F. Kennedy's style and charisma had been tremendous. He had instilled confidence in the people; under his leadership, it seemed a bright new world was about to dawn. But it was not to be so—at least not at that time. Further shock waves followed when, on the third day after the assassination, Jack Ruby shot Lee Harvey Oswald on live television. José knew that nothing would ever be the same again. Bob Dylan's song "The Times They Are A-Changin'" took on prophetic meaning. With Kennedy's assassination, the impulse to be a pacifist and devote one's life to creating a peaceful world that was awakened by the March on Washington became a living value for José.

Soon after, he attended a series of lectures on existentialism at the University of Chicago, given by Edward Conze, famous erudite Buddhist scholar. In some ways, José had been prepared for his encounter with

Buddhism during Mr. Bepler's existential theology class at Valparaiso. Now he was finally in the appropriate state of sobriety and personal disillusionment to clearly receive Conze's messages about the dharma.

The existentialists and Buddhists agreed on the first three of the Four Noble Truths, Conze said: life is suffering; the cause of suffering is desire; and the cessation of desire is the cessation of suffering. However, he said, the Existentialists leave it at that, while the Buddhists adhere to the fourth truth, which states that there is an actual way or path to follow, which they call the path of dharma. Conze said the path of dharma requires taking responsibility for your own life and laying no blame on anyone else. He said the cause of all suffering stems from personal cravings and desires. To José, these words were revolutionary. Never before had he heard these kinds of words spoken so plainly.

Conze explained that to follow the dharma is to follow the Eightfold Path: right view, right thought, right intention, right speech, right action, right livelihood, right effort, and right mindfulness. Until then, José had never considered the possibility of such a path. He was irresistibly drawn to this new way of thinking and knew it was the missing piece he needed to understand the workings of his own mind. He realized that to satisfy his inner seeking and yearning, he had to adopt some form of discipline or mind training. He was determined to learn everything he could about the path of dharma.

Chapter 12
Visions of Quetzalcoatl

And Quetzalcoatl sailed into the ocean on a raft of serpents, vowing to come back on the day sacred to his name, in the year sacred to his name.

—Laurette Séjourné

Plumed Serpent, Quetzalcoatl, Xochicalco. Photo courtesy of the Foundatino for the Advancement of Mesoamerican Studies, Inc. (www.famsi.org).

During the summer of 1964, José and Elena took a trip to Mexico with their friend Bob Ferry, whose parents had an apartment in Acapulco. To prepare for the trip, José read *The Plumed Serpent* by D.H. Lawrence, and absorbed as much as he could of Laurette Sejourne's writings about Teotihuacán and the religion of ancient Mexico. These lucid writings awakened in him a deep affinity with Quetzalcoatl, the Mexican prophet.

Mystified by the multiple qualities and characteristics of Quetzalcoatl, José spent many long hours contemplating this mythic hero. Was he the original cultural hero? Was there more than one Quetzalcoatl? Was Quetzalcoatl the prophet of ancient Mexico, the equivalent of a Buddha or Christ? How could his message become relevant again today? José identified with the enigma and the captivating power of Quetzalcoatl as a prophet; the symbol of the serpent with feathers represented the marriage of Earth and sky, of life and beyond. The opposites united in Quetzalcoatl, and that was what José was thirsting for most. Through the stories of Quetzalcoatl, José felt the possibility of human form embodying the grand, cosmic structure.

After the visit to Xochicalco, sacred to Quetzalcoatl, Bob drove José and Elena to Acapulco. José couldn't get the Quetzalcoatl story out of his mind. He spent his days body surfing and contemplating Quetzalcoatl, while Elena and Bob Ferry sat on the beach chatting about what José considered trivial matters. One day, after he had been body surfing for more than eight hours, fully absorbed in the contemplation of Quetzalcoatl, a great chill seized him, and he became very ill. Elena and Bob took him to the upstairs apartment. As he tried to resist succumbing to the waves of vertigo seizing him, he knew something was terribly wrong. Elena took his temperature; it was between 104 and 105 degrees.

Early the next morning, a worried Elena and Bob helped José into Bob's sports car and sped off to Mexico City at top speed. Bob's parents, American businesspeople living in Mexico City, saw to it that José was immediately put into a private hospital, where he was diagnosed with paratyphoid fever—a deadly virus. Elena flew back to Chicago to resume work, and Bob stayed with José, who was confined to the hospital bed for five more days.

For the first few days, he was covered with ice packs and fed intravenously. Lying in his hospital bed in a state of delirium and high fever, José heard ancient voices murmuring in other tongues. Then he saw the cosmic civilization of the Maya surrounded by great tropical flowers. Two people appeared above him, a man and a woman dressed in Mayan regalia. They beckoned him, calling, comforting; they began to move, to dance and chant. In his feverish state, José saw a clear image of himself returning from the jungle with some type of treasure or knowledge.

After coming to, José realized he had had a near-death experience, and that it was intimately connected with Quetzalcoatl and with his vision at Teotihuacán. The near-death experience caused him to re-examine his entire existence and led him into deeper mystical ponderings about himself, his own nature, and human destiny. After José had recovered from the virus, Bob Ferry drove him back to Chicago. As they passed through Texas and Oklahoma, José had an eerie sensation that all of the suburban tract homes he saw baking in the hot sun would someday be blown away.

He began his last year of graduate school at the University of Chicago in 1964 with his near-death experience at the forefront of his consciousness. A new determination filled his being; he felt a strong need to cultivate his inner will. He and Elena were now worlds apart.

José, graduate school, at his parents' home, 1964. Image courtesy of and copyright the José Arguelles Archive.

He realized their marriage had been born of insecurity and desperation, and he was increasingly aware that they had little in common. He knew something else was awaiting him.

José was unsure what would follow this second year of doctoral studies. The best fellowship available was the Fulbright, but the competition was high, and only one scholarship per year was awarded to the graduate studies program in art history. Should he stay with Elena and settle for the less-than-appealing job offer from Temple University in Philadelphia? (José equated taking this job with succumbing to a mundane, conventional existence.) He explored this option and even made a trip to Philadelphia, where he had lunch and martinis with a group of conventional university employees in the suburbs. This appeared to be the only opportunity presented to him, and he reluctantly resolved to accept the offer.

Fortunately, in the nick of time, a college mentor, John Rewald, presented another option. José felt a great rapport with Rewald, who was a practical and worldly man but, because he did not hold a PhD, was not regarded highly by many professors at the University of Chicago. Rewald helped secure a Samuel H. Kress fellowship for José, affording him a year of free study in Paris on the topic of Neo-impressionism, with no strings attached. José considered this a better deal than the Fulbright scholarship; he would get a stipend and didn't have to report to anyone. He felt something higher calling. The opportunity meant freedom, and he knew he couldn't take Elena. A painful break-up followed, for which José suffered greatly while in Paris.

Chapter 13
Alchemical Paris

An artist has no home in Europe
except in Paris.

—Friedrich Nietzsche

A tired José arrived in Paris in the fall of 1965. He thought the city, with its quaint urban architecture and very few tall modern buildings, looked like a big stage set from a 19th-century opera. Antiquarian bookstores full of esoteric literature gave him a mystical feeling of walking through a strange alchemical museum. Because many of José's favorite writers, as well as artists like Toulouse-Lautrec, Van Gogh, and Gauguin, had all lived in Paris, being in Paris felt like a waking dream. To José, Paris was the capital of the original bohemian. But he was arriving not as a bohemian, but as an academic who had just separated from his wife. It was the fall of 1965 and José, then 26, felt both a sense of excitement and an impending identity crisis.

A University of Chicago colleague, who was in Paris on a Fulbright scholarship, met him and helped him find a room—a sixth-floor walk-up in a small hotel on the Left Bank, one block from the River Seine. The narrow room was perfect for José. Looking out the window and craning his neck to the right, he could see the Eiffel Tower, which told him he was really in Paris. The room was equipped with a mini-sink, and the bathroom and shower were located on the floor below. Because it cost money to take a shower, José showered only once a week and the rest of the time cleaned himself at the sink. To him, the little room was his reward for having been a good student. He was now free to fulfill his bohemian dream—it was only a matter of when and how it would happen. Meanwhile, he felt obliged to fulfill his academic obligations.

While first in Paris, José spent most of his free time in his room, reflecting and writing profusely in his journal about art and alienation. He was later introduced to hashish and often rolled a hashish cigarette (European-style with tobacco), took a puff in his room, and drifted into an existential reverie that bordered on identity crisis.

He had heard about psychedelics and read about Timothy Leary, whom he would later meet. In 1960, Leary had had his first psychotropic experience in Cuernavaca, Mexico. After ingesting seven sacred mushrooms, Leary experienced conditioned layers coming off, causing him to feel revulsion with the current state of mind and consciousness. José admired Leary's psychedelic prayers and creative rendition of the *Tibetan Book of the Dead*. From reading Aldous Huxley's *Doors of Perception*, José knew there was something to psychedelics, and as soon as the opportunity arose in November 1965, he experimented.

He went to a friend's house and found a man at a table creating blotter acid. Another man and two girls were there. José ingested a tab of acid and went back to his hotel room to get some hashish for the French girls, who were afraid to try acid. He went back outside, only to discover that the streets were bedecked with dazzling diamonds and emeralds. "Oh my God," he thought, "this must be the experience Plotinus was talking about!" When he returned to his companions with the hashish, it was apparent to him that they were playing social games. Seeking a deeper experience, José returned to his own room alone with a few more tabs of LSD.

A few days later, alone in his room, he took a couple of LSD tabs. He felt the drug take effect as he lay on his long, narrow bed, which gave him the sensation of being in a wooden coffin that was floating in the South Pacific. Surrendering to the psychedelic impulse beckoning him to let go of all he had known himself to be, he felt layers of conditioning peel away. He drifted back to his childhood room on Seventh Avenue and flew through the portal of the painting of the South Pacific. Lying on his bed, he directly experienced his own death and rebirth, a phenomenon he'd only read about. He let himself float in bliss through the cosmic void.

As some semblance of a known thinking layer re-emerged, José realized he was experiencing what was written in neo-Platonist philosophy. He thought, "So this is what they are talking about when they talk about the One and all the mystical stuff." Re-entering his body, he felt a renewal of spirit and realized, for the first time, how precious was human life. He was filled with joy just to be alive and relieved to know there was much more to life than he had ever imagined.

It was after midnight. He went outside and walked the streets all night, feeling the whole of humanity to be a grand, theatrical event with all of the people playing out various archetypes. In his heightened state of awareness, civilization revealed itself as an elaborate game, a game most people weren't aware they were playing. This insight confirmed his deepest perceptions of reality: People are living a fake life. This was the same perception José had as a boy at Teotihuacán but couldn't articulate. Why did the normative values of modern society have to be so far from a true, genuine, everyday cosmic experience?

Morning found him still in an exalted state. Perusing the English bookstore, he found *The Life of Milarepa*, translated by Evans-Wentz, which told the redemptive story of the famous Tibetan saint. That same day, he was instinctively led to the Musee Guimet Museum, where he mused over a large collection of Tibetan paintings. He felt the LSD had put him in touch with states of consciousness akin to the mindset of the Tibetan paintings. Reading *The Life of Milarepa*, José felt certain he had been Milarepa in a past life. The book was a key that later put him on the search for a living Tibetan master.

The psychedelic revolution in the 1960s created a new wave of interest in esoteric or hermetic thought. It was in Paris that José first became interested in esoteric arcane studies, although he had become aware of alchemy as a graduate student when he studied iconography. In medieval art and the history of wooden engravings, etchings, and other media, José had discovered that much of what the West refers to as the "esoteric" or "alchemical arts" was actually transmitted through the medium of woodblock prints or copperplate etchings, and also could be found on gothic cathedrals, sculptures, and stained glass windows.

Access to this arcane information was limited in graduate school. But the few teachers who appreciated these themes allowed José to investigate the underground, invisible tradition from ancient times, continuing to Europe, through the Middle Ages, and into the Renaissance.

His study of symbolism prepared José to meet a mysterious American man in Paris who introduced him to the *I Ching, the Book of Changes*. The man told José that the *I Ching* was "a book that talks" and that, while he was serving a jail sentence for drug possession in Morocco, the *I Ching* kept him spiritually alive. José thought maybe there was a truth to the *I Ching* he had not yet perceived.

While in Paris, José came across the work of Swiss artist Adolph Wolfli in a magazine called *Art Brut*. He was struck by Wolfli's intricate work, which portrayed deep harmony with mandalic and archetypal themes. He appreciated that Wolfli viewed himself as a "creative channel of expression" rather than as a "modern" artist.

By contemplating Wolfli's work, José realized the initiatic aspect to art. From ancient to historic times, the creation of art was analogous to initiation into a mystery or a process that, through specific stages, revealed the divine process of creation. José felt this view was not present in most modern-day artists. Nineteen years later, José would travel to Switzerland and view Wolfli's original paintings in the state museum in Bern.

Each morning, he reported to the Bibliotheque National. He lined up to get one of the 400 available seats and continue his research on the Neo-impressionist painter Paul Signac, whom his mentor John Rewald had suggested he study. In the course of combing through literary journals of the 1880s and 1890s, José was struck by one character, Charles Henry, a French psycho-mathematician. By Henry's own self-definition, a psycho-mathematician was one who applied the rigors of mathematical analysis to the study of the sense experiences and their impact on the organs of perception. Henry was born in 1859 and, during the 1880s, his ideas of a "scientific aesthetic" greatly influenced what came to be known as "post-impressionist" painting, especially the work of pointillist Georges Seurat. José found Henry's work far ahead of its time; it would later become the topic of his PhD dissertation.

At this time, José was also researching the location of the original self-portrait of Van Gogh that depicted him with a bandaged ear. He had painted it after he was thrown into an insane asylum for sending a package with a slice of his ear to a prostitute who had rejected him. José had just read an essay, "Van Gogh the Artist Suicided by Society," by Antonin Artaud of France, who initiated the "Theatre of the Absurd."

After reading the article, José was astonished to discover that the portrait was in the possession of a steel millionaire, Leigh Block, who lived in a penthouse high above Lake Michigan in Chicago. José thought it ironic that this self-portrait by Van Gogh, painted when he was in a most desperate state, was now in the collection of a multimillionare who had the leisure to assemble a catalog of Van Gogh's private collection.

One day, while routinely gathering facts about the life of Signac, it suddenly dawned on José that Signac was just another fake artist; he claimed he was a Socialist and then adapted his art to modern styles. Continuing these studies suddenly felt meaningless. In a state of lucidity, José realized that he was spending all his time sitting in a library, piecing together a dead painter's life, while his own life was passing by. Looking around at the other 399 people in the bibliotheque, he couldn't help but wonder if they weren't all caught up in the same hypnotic farce. "How tragic," he thought, as he walked out of the bibliotheque, never to return. Under the Samuel H. Kress fellowship, he wasn't required to report to anyone, so he made a decision: "Now I'm going to live!"

With that thought and intent on changing his scene, he took his trusty journal and ventured to the Old Navy Café on the Boulevard St. Germain. No sooner had he begun writing in his journal than an Argentine man, Enrique, appeared and initiated a conversation. They became fast friends, and Enrique regularly took José to numerous cafes, introducing him to a wide array of eccentric people. Enrique also took him to Algerian and Moroccan clubs where hashish was readily available.

This experience gave José confidence; he had learned that, when he set his mind to change, he could simply change. He noted that, as his perspective and attitude changed, a whole other world opened up. By some standards, the world that had opened up was a degenerate world, but it provided the lessons he needed to learn at the time.

Chapter 14
Seeing the White Light

*Be thou the rainbow in the storms of life. The
evening beam that smiles the clouds away,
and tints tomorrow with prophetic ray.*

—Lord Byron

In late fall of 1965, José met Pamela Foley, a straight and serious student who had just earned an undergraduate degree in literature and philosophy. Tall, with dark hair and green eyes, Pamela came from a well-cultured family near Boston, Massachusetts. She was taking the year off to enjoy Paris and working part-time as a waitress.

By wintertime, Pamela was José's constant companion. He loved taking her to places such as Pere Lachaise Cemetery, where many famous 19th-century French artists and authors were buried. (Jim Morrison was later buried there, as well.) On cemetery visits, José consumed alcohol and over-the-counter drugs, and declaimed madly about art and society.

As the Americans began bombing North Vietnam in March, creating national and worldwide outrage, José experienced a near-fatal moment in Paris. Around the middle of March, after a prolonged period of drinking, smoking hashish, and ingesting an over-the-counter drug called Nubaren, José blacked out. He remembered boarding a subway train to visit Pamela, but he never made it.

Groggy and disoriented, José woke up in a pitch-dark room to the sound of rattling coughs and strange gurgling noises. He was in the throwaway ward at Lannec General Hospital, the place for people with no identification who are found in bad condition on the streets. The gurglings were the death rattles of several people breathing their final breath. "What is going on?" he wondered. "How did I get here?"

The hospital authorities told him that, when he got off the subway train at its last stop, he lurched forward, almost falling onto the tracks, but at the last moment, someone reached out and saved him. The police arrived and took him to the hospital.

After he had regained consciousness, a few psychiatrists examined him, asking rote questions: "What was your upbringing like?" and "How did your mother treat you as a child?" In deep despair and anguish over the direction his life seemed to be taking, José resolved to hitchhike to Afghanistan and become a hashish dealer.

On the second afternoon of his stay at the hospital, Pamela showed up. He wondered how she had found him. After he hadn't shown up for two nights, she knew something was wrong and went to his hotel. The concierge told her that he was in the hospital. But how did the hotel concierge know?

As fate would have it, the man who had saved José was a musical student from Harvard who had lived in the room just below him at the hotel. He had been on the same train as José and recognized him, even though they had never formally met. The man had noticed José's deteriorating, drugged-out condition and stayed on the train with him until the end stop to make sure he was okay. At the last stop, the man got off the train and then caught José when he almost fell onto the tracks.

José was released from the hospital after a few days. He was still shaky. Pamela accompanied him back to the hotel, where he immediately went to the concierge and inquired about the man who saved him.

"Not here anymore," said the concierge. "He checked out this morning to go back to the United States." José was in awe and was certain his guardian angels were watching over him.

"But," the concierge added, "there is a letter here for you, Mr. Arguelles." José took the letter and thanked the concierge. He glanced at the return address: Princeton University. He didn't know anyone at Princeton and wondered what this could be about. He and Pamela went to his room where he opened the letter. He was astounded to find he was being offered a job as an assistant professor in the department of art history at Princeton University, a position he had never even applied for! He sat on his bed in a state of complete astonishment.

As it turned out, his other graduate school mentor, Josh Taylor, a Princeton graduate, pulled some strings behind the scenes on his behalf, just as John Rewald had. José wondered if, despite all appearances, he wasn't leading some kind of charmed life. But why? And what did it mean? He accepted the job immediately.

In April 1966, Elena, who was living with a jazz critic in New York, came to Paris for a brief visit. The meeting was amicable, though bittersweet, as they both knew it was nothing but a friendly interlude to tie up loose ends. José took Elena to the south of France, where they stayed at John Rewald's 14th-century chateau. They continued to Barcelona, Spain, where José witnessed his first and last bullfight. The blood of the bulls made him sick to his stomach, but he closed his eyes and told himself, "My name is Arguelles. I can't possibly get sick at a bullfight."

From Barcelona, José and Elena made their way south, across the Strait of Gibraltar and into Morocco. Being in Arabic/Islamic country was thrilling for José. He found the land mysterious and the people warm and friendly. He and Elena enjoyed drinking tea in the teahouses and restaurants. From Morocco, they headed back up through the historical and picturesque city of Grenada, then on to Madrid, where they agreed to part ways. It was a sad moment, but they both knew it was for the best.

After saying goodbye to Elena, José took a train to the "Arguelles" subway station and found a bar called "Arguelles" on the "Arguelles" plaza. The next day, José contacted Pamela in London. They agreed to meet in Venice, Italy, and commence a historical art tour. He took a long train ride along the beautiful Rivera from Madrid, across Spain and Southern France, and then into Italy, where Pamela greeted him. Together they traveled to Florence and Rome. They found their way, by boat, to the Island of Corfu, where José was determined to re-read Homer's *Odyssey* on the beach.

One morning José arose early and, with a copy of the *Odyssey* in hand, rode his rented bicycle to the beach where Ulysses had supposedly been shipwrecked. Not long after he sat down to read, a Greek peasant woman appeared out of nowhere, and gave him some bread, cheese, and a bottle of red wine. By noon, he had drunk the wine and eaten the bread and cheese. He got on his bicycle and rode to the top of the mountain in the middle of Corfu. Already rather drunk and thirsty, he stopped at a tavern filled with little old Greek farmers drinking beer. He went to the counter, ordered a beer, and chatted with the farmers. They were delighted to know he came from Chicago and insisted he must know some of their relatives there.

The beer was too much for him. After leaving the bar, he flew down the mountain on his bicycle and, before he knew it, found himself lying on his back in a field, the bicycle some distance away, upside down, its wheels still turning. As he tried to sit up, a jagged pain shot through his left shoulder. A number of Greek peasant women came to help him, followed by an ancient-looking police van. He was taken to the men's hospital with a broken collarbone protruding from his left shoulder, where they told him the doctor would not be in until the morning.

That night, after the alcohol wore off, the pain became unbearable. He knew that in order to alleviate the pain he had to concentrate his mind in a way he had never done before. With that thought, he summoned all of his energy and instinctively focused his attention on understanding the nature of time.

He entered a profound concentration and saw a vast, all-encompassing spherical structure. Within the structure, he viewed the universe as different levels and workings of time. The degree of his mental absorption was so complete that he lost all awareness of pain and fully understood the power of the concentrated mind. He knew the insight he was receiving regarding the nature of time had many facets that he would later explore—when the time was right.

He later chalked up this experience as the high point of his mythic shipwrecked Odyssey stage and a precursor of what was to come. (In 1993, he received a mysterious text, *From Distant Tulan*, which began with a shipwreck. The members of the crew included many mythic figures from early history, including Homer.)

Pamela escorted José to Athens and then to Cape Sounion. His arm and shoulder were bandaged up in a sling. There on the wild rugged coast of Greece, José realized that this was the place he had visited in his astral body while in the dream lab. He must have been Lord Byron, he thought, who had been in Greece in the 1820s. From Greece, José and Pamela journeyed to Istanbul, Turkey.

José always had been greatly intrigued by the Islamic world and was excited to experience the culture firsthand. When he entered the ancient city of Istanbul, a great sense of mystery enclosed him as he viewed unfamiliar traditions and heard a language that sounded impenetrable. He visited the great mosques and was in awe of the overwhelming sense of sacred space they provided. He contrasted the mosques with Christian churches and cathedrals, which were filled with

José, "Lord Byron," Greece, 1966. Image courtesy of and copyright the José Argeuelles Archive.

images and intended for mass public events. The Blue Mosque, with its numerous Oriental carpets spread out across the floor, particularly affected him. Traditional Muslim Salat prayers were performed there five times a day. The intricate geometric designs in the carpets deeply impressed him; he felt that in their pure abstraction they were superior to the so-called abstract paintings of modern art. These carpets would later influence a series of his paintings known as the *Doors of Perception*.

From Istanbul, José and Pamela took the Orient Express to Belgrade, Budapest, and then to Vienna, where they separated. By this time, she was fed up with his intense lifestyle. He bought a copy of the book *Analects of Confucius* and then traveled to Amsterdam alone, before returning to Paris.

On one occasion, a bald, muscular Middle Eastern man approached José while he was drinking a bottle of wine in a Paris park. The man stared at José for a few moments and then said, "You are really a lot better than that. You shouldn't be doing that." It was a turning point; José knew he had to change.

From Paris, he flew to Minnesota for a brief visit with his parents. They were beside themselves with pride that their son had gotten his first teaching job at Princeton University. Almost speechless in his presence, they treated José like some enigmatic wonder boy who was finally redeeming himself for all the trouble he had caused.

While visiting his parents, he had a powerful dream in which he saw a print by hard-edge artist Ellsworth Kelly, which he'd had up on his wall in Paris. As he looked at the print, a voice said: "This is the way but this isn't it." He could not get this phrase out of his mind and pondered its meaning on the train ride from Minnesota to Chicago. He stayed in Chicago for four weeks with his old friends Martha and Norbert Scott while working at Kroch's and Brentano's bookstore to earn money to get to Princeton.

One day, while sitting alone contemplating his existence on a park bench in Grant Park facing Lake Michigan, he suddenly saw his entire life go by in a flash, from the time he was born on this planet, as well as parallel and future lives. Seeing the scope of his life from such a wide perspective, he realized he was already complete and therefore did not need anyone or anything to validate himself. His future self glimmered before him as he saw his streaming destiny pattern connecting his present self with who he was to become. This vision instantaneously transformed his mind, and he immediately bought art supplies.

Fourteen years later, in 1980, he would meet Buckminster Fuller, who shared with him that he, too, had a key visionary experience along the shores of Lake Michigan in Chicago. Fuller's experience led him into the realm of synergetics, geodesic domes, and new models of reality for a tired humanity. José's experience led him into the realm of time travel, parallel universes, and the discovery of a new galactic dispensation for the planet.

PART III

Through the Doors of Perception, See the Whole Earth

Chapter 15
Princeton and Visions of Venus

The purpose of art is to stop time.

—Bob Dylan

José's psychedelic painting "Mandala," 1968. Image courtesy of and copyright the José Arguelles Archive.

Arriving at Princeton in the fall of 1966, José moved into a studio apartment above a pancake house across the street from the university. He viewed Princeton as a gentle, yet elite, boy's school where there was an overall aristocratic atmosphere. Many of the students had graduated from prestigious prep schools, and an attitude of relaxed confidence pervaded the university. Because they were attending one of the nation's most respected universities, an unspoken feeling prevailed of everyone having "already made it."

Starting as an assistant professor in art history, his main duty was to moderate discussion groups initiated by the head professor. Though the job was easy and enjoyable, it was not entirely challenging. He soon met another young assistant professor from a different department, Ralph Abraham, who would later become a well-known mathematician and chaos theorist.

With his "outer world" in place, José's inner life flourished. Floodgates into more esoteric streams of thought rapidly opened, and he began the ardent study of Wilhelm Baynes edition of the *I Ching*, supplemented with studies of Tibetan mysticism, shamanism, and aboriginal thought. Study of the *I Ching* led him to the works of Carl Jung and Mircea Eliade, philosopher of comparative religion.

With his formative education complete, he was able to focus his acquired knowledge base and life experience on pursuing his visionary aspirations. He picked up his paintbrushes again after not having painted for six years. At first, he practiced improvised painting to activate his creative juices and loosen the creative flow. Before long, images appeared on the canvas, giving him instant feedback. He discovered his stored esoteric knowledge informed his paintings by means of symbols and forms.

Through painting, he sought to discover the universal foundation of symbolic structures before they splintered into different schools of thought. He determined to catalyze the original fundamental symbolic forms to establish the basis of a new universal symbolism. Faber Birren, an American art historian and prominent color theorist, declared José a "symbolist" after viewing his paintings on a visit to Princeton. These words greatly encouraged José, who admired Birren as a scholar. Birren wrote prominently about color, color theory, and color psychology, emphasizing in *Color in Vision*, which José was reading at the time, that "beauty is the result of a good ordering of colors."

When not at the university, José spent his time experimenting with drawing and painting images that gradually evolved into forms of mandalic art. He found the mandala a powerful cosmic art form that could be used as a tool to express the sensibility of longing for the return of cosmic vision. This was the key he had been looking for. During this time of creative exploration, José was deeply influenced by the paintings of Adolph Wolfli, a Swiss artist who painted vivid, psychedelic images on what appeared to be large doors or panels. At this time, José also steeped himself in the study of the *I Ching* and was immersed in the contemplation of cosmic, geometrical designs found on Islamic rugs. He felt the patterns in the rugs freed the mind, opening it to cosmic order.

These three influences converged in him one day in early fall of 1966; the result was four cosmic works of art, later dubbed the *Doors of Perception*, after Aldous Huxley's 1954 work.

José saw that all of the changing lines in the *I Ching* came about in eight three-line trigrams. This told him that if he wanted his paintings informed by the *I Ching*, he needed eight panels. Then he thought about Wolfli's double-sided art and decided he would paint on both sides of the panels in tribute to Wolfli; this way, he would need only four panels. Deciding that full-size doors were more exciting than panels, he went to the lumberyard and bought four unfinished 6 × 2 foot doors without doorknobs and painted them white.

He divided both sides of each door into three, 2-foot-square sections and determined that the top and bottom sections would create mirror symmetry, each with a common overall geometrical design: as above, so below. The middle section would represent the place of change or the zone of transformation. His intention was to create what he called the "cosmic change booth," where one could sit in meditation surrounded by these mind-altering paintings and allow their perceptual shifts to work on the subconscious mind.

José began playing a "hippie" bamboo flute and listened to a lot of rock and roll music and Tibetan chants. While painting the *Doors of Perception*, he entered into what seemed to be a "Venusian interplanetary" state, where he felt he was seeing through the lens of the Venusians. He was aware that Venus is the planet associated with Quetzalcoatl. While he was painting the *Doors*, images continually sprang forth onto the canvas in the form of Mayan hieroglyphs. Pausing before each image, he often felt he was traveling into the center of the painting. At the peak of his concentrated effort, he found the images turning into fantastic worlds of light, color, and sound. Sometimes he even saw groups of Mayans seated in a circle, visualizing and projecting a single thought-form into a crystal ball that transferred to his mind.

At this time, José was greatly influenced by Australian Aboriginal art. At one point while deep in the throes of painting, he became aware of the presence of an Australian Aborigine in the room. The visitation became frequent, and the Aborigine communicated many telepathic messages to José about "ancient, cosmic mysteries" embedded in the mandala forms of his paintings. The Aborigine also instructed José on the importance of yogic exercise and discipline.

To José, art represented the opportunity to participate in the mysteries of creation. He found that cosmic knowledge was revealed through exploring multiple creative outlets of artistic expression. Often, he tape-recorded spontaneous monologues with himself. As soon as he pressed "record," a surprisingly vast range of characters emerged, many of whom seemed Venusian and others of whom spoke in a strange language that even he didn't understand. Inspired by these monologues, he wrote a long treatise called the "Pepsi Cola Sutra," a compilation of his best recordings that he called "pop art Buddhism."

Thanks to his friend David Johnson, whom he had known since 1957 from the Libby Pea and Corn Packing Plant, he was able to get LSD. At this time, he felt that LSD opened a bridge between history and cosmos, or a bridge between the modern mind and the aboriginal mind.

From these experiments, he learned firsthand that there are visual patterns intrinsic to the optical nerve. He witnessed the universe consisting of one giant web of light connecting all material phenomena, from the tree to the rock to the stream to the human. He saw how this interconnected webbing of the different colored matrices is a function of the optical nerve and that in conditioned social life this perceptual understanding is inhibited and suppressed. He knew that a visionary artist must present the extraordinary in such a way that anyone with eyes can see.

He set to work to activate this vision through use of bright colors and cosmic forms. He sought to create a doorway that allowed the human organism to access the inner cosmic realm by evoking different perceptual responses. By using contrasting colors, such as red and green, he created optical flickers so those receptive could catch a glimmer of this always-existing interconnected reality. The ultimate purpose of his paintings was to raise consciousness in order that people might remember another reality—a higher reality of the sacred order.

Viewing himself as a cosmic channel, José never signed his paint-

Venusian Visions, 1968. Image courtesy of and copyright the José Arguelles Archive.

ings, but instead referred to himself as a "cosmic ballpoint pen," drawing down the visionary flow from the realm of endless archetypal forms. His working motto was "ownerless in the ownerless land of vision."

Chapter 16
Group Rug

*In art, all who have done something other
than their predecessors have merited the
epithet of revolutionary; and it is they
alone who are masters.*

—Paul Gauguin

On Thanksgiving Day in 1966, José met Miriam Tarcov, a 24-year-old intellectual, Jewish artist from New York City. He was introduced to her at a party hosted by Bob Solomon, a Princeton University philosophy professor, and his wife Elke, who worked as a slide librarian in the art history department.

Miriam made an immediate impression on José, with her hand-sewn psychedelic lime and purple knit outfit, spunky sense of humor, and quick wit. Recently graduated from the University of Michigan and earning an MA in art history, Miriam was newly divorced from engineer Michael Feldberger and was living with her mother, Edith, on the Upper West Side of New York. Edith was an assistant editor of a respectable Socialist literary magazine, *Dissent*. Miriam's father, Oscar, who had died not long before, had been a playwright and close friend of writer Saul Bellow. With much in common, José and Miriam became instant friends. Emotionally, however, he was still untangling from Pamela.

On January 24, 1967, Miriam called to wish José a happy 28th birthday. It had been a while since he had heard from her and, at this time, he realized they had an inexplicable connection. Soon after the phone call, Miriam visited José at his Princeton apartment. Upon viewing his *Doors of Perception* paintings, Miriam said, "Well, why aren't these in the Museum of Modern Art?"

Sometimes José traveled to New York to visit Miriam. On one of his visits, he discovered the Nicholas Roerich Museum on the Upper West Side. He fell immediately in love with the works of Nicholas Roerich, Russian painter, poet, and traveler of the Himalayas. José found Roerich's paintings highly inspiring with their universalism of cultural and spiritual values. He admired Roerich's writings on art that sought to restore the sense of the sacred to the modern world. Roerich's work played an increasingly significant role in José's life work.

꙳

After surveying the evolution of styles throughout the history of art, when he was 28 José concluded that he was living at the "end time." He contemplated the many mythic structures and determined it was indeed the Kali Yuga: the end of the Iron Age. In Hindu cosmology, the Kali Yuga is the fourth and last age, the Dark Age. This corresponds in Western tradition to the Iron Age. José intuitively felt the imminence of the end of a huge cycle.

While a graduate student, he had inklings of this notion after reading *Post-Historic Man (1957)* by Roderick Seidenberg and *The Myth of the Eternal Return: Cosmos and History* by Mircea Eliade. The latter defined history as a fall from

José's painting "Radiant Woman," 1970. Image courtesy of and copyright the José Arguelles Archive.

grace. The only hope was a renewal of vision, which Eliade called the Great Return.

José felt an urgency to communicate this message and so he envisioned a monumental literary work entitled *Art at the Dawn of a New Magic*. This idea first came to him while painting the *Doors of Perception*. Infused with a high vision, he saw the conventions and innovations of history had worn themselves out; something radically new had to be introduced to the human mind. There had to be a new magic to elevate humanity—a magic that transcended the logical rationality of technological thinking that was pervading civilization.

He envisioned a great race of artists, psychedelic magicians arising throughout the planet, transforming reality through the power of their arts and the evocation of their minds. Through conscious artistic creations, they would tap the potential of human spirit, change the way people perceived themselves, and ultimately inaugurate the dawn of a new magic, where the collective vision would change reality.

At Princeton, José met Humphrey Osmond, the man who introduced Aldous Huxley to psychotropic substances and the first to coin the word *psychedelic* (mind-manifesting). At this time, Osmond worked at the New Jersey State Neuropsychiatric Institute, just outside of Princeton. This was one of two places left in the country that conducted legal LSD research. At that point, the effect of LSD on the world soul was phenomenal. In one of Osmond's notes to Huxley, he wrote: "To sink to Hell or soar angelic, take a pinch of psychedelic."

Working with Humphrey was a young man, Jeff Linzer, a student of Alice Bailey, who turned José on to Bailey's esoteric writings in the fall of 1967. José also was studying the works of Carl Jung and had just stumbled upon Jung's idea of the "mandala in relation to the psyche." Jung wrote in his autobiography, *Memories, Dreams and Reflections*:

> I saw that everything, all paths I had been following, all steps I had taken, were leading back to a single point – namely to the mid-point. It became increasingly plain to me that the mandala is the center. It is the exponent of all paths.

Information about the mandala was scarce in 1967, and José was grateful for any he could find. He kept his findings in a file for later use.

By the end of his first year at Princeton, José had the opportunity to teach, which he enjoyed, and by his second year he was lecturing considerably more. He taught classes about Baroque, Modern, and Renaissance art, as well as medieval art and the ancient art of Greece and Rome. These were not his topics of choice, but he always challenged himself to learn something new.

In class, he often spoke out against the war to his students, and in the late spring of 1967 he attended the New York Be-In, a follow up to the previous San Francisco Be-In. This event drew thousands of people and surged with spontaneous artistic activity, big drumming circles, lots of marijuana smoking, and, in general, beautiful people demonstrating love for one another.

Following this event came the infamous March on the Pentagon. José boarded one of the many buses hauling thousands of peace activists from New York to Washington, where he marched with the masses across the bridge from Washington, D.C., to Arlington, Virginia. They approached the Pentagon, which was surrounded by protestors (known as yippies, the radical wing of the hippies) on flatbed trucks, who were painted like Aborigines, and chanting and reciting mantras to "exorcise the evil" within the Pentagon. As José and the rest of the peace activists ran toward the Pentagon to join the protest, led by Abbie Hoffman, helicopters swooped down, spraying the crowd with teargas. Shortly after, the police arrived and dispersed the crowd. After the military put an end to the Pentagon march, the participants retreated over the bridge back to Washington, with many saying, "Let's go home and watch this on television."

José concluded through his Alice Bailey studies that the March on Washington was an attempted act of seventh ray ceremonial magic to dispel hatred with love—and that this was the reason it attracted military opposition. He would have a similar experience with military control 28 years later when he organized a group of peace activists at Trinity Site in New Mexico to protest the 50th anniversary of the first nuclear explosion.

José and Elena's divorce was complete in the fall of 1967. Soon after, Miriam moved into his Princeton apartment. Having also studied art history, Miriam had similar feelings as José about modern art; the two enjoyed many long conversations about culture, art, and politics. Their intellectual discourse soon gave way to creative expression.

Immersed in the psychedelic subculture, José and Miriam found they loved to paint together, often on the same canvas, merging their styles to create a larger, synthesizing event. They sought to create a "transcendental anonymous art form," and the next few years proved a successful experiment of two personalities absorbing each other to create a higher vision. José and Miriam felt they were one being with four hands. They thought of themselves as a two-person rock band called "Group Rug." Soon, their paintings branched out into ceremonial art performances.

Unsatisfied with merely creating paintings to hang on a wall, José wanted to create whole environments where artistic forms would uplift people's perceptions and provide entry into a meditative world of higher cosmic mind. His first attempt to create an "art happening" came as a follow-up to the March on the Pentagon.

On March 25, 1968, 29-year-old José, with the help of Miriam, art critic Gene Swenson, and performance artist Ann Wilson, along with 20 of his Princeton graduate students, staged a street event called the Transformation. Held outside the Museum of Modern Art in New York, the intent of the Transformation was to draw attention to living art at the opening of the first retrospective entitled "Dada, Surrealism and Their Heritage." "Dada" was originally antiestablishment art with a revolutionary intention; it was art displayed in the streets rather than enshrined in museums. José's group, their bodies painted and wearing colorful masks, created a ritual ceremonial enactment, waving banners and gaily marching down the street wrapped in 19th-century quilts. They meant to illustrate that real living art was still happening on the streets and in everyday life, and was not confined just to museums.

A large antiwar protest was happening simultaneously outside the Museum of Modern Art, where rich, influential people were gathered. The protest was in response to the pro-Vietnam War stance of many of the board of trustees of the Museum, including the Rockefellers. Police were present to make sure no violence broke out.

José and his group were intent on creating a harmonious demonstration. The Transformation turned into a huge event and attracted a lot of press, actually diverting the attention of the media from the war protestors to the "pro-art, pro-life event," as José referred to it. *Time* and *Newsweek* covered it, as well as the local New York press, which portrayed José and his group as "radical, psychedelic hippies."

Although a good portion of the media sloughed off the event as "farcical," Salvador Dali, the leading surrealist artist at the time, declared his support for the demonstration in a *New York Times* article that appeared the morning after the event. "Those hippies had the right idea," Dali stated in the article.

This marked the beginning of José's interest in ceremonial, theatrical performance art, and, in April 1968, he and Miriam would have a show displaying their mandalas at the Princeton Art Museum.

On May Day of 1968, José and Miriam married at the Princeton County Courthouse. Because of Miriam's background, José quickly became educated in the subject of Jewish religion and culture, and the knowledge sparked in him a desire to learn about all other religions. This marked a time of great creativity. José and Miriam spent much time in New York, where they were active in the art scene of the city, meeting and sharing time with various artists, many of whom were mainstream.

José's University of Chicago colleague Robert Pinkus-Witten had become a prominent art critic. José sent photos and slides of his work to Robert. When he called to see if Robert would review his show, Robert replied, "I don't know what happened to you. You used to have a fine analytical mind, and now you are running

José and Miriam, art exhibit, 1969. Image courtesy of and copyright the José Arguelles Archive.

around like some turned-on Tibetan. I couldn't possibly review your show!"

Most mainstream modern artists were horrified by his paintings. From his point of view, José was attempting to depict the sacred order of reality, while the others were building on a vocabulary of modern art styles. Many told him his work didn't look "polished" or "finished." But José knew that a true visionary crosses the line and says, "No. I dare to say that there is a sacred reality and you, who call yourselves artists, are cowards because you have an artistic gift that you refuse to own."

Chapter 17
California

California, preaching on the burning shore;
California, I'll be knocking on the golden door.

—The Grateful Dead

Although it was comfortable and prestigious to teach art history at Princeton University, José realized that his thinking and lifestyle were too radical to allow him to remain at such a conventional institution. He wanted to go where the action was. All signs pointed to California. It was evident from hearing the new music and reading journals such as *The San Francisco Oracle* that California, especially northern California, was the place to be. He viewed it as the epicenter of the world revolution of consciousness. José resigned from his position at Princeton and sent resumes to many colleges in California. The University of California at Davis soon hired him.

In the summer of 1968, before moving to California, José and Miriam took a four-week trip to Mexico, driving to the Gulf Coast and Monte Alban in Oaxaca. He knew Monte Alban was a great place of power and one of the earliest centers of high civilization in ancient Mexico.

He was amazed to view the famous sculptures, the Danzantes, which were inscribed with some of the earliest hieroglyphic writings and calendrical notations, dating as far back as BC 550. He admired the skill with which these low-relief stone figures had been sculpted, so that, even after 2,500 years, they remained vivid and animated representations of what appeared to him as beings emerging from other worlds.

While contemplating these stone sculptures, an otherworldly sensation seized José, and he felt large presences—etheric beings—from other dimensions. The large sculptures now appeared as mere third-dimensional imprints of higher dimensional beings penetrating this reality. The sculptures seemed to hold the memory of a greater galactic origin, and he felt deep comfort in their presence.

José and Miriam proceeded to Teotitlan del Valle, a dusty little village famous for its tapestries and rugs. A proprietor in a small shop, noting José's fascination with the geometrical rug designs, approached him and said in English, "I have something special for you that was just made today." He brought out two weavings of the same design, one in red and black, the other in blue and orange. The design consisted of a single line with two yin/yang spirals at the center, creating four sets of antennaes and four rays extending out. Jose recognized the image from ancient Mexican design work, but found it breathtaking to see it reproduced in these two beautiful rugs. Jose chose the blue and orange rug, as he admired how the constrasting colors created a shimmering effect. Upon purchasing the rug the proprieter winked at him and said, "See, the ancient Mexicans knew all about the yin and yang!" With that, the proprietor broke open a bottle of Corona in honor of José being the first to purchase one of these rugs. This design would become the motif for *The Mayan Factor* (1987) and later popularized around the world by José as the "Hunab Ku."

Soon after their trip to Mexico, José and Miriam moved into a little house in Woodland, California, not far from the university. Miriam told José she was ready to start a family. Though he didn't view himself as a family man, José didn't resist her desire. Becoming pregnant proved difficult, but after four months conception was accomplished.

At this time, José found himself at the forefront of the West Coast psychedelic art culture. Upon José's departure from Princeton, Humphrey Osmond had given him a list of people to contact in California, including Aldous Huxley's widow, Laura; Charles Tart, author of *Altered States of Consciousness*; and Ralph Metzner.

Metzner was the lesser known of the famous three Harvard professors who, in April 1963, were fired from the university for experimenting with psychedelics and encouraging their students to do the same. The other two professors were Timothy Leary and Richard Alpert, later known as Ram Dass. This incident launched the "psychedelic movement."

Ralph Metzner and José became fast friends; they shared many long discussions about psychedelics and esoteric studies. José provided the drawings for Metzner's book *Maps of Consciousness*, which had as its theme the integration of alchemical studies. José also provided one of his psychedelic paintings for the cover of Bernie Aaronson's book, *Psychedelics: The Uses and Implications of Hallucinogenic Drugs*.

In the fall of 1968, José and Miriam painted a mural of a dragon slithering its way up the stairwell from the first to second floor in Young Hall, which housed the psychology department at U.C. Davis. By this time, psychedelic use had lost its fizzle for José, who witnessed it increasingly used for frivolous purposes rather than as a sacred substance to explore mind and consciousness.

In October 1968, five years after the death of Aldous Huxley, José had an initiatic dream experience in which he visited Huxley in his octagonal dome on Uranus. Huxley asked José to climb the staircase "to experience the sound that matter makes when it creates itself." Huxley said this sound was "bhakti."

José climbed the stairs to the second floor of Huxley's dome, which had a spiral roof reaching into infinity. Upon entering Huxley's room, José saw the swirling psychedelic walls vibrating with color, and he could see, hear, feel, taste, and smell the sound of matter creating itself: "bhakti...bhakti...bhakti." José asked Huxley what he was doing on Uranus.

"Life as we live it is the ritual we are looking for," Huxley responded. At that point, José noted that the shifting psychedelic walls transformed into a frozen image of his *Doors of Perception*.

After this experience, José immediately called Laura Huxley, who invited him and Miriam to her home on Mulholland Drive in the Hollywood Hills. Laura, who was in her mid-50s, graciously welcomed José and Miriam. She listened with great interest as José told her his dream of her late husband. He then left her with the drawing he made of Aldous's psychosensory, octagonal dome with its roof spiraling into infinity.

Laura supported José and Miriam's work and even arranged a public art exhibit of their paintings at the Inner City Gallery in downtown Los Angeles. In the fall of 1968, she suggested that José meet her friend Khigh Diegh, an avid *I Ching* scholar and Hollywood actor. José contacted Khigh Diegh, who ran a Taoist Sanctuary in Topanga

Canyon in addition to playing bit roles in movies and television programs. His most notable role was as Wo Fat, the Chinese villain in *Hawaii Five-O*.

Born in Brooklyn, Khigh Diegh was African-American on his father's side and Turkish-Mongolian on his mother's side, giving him a chameleon-like quality. José found Khigh Diegh a mysterious paradox of ancient wisdom and Hollywood glamour. He was amazed at Khigh Diegh's level of insight and knowledge regarding the *I Ching* and learned much from him.

Following his renewed studies in the *I Ching*, José's interests expanded into alchemical thought, theosophy, and the works of Alice Bailey. He spent a lot of time perusing the shelves at Shambhala, a bookstore on Telegraph Avenue in Berkeley, the prime hotbed of esoteric literature along the West Coast. It was here that he met Sam Bercholz and Michael Fagan, the owners of the store and of Shambhala Publications. Later, Bercholz and Fagan published his books.

The remainder of his free time was spent in the library at the University of California at Berkeley, researching Charles Henry for his PhD thesis. José viewed Henry as a mythic, French-born bodhisattva, carrying the tradition of the "Invisible College." He was fascinated by Henry's notion of a "scientific aesthetic" that emphasized synergy and synhesthesia. He had an uncanny feeling that Henry set out a bunch of clues for him to decipher. Henry's last published works were on the nature of consciousness, specifically "Postmortem Survival and the Nature of Consciousness," in which he wrote: "Death is but a physiochemical change. It is only after death that I will truly begin to amuse myself."

José found Henry, with his elaborate notions on synergy and synergetics, a predecessor to Buckminster Fuller. He brought this to Fuller's attention through correspondence in 1969. Many of these correspondences were published in the philosophical journal *Main Currents of Modern Thought*. Fuller agreed that it must have been Charles Henry's postmortem synergetic thought form that he received in 1927 when the idea of synergetics came to him.

In these correspondences, Fuller suggested to José that there was a "thinking band" around the planet that contained all of the thoughts a human ever had or could have throughout the ages. He said these thoughts were continuously recirculated. This "thinking band" planted the seed for what José would later refer to as the *psi bank*.

In contemplating Fuller's "thinking band" and Henry's "scientific aesthetic," José began to perceive himself as an "omni-resonant field organism"—that is, an organism attuned to all resonances in the field that the senses and mind encompass. He discovered that information was everywhere. Space was saturated with information. He often told his students that he was a "cosmic tuning fork," which was a role potential for everyone. He told them that becoming a clear channel for the cosmos was the highest aspiration of the human race.

Chapter 18
Dates of Destiny

The riddle of the thirteen heavens and nine hells
has challenged the imagination of man since
first it came to light.

—Tony Shearer, *Lord of the Dawn*

As the birth of their first child approached, José became increasingly excited and spent much time preparing the child's room. He bought unfinished furniture that he painted in bright colors. He also made an altar box with paintings on all sides. At this time, he and Miriam began giving workshops on the mandala and art as tools for expanding consciousness. Beginning in 1969, they often taught together at Esalen Institute, and that continued through the mid-1970s.

On June 13, 1969, José received his PhD for his thesis on Charles Henry. The first version of his work was submitted as his doctoral dissertation to the University of Chicago and was accepted that same year. His professors, namely Joshua Taylor and John Rewald, were intrigued by his unusual subject matter. Rather than conducting a formal oral exam where professors ask questions to put the student on the defensive, Rewald, Taylor, and another professor questioned José about his dissertation to satisfy their own curiosity. It was a highly congenial event.

The University of Chicago Press published José's thesis in 1972 as a book, *Charles Henry and the Formation of a Psychophysical Aesthetic*. This book started his career as a writer and emphasized the theme of harmony that would carry on through his life work. The first lines from his first book state:

109

Many are the attempts that are made and the words that are spoken with regard to the age-old ideal of harmony: the union of all faculties, of all senses, of all knowledge. The highest dreamers would proclaim that the true art and science are one.

A few weeks after receiving his PhD, he had a powerful dream of a vast, sweeping landscape that was rapidly changing through cycles of birth and destruction. In the dream, a mage appeared bringing the news that only when the old had completely worn away would the new appear. In the dream, José witnessed the birth of a new man, a man born from the center of the Earth, signifying an entirely new cycle of evolution. This "new man" moved swiftly across the rotating Earth as a voice whispered: "In order for there to be new birth, the mage must move across the Earth."

On July 13, 1969, Joshua Maitreya Arguelles was born. Like his conception, Josh's birth was difficult. After 20 hours of intense labor, Miriam had a Caesarean section. José waited, anxious, and was finally able to see his son through a thick glass window in the newborn nursery. He was shocked. The baby looked Asian. He had a full head of dark hair. Blood still covered his tiny hands and face. José felt an immediate connection with his son; he thought his son looked quite mature.

José and Josh, 1970. Image courtesy of and copyright the José Arguelles Archive.

Josh's birth was followed by the *Apollo 11* mission to the Moon. People saw the whole Earth on television, live from space! Upon first seeing the image of the whole Earth, José knew it was a momentous event, signaling the beginning of planetary consciousness. What would life be like if we all recognized ourselves as planetary beings?

His son's birth, and the sight of Earth from space for the first time, combined to create one of the most naturally mind-altering times of José's life.

After Josh's birth, Miriam and José felt like a little, holy family. They loved taking care of him and seeing how he responded to their affectionate gestures. José loved making up songs to put him to sleep at night. José considered Josh a great gift and was very close with him.

Later, José reported that, when Josh was 2 years old, after being tucked into bed one night, Josh called José back to his room. "Daddy, you know what I see when I close my eyes?"

"No. What do you see, Josh?"

"I see the whole universe, everything—it's all there."

🎵

Following the "man on the moon" event was Woodstock, which created a vision of a new sub-culture based on music and love. Like seeing the Earth from space, Woodstock was a huge media event. José watched as much as he could of the event on television. Nothing like it had ever happened before. A feeling of great power arose out of seeing so many people willing to live in the rain and the mud, dancing, loving each other, and loving the music that made them love each other. For José, nothing captured the feeling of the music at Woodstock better than Jimi Hendrix's wild guitar rendition of *The Star-Spangled Banner*.

A few weeks later, José met Tony Shearer, a Native-American poet and storyteller with a special interest in Quetzalcoatl and the sacred calendar of ancient Mexico. Tony was with a number of other Native-American and Chicano activists attempting to acquire unused military land near Davis. This land was converted into a Native-American learning center called Deganawida-Quetzalcoatl University.

On their first meeting, Tony revealed to José the prophecy of Quetzalcoatl, Thirteen Heavens, and Nine Hells. Tony explained that each of the Thirteen Heavens and Nine Hells refers to a 52-year cycle. Thirteen 52-year "Heaven" cycles took place between 843 and 1519 AD, the beginning of the conquest of Mexico. Eight 52-year "Hell" cycles occurred between 1519 and 1935.

"This ninth hell," Tony told José, "began in 1935 and ends August 16, 1987. Thirteen heavens of decreasing choice, nine hells of increasing doom."

"But then what?" José asked.

"We must get ready for the cleansing of the world and for the end of the Great Cycle."

Chapter 19
Whole Earth Festival

Who will speak for Planet Earth?

—Carl Sagan

T he birth of Josh, the vision of the whole Earth from outer space, the prophecy of Quetzalcoatl, and Woodstock all blended into one. When the school year began in September 1969, José was highly inspired. He taught a yearlong sequence of classes in the history of modern art, from the beginning of the Industrial Age to the present. More than 180 students enrolled in his main course, History of Modern Art, making it the largest class he'd ever had. His students were restless. The thought of giving them a traditional final exam—asking them to identify artistic styles from slides—seemed tedious. It was 1969. Revolution was in the air. He wanted to bring the feeling of Woodstock and the Whole Earth into his classes, but how?

Two books he was reading at the time gave him the answer. The first book was *The Pulse of Life* by Dane Rudhyar. The second was *Education for the New Age* by Alice Bailey. Rudhyar's book stressed the psychological qualities of the different astrological houses; Bailey's book emphasized group activity as the key to education in the new age. That settled it: He asked his 180 students to identify their astrological Sun signs and then form into their 12 zodiacal groups. For their final winter exam, José told his students to do something they "believed in," with an emphasis on ceremony and ritual.

With this freedom, the 12 groups decided to stage a "Believe In." The students immediately put their creative intelligence into action and began to ask questions such as "what kind of costume would an Aquarius wear?" or "what kind of ceremony would a Piscean have?"

They acquired use of the Experimental College Coffee House for four hours one afternoon in December 1969, just before Christmas. What occurred was a spontaneous mini-Woodstock. Each group designed its own hand-sewn costume to complement its Sun sign. There were creative ceremonies, musical demonstrations, artistic food creations, and gift-giving events. Other students wanted to join in their final exam. In order to gain admittance, José's students made them divulge their Sun sign as their initiation.

In January 1970, after the two-week Christmas vacation, José's next History of Art class (which he now deemed History of Media and Visual Perception) met for the first time. Now there were more than 400 students. In his other class, Visual Symbols, he had another 120 students. Word had spread, and all the new students came with the same expectation. "What are we going to do, José?" they all wanted to know.

Because the second quarter ended at Spring Equinox, and the historical frame of his teaching ended at World War I, he told his class they needed to do a "Rite of Spring" (after Stravinsky's famous musical performance of 1913). One of the students spoke of plans for an Earth Day that was being formed for April 22, 1970. After several classroom discussions regarding the implications of the whole Earth and human consciousness, and the rise of the ecology movement, José's students determined to prepare the ground for Earth Day and create the First Whole Earth Festival right on the University of California Davis campus!

The 180 core students, veterans of the "Believe In," organized the new students according to their astrological Sun sign groups. In his Visual Symbols class, José organized the Sun sign groups into four larger elemental groups: Earth, Air, Fire, and Water. As with the previous quarter, the students began meeting in their groups with great regularity and purpose. José's reputation as a "radical" professor had attracted to his classes all of the most active and radical students of the campus, and they went to work right away to make their final exam, the first Whole Earth Festival, a complete success.

This time the students decided their final exam would span the entire week of March 17–21, 1970. The students managed to convince the university officials to let them use the center of the campus, the Quadrangle, a park-like area of grass and trees with two major walkways. As the time for the event drew near, everyone was amazed how smoothly it was all going. Everything clicked. Students spread the word all over California and the West Coast. They sent invitations to all ecology groups, artists, spiritual groups, and alternative communities. Some students contacted the organizers of Earth Day, including John McConnell, to inform them of the preliminary Earth Day activities of the first Whole Earth Festival. Not only did John McConnell attend the event, but the renowned psychedelic artist Peter Max designed the poster for the event.

Dressed in psychedelic clothing, José, Miriam, and Josh arrived early to the campus on March 17th for the first day of the first Whole Earth Festival. Nothing could have prepared José for what he saw: Scattered around the edge of the Quadrangle were teepees, geodesic domes, tents, and yurts; a global village had sprung up overnight. The two main walkways had been transformed. One was now called the "Street of the Mysteries," the other the "Street of the Magicians." Tie-dyed banners were stretched between the trees and, in some cases, over the walkways, which were lined with booths.

The Street of Magicians hosted crafts people, musicians, artists, and merchants. On the Street of the Mysteries were booths offering tarot and astrology readings, as well as spiritual groups practicing yoga and meditation, alongside exhibits of alternative energies. Over five days, ongoing public events took place, either at the main speakers' stand or in the Experimental College building and Coffee House. Because the Whole Earth Festival took over the entire central campus, no one attending the university could avoid the event.

At this time, the "hippie" movement was termed the "counter-culture," and it seemed as if everyone over the entire West Coast who belonged to it had arrived for the grand event: the first Whole Earth Festival in Davis, California.

Large Earth flags billowed around the outdoor stage set up for the public events. José initiated the event with a short, opening speech: "We are here today to remember the Earth, to know that the Earth is a living being and that we are the Earth's spiritual children."

Other speakers included Yogi Bhajan, John McConnell of the Earth Day Committee, Swami Satchidanada, and representatives of different environmental and ecology groups and from the United Nations. Also in attendance were Tony Shearer and Sun Bear, a medicine man of Chippewa heritage.

Poster of Whole Earth Festival, 1970. Artwork by Peter Max. From the photo collection of José Arguelles.

Alongside the scheduled speakers and events were countless musicians, street theater performers, and mimes. Many spontaneous artistic "happenings" took place. In a grassy area surrounded by teepees and redolent with the scent of burning sage mingled with incense, great circle dances arose. The beat of the tribal drum was constant, and different forms of music, singing, and Hare Krishna chanting cascaded through the din of people surging over the two main walkways.

On the first afternoon of the Whole Earth Festival, a student called José over to the Experimental College, where he said a letter was waiting for him.

José opened the letter. It was from Dane Rudhyar! For some reason, when reading his books, José had imagined him to be dead or in another world. The last thing he expected was to hear from him. In his letter, Rudhyar told José that he heard about the Whole Earth Festival from a mutual friend, Stephen Levine. In the letter, Rudhyar congratulated him and his students for fulfilling a vision he'd held since the 1920s: a vision of the "whole Earth celebrated as a work of art." Rudhyar wrote that the Whole Earth Festival marked the beginning of a new stage of spiritual consciousness, what he referred to as the "planetarization of consciousness."

For José, this letter confirmed, as well, the notion of a planetary consciousness and the possibility of a truly planetary being. It also affirmed the correspondence he had exchanged with Buckminster Fuller on the matter. Now, he was certain it was real and that the Whole Earth Festival was more than just a passing scene.

On the last day of the event, Spring Equinox, a global peace meditation was held, synchronized with spiritual and Earth Day groups in India, Australia, Europe, and North America. One month after the first Whole Earth Festival came the first Earth Day, on April 22, 1970. Despite the controversy that ensued over José's educational vision, the momentum of the first Whole Earth Festival continued into 1971 and came to be known as the Whole Earth Festival, which has continued every year thereafter.

Chapter 20
Radiant Seed Man

*The future possibility and ideal image
becomes the present fact in terms of inherent
ability to overcome the inertia of the past.*

—Dane Rudhyar

T he first Whole Earth Festival was a milestone, and it cost José
his job. After the Festival, he wrote a summary of his initial educational experiment, entitled "The Believe-in, an Aquarian Age
Ritual." Besides describing his experiment, the article also examined
educational values in the "incipient" age of the computer, arguing for
a more humanistic, experiential approach. This was published in the
summer of 1970 in *Main Currents of Modern Thought*. When the president of the Academic Senate of the University of California, Davis,
read the essay, she decided José's methods would destroy traditional
education. She said he was a threat to the university community and
that he should be severely reprimanded, or, better yet, relieved of his
duties.

When word reached José's students, they became upset and angry,
and wanted to take action. It was a time of great social unrest in America,
especially because of the Vietnam War. José's colleague Angela Davis,
from the University of California, Los Angeles, had just become a fugi-
tive because of her radicalism. Timothy Leary was also in exile.

In August, José was invited to speak at an educational conference
at Washington State University, sponsored by *Main Currents of Modern
Thought*. On the drive to Washington, he contemplated his predicament. Winding through Northern California, he decided to visit Mount
Shasta for the first time. He had heard many mystical stories about the

mountain and knew some people considered it a type of "higher-dimensional vortex." As he drove up the mountain, it didn't take him long to realize that the most peaceful resolution was to resign; his inner calling was beyond this type of politics. He saw the potential for a confrontational crisis at the university and knew he didn't want conflict to be associated with the Whole Earth Movement.

He felt that what had happened to him because of his activities in creating the Whole Earth Festival only demonstrated why people don't change: They were not ready to change. The vision of the whole Earth was too far ahead of the mainstream, especially those in charge of institutions. For these people, the idea of an Earth without boundaries, where all people live in peace and harmony, seemed threatening to their belief system. He knew he had to leave his position at the university and think deeply about these matters.

The first week of the fall quarter of 1970, amid a campus-wide controversy, he submitted his resignation, although he stayed on to complete his last year in the spring of 1971. More than 1,000 students enrolled in his classes with high expectations, wanting to know what he would do next. He told them everything had already been done. He didn't feel he had the wherewithal, at that time, to meet the expectations of producing something as creatively monumental as the Whole Earth Festival.

Inevitably, much speculation was circulating around campus regarding his five-day final exam; it had become quite a controversy. To top it off, his superiors were less than pleased to find him playing John Lennon for the students in his Humanities class.

José, who was 31, was finding life in an academic institution a constant struggle—he was always "too creative," "too active," and "pushing the edges just a little too far." To offset his frustration over formal academic regime, he sought a creative outlet in studies outside of the usual disciplines. At that time he was studying *The Secret Teaching of All Ages*, Manly Hall's compendium of esoteric knowledge.

Through this book he realized the power of the mandala within different symbolic systems, including astrological symbols, the chakra system, and esoteric symbolism. As he contemplated these systems, he conceived of two paintings (male/female) depicting the image of the new human as the microcosm synthesis of different symbolic systems. He told Miriam his vision. She was inspired, and the two set out painting each other in their etheric/astral forms.

To begin the project, José and Miriam purchased two 6-1/2 by 2-foot doors. In turn, each lay down on a door while the other outlined his or her body in the same yogic style posture, hands in the air and thumbs and index fingers touching. José then outlined Miriam's hands and footprints in invisible, glow-in-the dark acrylic paints for what would be known as "Radiant Woman," and Miriam likewise outlined José's hands and footprints for what would be known as "Radiant Man."

For nearly a year, José and Miriam painted together side by side in a little art studio in their Woodland, California, home. Designed using visual/perceptual effects influenced by the psychedelic experience, these paintings incorporated esoteric and symbolic systems in a type of yin/yang crossover, emphasizing the Hindu and mantric systems of the chakras. The paintings also highlighted astrological signs and Taoist writing and symbolism. This marked the high point of José and Miriam's work together as painters.

Through the early 1970s, José intensified his study of the *I Ching* and began writing prefaces and forewords to *I Ching* books, including the annual *Taoist Book of Days*. In January 1971, Dane Rudhyar came to Woodland to meet José. Rudhyar, who was then in his mid-70s, seemed to embody the living hermetic tradition. He introduced José to many esoteric streams of thought, confirming in him many inner knowings.

Rudhyar was well acquainted with the work of both Madame Blavatsky and Alice Bailey, whom he knew personally. Bailey's publishing company, Lucis Trust, had printed some of Rudhyar's first books. He told José that the notion of Shambhala, derived in modern times from Blavatsky and Bailey, was accredited to their telepathic access to Ascended Master Koot Hoomi.

At their first meeting of many, Rudhyar and José discussed the planetarization of consciousness, the difference between Eastern mysticism and Western occult traditions, the role of art, and the creation of the future. Rudhyar told José that it was essential for every household on the planet to have a globe. He gave José a copy of his article "Artist as Avatar," which had been published in 1939 in the *Theosophical Journal*.

"The greatest avatars," Rudhyar told José, "come at the closing of a cycle.... This means they have to exemplify the whole life of the new cycle."

At this meeting, Rudhyar expressed eagerness to form conscious "seed groups" as the basis of a new civilization. These initial "seed groups," Rudhyar said, were the "lenses, giving existential form to seed ideas and new aspects of archetypal man."

Rudhyar recognized José as the "artist as avatar" and the Whole Earth Festival as an example of "seed group work." Rudhyar deemed José a "seed man" and encouraged him in the direction of forming art communities or "seed groups" as the basis of a new civilization. In *Seed Man*, Rudhyar wrote:

> We therefore need men of vision, men who are not specialists, men who have the vision and courage to wait and to in some way, through their lives and example, through whatever they leave after their death, become the seeds of the future world. This is the great choice we all have to make and we all have to make it. We can follow the mass vibration and decay like all the leaves of the world in the Fall, they all have to be changed to become the new of the future civilization…. The seed men are the only insurance to the future rebirth of humanity.

Chapter 21
Mandala

> *Mandala means a circle, more especially a*
> *magic circle, and this form of symbol is*
> *not only to be found all through the East,*
> *but also among us....*

—Carl Jung

On José's 32nd birthday, he appeared on the front page of the *Sacramento Bee* newspaper. The photo depicted him sitting in his living room in front of the *Doors of Perception* with the headline "Artist as Psychic: What is Psychic Art?"

The article expressed his perception that art was meant to evoke the contents of the psyche and communicate psychically to the viewer. He explained that his art was meant to "reach subtle, subliminal psychic levels to penetrate the conceptual mind and enter a deeper cosmic level."

In early 1971, José found out that his PhD dissertation awarded in 1969, *Charles Henry and the Formation of a Psychophysical Aesthetic*, had been accepted by the University of Chicago Press for publication in 1972. At that time, José was maintaining a steady mental diet of Hindu and Buddhist books, Sufi writing (especially the poetry of Rumi), and Taoist texts. While lecturing at Integral Yoga Institute in San Francisco, he was introduced to the works of Sri Aurobindo, modern Hindu mystic and founder of Integral Yoga. Sri Aurobindo's writings opened a window of fresh perceptions for José, indicating that evolution is possible and immediately attainable through pursuit of the correct spiritual goal. José was particularly inspired by Sri Aurobindo's books *Life Divine* and *Future Evolution of Man*, which he found complementary to Rudhyar's *Planetarization of Consciousness*.

Encouraged by Sam Bercholz and Michael Fagan of Shambhala Publications, José and Miriam set to work on their artistic collaboration for the book *Mandala*. Having already given a number of workshops and lectures together on the mandala, José and Miriam were excited at the prospect of synthesizing their knowledge and experience into book form. Their many workshop and lecture notes formed the foundational structure of the book.

Together, José and Miriam designed page borders and collaborated on many original black-and-white drawings. José did much of the research and writing of the book, and Miriam was largely responsible for the overall artistic design and layout, as well as some writing assistance. Together, they obtained reproductions of the front cover of the book from the curator at the San Francisco Museum of Art. They wanted the book published in 1972 and so employed a few of José's students to help expedite the process.

For José, *Mandala* was a vehicle for synthesizing his psychedelic experiences. Working on the book allowed him a more in-depth exploration of questions such as "what is sacred art?" and "what are sacred structures?" His intention was to inject the sacred into a stream of modern thought and also to explore the theme question: What is the relationship of vision, the optical nerve, seeing, and the depiction of sacred structures? This became an all-absorbing investigation. In this book, he also made his first reference to Pierre de Chardin's *noosphere*. The noosphere would be a continuing theme throughout his life's work. In *Mandala*, he wrote:

> To project into the future is only to speak of the potential of the present. If man can mandalize himself, there will be a resulting deployment of now unused energies within his bioorganic structure. These energies are what will be most instrumental in creating a radiant—radiating from multiple centers—planetary sphere. This is what is implied in Teilhard de Chardin's *noosphere*: a glowing, pulsing aura, a phosphorescent psychic plasma, Earth's last sheath expanding and opening in her mating with the reaches of cosmic space. To realize this vision, courage to change is the chief prequisite; to simplify and yet expand, to purify and integrate, to individuate and interrelate with all other forms and evolutionary possibilities—*this* is the destiny of man.

The final year at Davis was a struggle for José, and he wasn't sure what his next step would be. One day, in the spring of 1971, while working in his university office, José got an unexpected visit from Merv Cadwaliter and Don Humphrey, two deans from the soon-to-be-opened experimental college in Washington State. The deans heard about his work with the Whole Earth Festival and were searching for "innovative" professors to work on the faculty at Evergreen State College in Olympia, Washington. Though grateful for the offer, José's feelings were mixed. On the one hand, he thought that maybe an experimental college would accommodate his radical educational vision. On the other hand, he had misgivings about any institution, even one that boasted it was "experimental."

After talking it over with Miriam, he decided to accept the offer and not think too much about the actual move until the time came. He called the deans and formalized the position.

Soon after, and without warning, his landlord gave him and Miriam a 30-day notice, telling them he planned to turn their home into a real estate office. Because they would have to move soon anyway, José thought it pointless to try to find another house. His coworker, Ruth Horsting, a sculpture professor, heard of his plight and offered his family a room in her house-turned-ashram for the remaining three months of the school year.

In the summer of 1970, Ruth had traveled to India, where she met Baba Hari Dass, the Ashtanga yoga master acquainted with Baba Ram Dass. Initiated in the Vairagi Vaishnava order in 1942, Baba Hari Dass was just beginning to gain notoriety as a yoga master and had a number of American students studying yoga with him. Ruth invited Baba Hari Dass and his small entourage to move to America. He accepted, and immediately her suburban home was converted into a Hindu Ashtanga yoga ashram.

In March 1971, José, Miriam, and their almost-2-year-old Josh moved into the ashram. José found Baba Hari Dass a charming enigma with his long braided hair wrapped in a coil on top of his head, his sparse beard, and a chalkboard around his neck. The man had taken a vow of silence in 1952 and lived on nothing but *prana* and a glass of milk a day.

José felt fortunate to receive a direct initiation into Ashtanga yoga from a real Indian yogi. Every morning he practiced yoga with Baba Hari Dass, who wrote his teachings on a chalkboard. He also read as much as he could about yoga, particularly Patanjali's *Yoga Sutras*. In his later work, José would further discover yogic discipline as the essential foundation for evolutionary cultivation.

While living at the ashram, José had a dream that he was supposed to teach but couldn't find his notes. He pulled out a scroll with a picture of a Shiva dancing on the body of the whole Earth (as seen in *Mandala*). José showed this picture to Baba Hari Dass, who immediately went to his chalkboard and wrote: "This is the mahapralaya."

The mahapralaya is the dance of the great seed time, or the time at the end of the cycle. It was a peak experience for José. It set the standard of his vision to unify the human race in the understanding that the whole Earth is one vast work of art, or, as Rudhyar put it, the Earth is an art-whole.

Often on the weekends, José, Miriam, Josh, Baba Hari Dass, and a few of his devotees stayed at Ruth's second home in Sea Ranch near Mendocino on the coast in the northern part of Sonoma. These times were extraordinary. José considered Ruth a most gracious host. Ruth continued to devote her life to Baba Hari Dass until her death in 2000.

José, Miriam, and Josh with Baba Hari Dass, Sea Ranch, California, 1971. Image courtesy of and copyright the José Arguelles Archive.

Around this time, José also met poet Gary Snyder, known as one of the most lucid writers of the Beat generation. A Zen Buddhist practitioner, Snyder advocated community living and active engagement in ecological concerns. José and Miriam traveled to Snyder's elegantly rustic home near Grass Valley, California, where he lived in a loosely formed community with his Japanese wife. José was impressed by his Zen approach to life and admired his conscious, close-to-the-Earth living.

In late March of 1971, José reunited with Sun Bear at the first annual Whole Earth Festival and was struck by his warmth, innocence, and sincerity. Of Ojibwa-Chippewa descent, Sun Bear was born in Minnesota on the White Earth Reservation. A friendship was kindled, and Sun Bear gave José some of his writings on self-sustaining communities and the importance of living in nature. Sun Bear had been in Hollywood playing bit roles as an Indian, but was then dedicated to fulfilling his vision of creating a new tribe; he felt the traditional tribes were not strong or clear enough. He knew there had to be some kind of new tribe based on Mother Earth and the Native American ways, and so was born the Bear Tribe, with its open invitation of membership to people from all walks of life.

José also met Allen Ginsberg and his partner, Peter Orlovsky, at the first annual Whole Earth Festival. José found them warm, folksy, and easygoing. Allen was excited to hear that José was living with Baba Hari Dass and was enthused to meet him. The following day, José took Allen and Peter to Baba Hari Dass's ashram, where the yogi held a brief darshan for the three in his bedroom. Allen eagerly asked Baba Hari Dass questions pertaining to the practice of bhakti yoga. José observed a deep level of recognition and affection between Allen and Baba Hari Dass. Allen asked the yogi whether or not it was alright to smoke "ganja" while practicing bhakti yoga, as he had seen so many yogis do in India. Baba Hari Dass smiled and scribbled something on his chalkboard that delighted Allen.

PART IV

Beating the
Drum of
Dharma

Chapter 22
Treasures From Tibet

To indulge in worldly things stirs up misery at its very source.
Swirling continuously, one is thrown into the pit of samsara.
What can they do, those trapped by sorrows and tribulations?
There is no other course than devotion to the Dharma.

—Milarepa

José had been on the lookout for a Tibetan teacher since the LSD experience that led him to *The Life of Milarepa*. He felt a strong past life connection with the Tibetan saint who lived in the 12th century.

Milarepa began his career as a black magician but later felt deep remorse for his actions, leading him to seek out his teacher "Marpa the Translator." The first instruction Marpa gave to Milarepa was to build a stone structure on a high rocky ridge. After much strenuous physical labor, Milarepa completed the project. Marpa told him to tear it down and build a new structure in a different location. So Milarepa took all the rocks and boulders back to where he had found them and patiently began again. This happened nine times before Milarepa got it right.

After his apprenticeship, Milarepa moved to a solitary cave where he practiced strict asceticism until he reached a state of enlightenment. His teachings were passed down through songs and poems. After hearing this story, José formed a strong mental picture of finding a Tibetan teacher. Regardless of his eclectic taste, he knew that to learn something serious about spiritual matters it was necessary to commit to a good teacher. He felt the Tibetans had an expanded view of mind, spirituality, and higher consciousness, and he was determined to learn how to access it.

In the late 1960s and early 1970s, finding a teacher or guru became stylish after the Beatles traveled to India to study Transcendental Meditation with the Maharishi. In early 1970, José's friend Charlie Tart was also searching for a Tibetan guru. They checked out a few potential teachers, but none felt right to José. One teacher told José he'd have to wear robes every day; another said he had to learn Tibetan before he'd teach him anything.

Chögyam Trungpa Rinpoche, early 1970s. Printed with permission from Shambhala.

In late 1970, José received the book *Born in Tibet* from Sam Bercholz. *Born in Tibet* is the autobiography of Vidyadhara Chögyam Trungpa Rinpoche, the 11th descendent in the line of Trungpa tülkus. In his late teens, Chögyam Trungpa became the head of the Surmang monasteries in eastern Tibet.

In 1959, when Chögyam Trungpa was 20 years old, he led a group of monks on horseback and foot on a risky journey over the Himalayas to India to escape Chinese invaders. He stayed in India for four years before receiving a fellowship to study Western history and culture at Oxford University in England. While in Europe, he helped open a Buddhist center in Scotland before heading back to Nepal, where he retreated to the Tagstan Cave, famous for housing Padmasambhava. Here, Trungpa had many realizations, which he compiled into one of his first works, *Sadhana of Mahamudra*. In this pithy text he wrote of civilization sliding into the "dark ages of materialism."

After this experience, Trungpa returned to Great Britain, where he was seriously injured after crashing his car into a joke shop. His left side was partially paralyzed, causing him to walk with a limp. He married Diana Pybus, a 16-year-old Scottish girl from an aristocratic family. As a yogi in the tradition he came from, Trungpa was supposed to marry someone who was 16 years old.

In 1969, Trungpa received a postcard of the Rocky Mountains in Colorado. He thought it looked like Tibet and decided to move there.

By 1970, he and Diana had moved to Colorado, and Trungpa took off his robes and became a lay yogi, as he thought that would make him more effective in the United States. In Colorado, Trungpa was put in touch with Sam Bercholz, and soon Shambhala Publications published his autobiography.

After reading *Born in Tibet*, José assimilated all his esoteric studies, and he began studying Vajrayana Buddhism, of which Trungpa was a master. He found it fascinating that Chögyam Trungpa was born on February 19, 1939, New Year's Day on the Chinese Tibetan lunar calendar, and exactly 26 days after his own birthday. José immediately knew that Trungpa was the teacher he'd been searching for. He was further impressed that Trungpa, like Milarepa, was of the Kagyu lineage: one of four main schools of Tibetan Buddhism known for its strong emphasis on meditation practice.

In May 1971, with Ruth Horsting's blessing, José and Miriam invited Trungpa to Baba Hari Dass's ashram in Davis. The night before Trungpa's arrival, José had an auspicious dream. In the dream, two giant creatures appeared. They were so large that he could see only their big boots. One creature said to the other, "Are you with the World Union of the Guardians of Sufficient Evolution?"

"Yes," the other responded. "We will meet again when the Eastern Sun meets the Western Sun at the 33rd degree."

José woke up feeling a strange power. As mysterious as the dream was, he knew it was true. Contemplating the phrase *sufficient evolution*, he concluded that this referred to the Middle Way, described by the Buddha. From his esoteric studies, he knew that the 33rd degree was the most exalted level of the Masonic order and the key number of initiation.

José met Chögyam Trungpa at the Sacramento airport. Dressed in Western clothes and walking with a heavy limp, Trungpa was accompanied by his wife Diana and an entourage of earthy Westerners. In the car, José told Trungpa about his dream the previous night. Trungpa listened silently, looking curiously at José with a calm smile. At this time, Trungpa was in his high hippie phase: He dressed casually, smoked cigarettes and marijuana, took LSD, and consumed lots of Johnnie Walker whiskey. He often referred to himself as a "crazy wisdom teacher."

That evening José and Trungpa shared a bottle of scotch. Talking animatedly, Trungpa caught sight of one of José's large psychedelic paintings. After studying the painting for a few moments, Trungpa turned to José and said with a sly grin, "I see you already know all about tantra, don't you?" At this remark, José's mind flashed to an image of Padmasambhava in full Tibetan regalia. On either side of Padmasambhava were a man and a woman wearing Mayan turbans and dressed in royal finery, conversing intimately with mudra-like hand gestures. Was this a memory flash? What was it?

The next evening, Trungpa gave a dharma talk at U.C. Davis. José opened the talk by playing his bamboo flute. Upon hearing his flute, Trungpa said, "Sounds like Milarepa in the cave." José knew he had found the right teacher. At the talk, a woman asked Trungpa: "You Tibetans are supposed to know all about reincarnation. What can you tell me about it?" Trungpa leaned forward with characteristic humor and replied, "I'm here."

Not long after José met with Trungpa, Sun Bear invited José to one of the Bear Tribe's base camps in the Sierra Nevadas. The initial Bear Tribe began in California in 1970 when Sun Bear took the message of his vision to several universities and colleges in the Sacramento area. The response was great, and soon he had 200 people living in 17 different base camps.

José found Sun Bear's camp refreshing and simple, with its strong back-to-the-Earth philosophy. Sun Bear told José he liked the direction he was going with the Whole Earth Festival and felt he'd be a valuable addition to the Bear Tribe. Sun Bear also told José to invite Dane Rudhyar to join the tribe. "I really like that French philosopher brother," Sun Bear told José, referring to Rudhyar. "It would be wonderful if you and the philosopher brother could live here and join the Bear Tribe." José was moved by Sun Bear's pure heart and the sincerity of his vision, but he told him he'd have to decline; he had already accepted Trungpa as his teacher.

Chapter 23
Planetarization of Consciousness

*A great avatar refers to the beginning
of a phase of the cycle of evolution of
the whole planet and humanity.*

—Dane Rudhyar

José, Miriam, and Josh moved from their temporary ashram dwelling with Baba Hari Dass into Dane Rudhyar's summer home in Palo Alto, California, in June 1971. Here, with Rudhyar and his Canadian wife, Tana, they stayed three months, completing the illustrations and manuscript for *Mandala*.

Believing in non-possessive love, Rudhyar proposed that the four of them have a "free" living arrangement. The idea did not go over well with Tana, so nothing came of the proposal. Rudhyar believed that modern monogamous relationships and the nuclear family created far more possessiveness and neurosis than spontaneous love and compassion. He felt the lens should be expanded through experimentation with different kinds of conscious, tantric arrangements in order to dissolve possessive human barriers.

During this time, José had many long conversations with Rudhyar about his life, his views, and his experiences. His work and friendship watered the seeds of prophecy planted in José by Tony Shearer and vastly expanded his vision.

Born in Paris, Rudhyar studied in France during World War I and, in 1917, moved to California, where he believed the "New Age" was to emerge. Being well studied in the works of Madame Blavatsky, predominantly *The Secret Doctrine*, he traveled to Ojai, where he encountered Alice Bailey and Krishnamurti, and became an esoteric initiate of the Western occult tradition (the White Brotherhood). Alice Bailey saw to it that some of Rudhyar's first books were published by her own organization and publishing company, Lucis Trust.

For a short while, Rudhyar lived in Santa Barbara, not far from Krishnamurti, who had been set up by Blavatsky's Theosophical Society to act as the new avatar. Krishnamurti realized he was not the one they were looking for, but became a great teacher in his own right, with a teaching style akin to existential Buddhism.

Dane Rudhyar, Miriam, and José, 1972. Image courtesy of and copyright the José Arguelles Archive.

Through Rudhyar, José became aware of the Theosophical Society and the work of Madame Blavatsky, whom he highly regarded. In addition to esteeming her as the founder of the New Age, Rudhyar saw the date 1875, when the Theosophical Society was founded, as the actual beginning of the New Age. The Theosophical Society was based on the tenets of a universal brotherhood of humanity, which sought to study ancient wisdom and to explore the hidden mysteries of nature and the latent powers of man. It established an occult hierarchy drawing from the Hindu and Buddhist traditions—in particular, the Tibetan tantric texts and teachings.

José's impression of reading Blavatsky's work was that she was a very serious, encyclopedic, and comprehensive thinker. Her works were vast, and he held her in high regard for having brought Eastern thought to the West.

Rudhyar spent much of the 1920s in Hollywood, practicing piano, painting, and studying astrology, all of which would blossom into a planetary global vision that he referred to as the "art-whole."

His vision of art was that it would absorb the living cultural communities so that each whole community was immersed in the same artistic vision. In this way, whoever came from a specific community would express the art-whole blueprint of that particular community.

In the 1930s Rudhyar's astrology became prominent, and in 1936 he published *The Astrology of Personality*, which included his Jungian analysis of the archetypes and his interpretation of the 360 Sabian symbols. The Sabian symbols are a set of 360 symbolic images, each symbol depicting a particular degree of the zodiac.

Rudhyar moved to New Mexico in the 1930s and was part of a visionary artist group located between Taos and Santa Fe. He continued to paint his harmonious semi-abstract paintings that looked, to José, like visual music. He also pursued his unique style of piano music, breaking down traditional chords in unusual ways that could potentially create a type of evocative tone poem.

José attended one of his concerts at Berkeley in the early 1970s, where Rudhyar played the piano by banging his fists on the keyboard a lot. Rudhyar believed music should be reduced back down to a kind of primal scream. José found Rudhyar's music curiously dissonant with an almost jarring quality. He understood this as the intentional breaking of old molds, but as yet the music didn't have the harmony depicted in his paintings, which were symbolic, archetypal abstractions, warm and evocative, with luminous colors expressing hitherto unseen harmonies.

Rudhyar's major philosophical, metaphysical, and psychological work from 1970, *Planetarization of Consciousness*, had just been published in Holland. The book had a deep influence on José, who was struck by Rudhyar's themes, one of which was that evolution would reach the stage where consciousness would become planetized. He described the importance of the influence of the Sun as a star on the entire galaxy. These ideas resonated deeply with José, who was highly influenced by Rudhyar's vision of higher dimensional, whole system astrology, inclusive of galactic dimensions of stars, galactic beings, and galactic culture.

Rudhyar likened the planetary unfolding to that of a vast ritual. He believed that, in the next stage of evolution, consciousness would be fully realized as a planetary phenomenon, the *noosphere*. He wrote the following in *Occult Preparations for a New Age:*

The planetary crisis mankind is now experiencing, if seen from an occult-spiritual point of view, is truly a vast ritual. In this planetary ritual, great personages, some visible but many more invisible, are performing their acts of destiny according to cyclic rhythms…. The Age is dark with blatant pride, violence and greed. Passions are wild, after a period of artificial containment. We worship success, comfort, material possessions. Confusion is in every soul and mind. How could the great "rite of passage" to a new humanity, or at least a new consciousness of the meaning of being human, be anything but a mysterious performance in the crypt of the human temple, while on the floor above nations as well as individuals indulge in mock trials, and devastating and absurd wars? Yet the ritual unfolds its potentialities of human renewal as ineluctably cosmic time moves on toward its fulfillment.

Later that year, Rudhyar dedicated his new book, *Directives for New Life*, to José and Miriam. This little book contained chapters such as "A Re-evaluation of Man's Relation to the Earth" and "Principles for the Structuring of a Harmonic Society."

Many of the fundamental notions of José's initial impetus to create the Planet Art Network (1983) derived from Rudhyar's assessment of the role of art in the coming new age. A decade later, José would write the "Planet Art Report for Desperate Earthlings of the Past" (an appendix to his 1984 book, *Earth Ascending*), in which he would expand on this theme.

After spending the summer with Rudhyar in Palo Alto, José, Miriam, and Josh drove to the Lama Foundation about 20 miles north of Taos, New Mexico, where they stayed for two weeks on their way back to Washington State. Founded in 1968, the Lama Foundation is about 109 acres, bordered by Carson National Forest to the north, east, and south. At that time, the Lama Foundation had a reputation as the most spiritually oriented of the hippie communes and was one of the first spiritual retreat centers to welcome all spiritual traditions. Ram Dass was staying at the Lama Foundation at this time, collaborating with Lama residents to create his seminal volume *Be Here Now*.

Coordinator Steve Durkee and his wife immediately put to work everyone who arrived at the Lama Foundation. There was much work to be done: constructing geodesic domes, making adobe plaster, putting up adobe walls, farming, and gardening. José's afternoon assignment was to milk the goats. No matter how many showers he took during his stay, he could never seem to wash the goat smell off. As a result of that assignment, he developed a great distaste for goat products.

In the evenings, everyone staying at the Lama Foundation gathered to work on *Be Here Now*, which would become a spiritual cult classic, opening many Westerners to the teachings of the East. José looked forward to these evenings and found the work an exciting, almost medieval, group project. He happily provided some of the black-and-white drawings for the book. The first edition of *Be Here Now* was handmade and hand-printed, bound with rope and twine. This inspired both José and Miriam, who wanted *Mandala* to have the same homegrown, handcrafted feeling.

One day, José overheard Ram Dass and Steve Durkee in a room listening to what sounded like interesting etheric piano music. He later found they were listening to original recordings of Russian mystic G.I. Gurdjieff playing the harmonium. (Years later, jazz pianist Keith Jarrett would make a recording of these same pieces.) Though José met Ram Dass briefly, he didn't have the opportunity to connect with him until 32 years later in 2003 at the 33rd annual Whole Earth Festival.

Chapter 24
Evergreen State College

> *Art degraded, imagination denied,*
> *war governs the nations!*
>
> —William Blake

José, Miriam, and Josh drove to Washington State in September 1971 to find a house. Bob Morris and his girlfriend, Patty, José's former students, accompanied them. The students had offered to move with them to Washington to help with domestic duties, including the care of Josh. José and Miriam were happy for the help. Bob and Patty had been instrumental in organizing the Whole Earth Festival. They had a deep curiosity about life and a passion for the Grateful Dead.

It didn't take them long to find a large two-story house in the woods on Country Club Road, not far from Evergreen College. Soon after they had moved in, Gary Snyder came for a visit. He looked around at the middle-class suburban home and said, "Oh, I get it: suburban hippies!"

José and Miriam found living with Bob and Patty a harmonious arrangement. Even though they weren't enrolled at Evergreen, Bob and Patty spent much time on campus mingling with art students.

José's first year as an art history professor and head of the Man and Arts Program at the experimental college provided many challenges. He had many creative students but no paints, no canvasses, no musical instruments, and no facilities for art projects—nothing. For the second-year budget, José recommended $750,000 to get the Man and Arts program off the ground. In early January, the governor of Washington, Dan Evans, sent back the budget indicating zero funding for the arts. The majority of the second-year budget was given to Science Phase II to build laboratories, and the parking lot project received as much as José had requested for the art department.

Frustrated, José went to the library building (which is now named after Dan Evans) and, with a can of red paint, spray-painted: "No construction without destruction!" on the bottom of the stairwell. No one knew who had done it.

As was true in many academic institutions, there were many polarized feelings among the administration, the faculty, and the students. José did his best to get along, but it wasn't easy. A deep personal disquietude and inner dissatisfaction grew. Still, he felt he needed to gain more academic experience, and working as a professor at a college at least offered some amount of leverage in the world, which he would later need.

At this time, Miriam was busy working on completing the design aspects and editing of *Mandala*, and often traveled to Berkeley to complete the editing with Shambhala Publishing. This only highlighted his feelings of confinement within the shell of an institution and also within the frame of the family unit. Much friction and tension arose between José and Miriam at this time. He knew the state of his marriage was an outer manifestation of a much deeper dissatisfaction within himself. He was impatient with himself and knew there was much more he needed to learn before he could really accomplish his life mission, whatever it was.

In late January 1972, Governor Evans invited the entire faculty of Evergreen to the governor's mansion for the annual open house Washington State art show. Because Dan Evans had granted zero funding for the college art program, José organized a protest demonstration at the open house event. He and his colleagues showed up holding a banner bearing the William Blake inscription: "Art degraded, imagination denied, war governs the nations!" They each pinned a copy of the budget onto their jacket showing that everything was funded except the arts, and here was the governor hosting an art event at his mansion and inviting everyone from the new college! An old, well-to-do woman tore the Blake banner out of José's hands, but, after he explained what had happened, she immediately wrote a $10,000 check for the arts program.

The next day, José bought musical instruments and paints. Because there were no art facilities available, José and his students used the four-floored stairwell as their visual arts studio, painting a four-story mural. José hired Miriam to oversee the project, a group effort that included José, his colleague Cruz Esquivel, Miriam, 17 art students, and Bob and Patty.

Drawing upon the four elements, José conceived of the mural as a "transformative art piece," It depicted a dragon transforming itself from earth to water to air to fire. The mural appeared on each of the three stairwell landings. On the top landing, located directly outside the president's office, the painting depicted the transition between the air dragon ascending into the fire dragon. For this image of transformation José chose a hydrogen bomb test with a brilliant phoenix rising from the mushroom cloud. This climactic image was based on an actual photo of a French hydrogen bomb test in the South Pacific.

In February 1972, José and Miriam were just finishing *Mandala* and, at the suggestion of Sam Bercholz, they sought Trungpa Rinpoche to write the foreword. Though their relationship was still strained, José and Miriam traveled to California together to attend Trungpa's "Dawn of Tantra" seminar and to ask him to write the foreword. Upon arriving in Berkeley, José and Miriam met up with Gary Snyder, Allen Ginsberg, and Allen's partner, Peter Orlovsky. Here, they also met Herbert Gunther, a leading scholar of Tibetan Vajrayana Buddhism. After the seminar, José sought out Trungpa and found him at a wild dharma party in Berkeley. As José approached Trungpa, who was sitting at the kitchen table, a visibly intoxicated woman named Ruthie grabbed him, put him in a "scissors hold," and tried to take him down to the floor. Through all the wildness, he finally reached Trungpa, who dictated the foreword as José scribbled it down:

> The search for knowledge and wisdom by concepts is part of man's confused struggle. Nevertheless using ideas as a stepping-stone is necessary for the student as a starting point.... In this book the authors have worked diligently, delving into many different cultures and studying the expressions of Buddha nature in each tradition, particularly in terms of the Mandala principle. As such, their work is itself a demonstration of Mandala in action.... It is my hope that this book will give you new insight in transcending the world of psychological and spiritual materialism....

In the early summer of 1972, José and Miriam again visited Rudhyar, now living in the mountains outside of Idyllwild, California, near Palm Springs. During the visit, José learned Rudhyar's books had fallen out of print. José immediately contacted Shambhala Publications, which reprinted some of his books, making his works prominent in the late '70s and early '80s.

Mandala was published in June 1972. The feedback was phenomenal. Illustrated throughout with examples of mandalic symbols, architecture, and artifacts, *Mandala* was the first book of its kind to document historical and cultural mandala use. The opening chapter starts with a vision of the whole Earth, describing it as a living mandala. This book, with its colorful descriptions of the creative process and the spiritual and transformative power of mandala as art form, proved to be a cult classic among many artists.

Published simultaneously was the revised version of José's PhD dissertation, *Charles Henry and the Formation of a Psychophysical Aesthetic*. Suddenly, with two books in print, José felt a new sense of accomplishment, though he knew he had a long way to go.

Not long after *Mandala* came out, José stopped painting mandalas for fear they would become another "modernist gimmick." Instead, he turned his focus to the study and practice of Tibetan Buddhism. He felt the only way to reach a higher level of artistic creation was to discipline himself in study and practice of a formal spirituality. Twenty years passed before he painted again.

The second year at Evergreen proved better than the first. He felt satisfied having at least been able to acquire minimal funds to launch the Man and Arts Project and complete the mural project. With his colleague Cruz Esquivel, he administered a Chicano study program a few times a month with Mexican-American prisoners at the federal prison on McNeill Island, Puget Sound. He stepped down from being lead in the Man and Arts Program and was free to organize tutorial programs on any subject he wished. Especially gratifying was designing the class "Impact of Buddhism on the West," which allowed him time to research how Buddhism came to the West. He studied the works of Chögyam Trungpa, Madame Blavatsky, Walt Whitman, Allen Ginsberg, and Gary Snyder. He also taught a seminar on Quetzalcoatl. This was a time of great creative fulfillment.

Chapter 25
Seeds of Prophecy

In the coming Earth changes and time of
prophecy, only a people who are
spiritually strong will survive.

—Thomas Banyaca, Hopi

At José's invitation, Tony Shearer gave a talk at Evergreen State College in the fall of 1972. At the time, Tony was working as a guest lecturer at a small nearby college outside of Tacoma. Deeply passionate, Tony explained the prophecy of Quetzalcoatl in great detail to José and his students. Everyone was captivated by Tony's colorful stories of the magic of the ancients and the Mayan sacred calendar.

Tony said the prophetic dates, August 16–17, 1987, were revealed to him by a mysterious female *curandara* (shaman) in Oaxaca, who came from a "long lineage of shamans." He said she also transmitted to him the knowledge of the calendar with its special, interwoven, 52-unit design, published in his 1971 book *Lord of the Dawn*.

Over the course of several visits, Tony explained to José in detail about the Tzolkin, the 260-day sacred count of the Maya. José remembered the 260-day cycle from Morley's *Ancient Maya* book, and knew it was the basis of Mayan time knowledge.

Tony showed him the Tzolkin's central "magic number pattern" that revealed the 13 moons. José would later refer to this "magic number pattern" as the Loom of Maya in his 1987 work, *The Mayan Factor*. Tony showed José the intrinsic numerology and mathematics of the radially opposite quartets contained within the Tzolkin, which all add up to 28. He also pointed out how the 52 days of the "magic number pattern" constitute 13 sets of four, each set adding up to 28, which is the basis of the 13 Moon calendar: $13 \times 28 = 364$ days.

Tony also told José for the first time about the tomb of Pacal Votan, discovered in Palenque in 1952. When José heard this, he felt like he was remembering something he had long forgotten. Tony told him the great Votan lived in "the dark house beneath the Tower of the Winds." Tony associated Votan with Joseph Smith, founder of the Mormon religion. He believed the basis of the Mormon prophecy, the 22 plates of gold discovered by Smith, were actually the plates Pacal Votan had entrusted to his son, Chan Balum, whom the Mormons call the angel Moroni.

According to Tony, Pacal Votan was the mysterious inspiration behind the angel Moroni, who directed Joseph Smith to these 22 plates. Tony related the 22 plates to the numbers 9 and 13, claiming the actual source of the Quetzalcoatl prophecy of the 13 Heavens and 9 Hells was well known by Pacal Votan. He believed this knowledge originated with Tetzotlipoca, one of the chief architect designers and rulers of Teotihuacán around the second century BC.

After his meeting with Tony, many things fell into place for José. With Tony's inspiration, José concentrated deeply on the Tzolkin, exploring and meditating upon all of its magical number patterns. (See image on page 144.)

José and Miriam's relationship continued to improve, and in May 1972 they conceived their second child. This was followed by their first trip to Hawaii to give a mandala workshop in Honolulu.

After arriving back in the continental United States, they drove through the Southwest Indian country to Santa Fe and then made their first visit to Boulder, Colorado, to Trungpa's headquarters at 1111 Pearl Street. They also visited the recently acquired Rocky Mountain Dharma Center (now known as the Shambhala Mountain Center), where they camped for 10 days while attending Trungpa's first seminar on the land, the "Ten Bhumis." At the seminar, Trungpa described the 10 bhumis as the 10 stages of the development of the bodhisattva; he emphasized that "bodhisattvas could not leave Earth" until they "picked up every last piece of plastic off the ground." This struck a deep chord in José.

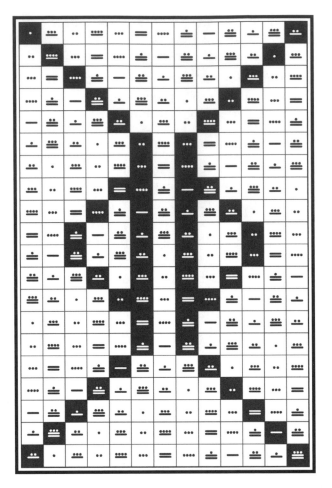

260-unit Tzolkin/Harmonic matrix. From The Mayan Factor *(Bear and Company, 1996). Reprinted with permission of José Arguelles.*

During this event, José received his first meditation instruction from Trungpa. Sitting face to face in Trungpa's small camp trailer, José learned the proper sitting posture and the "clear meditation" technique of "mixing mind with space."

"Remember to dissolve your thoughts with the out breath," Trungpa told him. José realized it was not just meditation instruction he was receiving, but rather an entire mindset that was being transmitted. For José, this was an indestructible enactment sealed in Eternity, and one of the most important moments of his life.

After receiving the instruction, José meditated whenever he could, particularly early in the morning when everyone was asleep. This practice brought him great inner relief. The opportunity to sit with himself, release his thoughts, and experience the fundamental void space was a great comfort to his soul. He became aware of many habitual patterns, particularly his tendency to create elaborate, complex thought forms regarding the nature of history. As pleasurable as he found it to create these thoughts, he persistently worked to dissolve them and enter into pure mind awareness. Through this initial meditation experience, he realized how active his mind was, churning out thought after thought, whether he liked it or not.

Toward the end of 1972, Thomas Banyaca of the Hopi Nation accepted José's invitation to deliver the Hopi Prophecy to his students at Evergreen. Banyaca came with a small entourage and carrying a large white banner with a pictograph of the Hopi Prophecy as depicted on Prophecy Rock in Hopi Mesa. The pictograph showed the two paths open to humankind. One was the straight, sacred path (Red Road) and the other was the zigzag path (High Road).

Banyaca said the human race had reached a crossroads and taken the High Road, or the troubled path. Above the disintegrating High Road, the pictograph showed a gourd of ash, representing the Third World War or final cataclysm. He explained that the gourd of ashes had been shaken twice, by the two atomic bombs at Hiroshima and Nagasaki. The prophecy said the gourd of ashes would shake a third and final time, leading to the final disintegration of the High Road. This coincides with the prophecy of the Blue Star Kachina, due to appear in 2012.

As Banyaca was delivering the prophecy, a snowstorm broke out without warning, and all the lights went out. "In the coming Earth Changes and time of prophecy," Banyaca warned, "only a people who are spiritually strong will survive!"

Banyaca said that, after the final cataclysm, only the straight Red Road, which was shown at the bottom of the pictograph, would remain. At this point, Banyaca said, the Hopi with their planting sticks would still be there, planting new corn.

From that time on, José carried with him the little booklet by Hopi elder Dan Katchongva that told about the creation of life to the Day of Purification. Katchongva had first revealed the Hopi Prophecy in 1949 and had spoken words transcribed in this little book that José regarded as a sacred treasure. José would meet Banyaca again in 1995 and inform him of the Prophecy of Pacal Votan.

Soon after Banyaca's visit, Khigh Diegh came to Olympia and made an *I Ching* presentation to José's students. José gifted him two of the four original *Doors of Perception* and another painting called *Mandala of the Void*, a colorful piece of wood with a huge circle void where a coffee table had been cut out. Khigh Diegh strapped the three paintings on top of his station wagon, said goodbye, and drove off to California. When he got home, he called José and told him he lost Mandala of the Void somewhere between Grants Pass and Ashland, Oregon. He couldn't find it anywhere.

"Don't worry," José told him. "There are a lot of hippies in those hills down there, and one of them will find it and think it fell from the sky."

Chapter 26
The Transformative Vision

*The vision of what we are to become is
already within us, awaiting the proper
discipline through which it might be
appropriately expressed.*

—José Arguelles, *The
Transformative Vision*

On January 26, 1973, Tara Oriana Arguelles was born by Caesarean section at a hospital in Olympia, Washington. She had been due on January 24th, José's birthday, but he and Miriam didn't want that and asked Dane Rudhyar for his astrological advice on a favorable birth date. They chose January 26th because of the particular Sabian symbol associated with the day. Remembering Josh's birth, José stood outside the operating room, chanting the Tibetan heart sutra: "*Om Gate Gate Paragate Parasamgate Bodhi Svaha!* (Gone, gone, gone beyond, gone totally beyond, hail to the enlightened one!)"

José saw Tara for the first time in a hospital elevator. It was 30 minutes after her birth, and the nurse was taking her to the nursery. He was amazed at how perfectly formed every part of her body was. She was so silent that he wondered if she was breathing. The nurse assured him that she was just fine.

The first six months of Tara's life was the worst time of Josh's. Three-year-old Josh was congenitally rundown and confined to an oxygen tent in their small duplex in the middle of the woods outside of Olympia. The Western medical doctors strongly suggested that Josh might have leukemia, but José and Miriam did not feel this was a correct diagnosis and sought alternative help.

In the spring of 1973, Ethel and Enrique traveled from Minnesota to Olympia to see their grandchildren. During their visit, José and his Evergreen students performed *Lord of the Dawn,* a mystery play based on Tony Shearer's book. The play was performed in a forest clearing near the college. José played Quetzalcoatl. After the performance, Ethel remarked to José, "I used to think there was just the Christian religion, but after seeing this, I think religion might be bigger than that."

By the spring of 1973, *Mandala* had been out for nine months and was doing phenomenally well. Though pleased with the book's success, José and Miriam had other concerns. Josh had been sick for months and was showing little improvement. José and Miriam grew increasingly concerned and felt they might find a better alternative therapy for Josh in California. Living off royalties from *Mandala,* José was able to take a yearlong sabbatical from Evergreen beginning in June 1973. They could move back to California and find help for Josh, and José could continue his focus on research and writing *The Transformative Vision.*

Before leaving Evergreen, José presented a long-term academic vision and plan for the school to the entire faculty and the deans at his last breakfast meeting. The college was having difficulty defining its unique niche in the eyes of state government. José proposed that the college focus on developing alternative environmental technologies, with the arts and all other subjects revolving around the environment. He suggested that Evergreen State College be renamed "Washington Institute of Technology (WIT)." His proposal didn't go over well.

In June 1973, José, Miriam, Josh, and Tara moved back to California. They rented a house in the older north side of Berkeley, at 1404 McGee Street. Both José and Miriam were happy with the move. The urban Bay area felt fresh and inspiring. At the time, the war was winding down in Vietnam and, in 1973–74, there were a big gas shortage and a scarcity panic in America. José and Miriam bought a lot of dry food and stored it, just in case there was a gas shortage and food supplies weren't readily available. As it was, the gas lines were long, with only a few gas stations open. This was the beginning of the formation of OPEC (Oil Producing Energy Cartel), which mostly represented Arabian countries, but also included Venezuela.

During this time, José managed to slowly begin research and writing for what would be known as *The Transformative Vision: Reflections on the Nature and History of Human Expression.* His free time was spent piecing together notes and ideas that he'd gathered over the previous seven years. He had stacks and stacks of notes and loose papers with all of his art history research and reflections about art.

He first thought the book would be called *Art at the Dawn of a New Magic.* As his research deepened, however, he realized that first he must create a thorough understanding and analysis of the artist and the visionary in history. He felt that, ultimately, history had to end before the new magic could dawn. Therefore, *The Transformative Vision* evolved into a foundational, encyclopedic study.

Josh's health worsened, and José and Miriam did their best to care for him while seeking the right alternative healer. They soon found Dr. McKimmey, a psychic chiropractor in Palo Alto. After examining Josh, Dr. McKimmy concluded that his entire nervous system had been stripped down from too many drugs during his traumatic birth. He said Josh's system had to be rebuilt. This diagnosis felt correct to José and Miriam, who spent much energy administering Josh's treatment and diet.

At Dr. McKimmey's suggestion, José and Miriam put their son on a strict diet of tomato juice and ground beef liver. They were told this would build up his nervous system and red blood cells. Though the diet seemed strange, José and Miriam were willing to try anything at that point. Josh had also become anemic, and his spleen had weakened. They treated him by dipping a heating pad in castor oil and placing it over his abdomen, daily. He began to recover quickly.

During his convalescence, 4-year-old Josh spent much time indoors, drawing pictures. José established a strong bond with Tara, who was an exceptionally healthy baby. Between ages six and 12 months, Tara established a way of blinking at her father to communicate.

On one occasion, José and Miriam took Josh and Tara to a Chinese restaurant, where Josh spilled boiling tea water all over his abdomen, resulting in second-degree burns. Because Josh was just recovering from a long illness, this particularly disturbed both José and Miriam. In retrospect, the event seemed to be an omen indicating Josh's fate.

José visited Rudhyar again in 1973 at his home in San Jacinto. They went for a long walk behind his house in the mysterious high desert mountain country outside of Palm Springs. Rudhyar asked José if he would consider being his successor to carry on his esoteric stream of knowledge. Deeply touched by the proposal, José declined the offer, telling Rudhyar he'd already accepted Chögyam Trungpa Rinpoche as his teacher. Rudhyar respected José's decision but expressed skepticism about Eastern thought. Nonetheless, the connection between the two was undeniable.

Rudhyar told José, "Even though you won't accept being my successor, I have to let you know that I know who you are." Rudhyar gave José the transmission of St. Germain and seventh ray ceremonial magic. (St. Germain lived in the 17th and 18th centuries and is credited with mysterious activities associated with the seventh ray: the will toward expression to produce new forms of civilization.)

Rudhyar, who had received the transmission from Master Morya, told José he felt him to have a special connection with Count Rakoczy, a 19th-century emanation of St. Germain. Count Rakoczy was a Hungarian mystic aristocrat and friend of Beethoven, commissioning him to write much of his music. Rakoczy was also said to have strong influence on Hungarian composer Franz Liszt, whom Rudhyar thought himself an emanation of. In *The Rays and the Initiations*, Alice Bailey, a personal acquaintance of Rudhyar, described Count Rakoczy, whom she referred to as Master R, as "a master of civilization and one of the presiding members of hierarchy that operates throughout the planetary and the solar logos."

Rudhyar went on to tell José that he considered him a carrier of the seventh ray ceremonial magic. He believed the Whole Earth Festival was "an act of seventh ray ceremonial magic." Rudhyar told José not to forget this responsibility of his destiny and character unfoldment.

Rudhyar and José discussed the meaning of humanity moving from the sixth ray (Piscean Age) to the seventh ray (Aquarian Age). The sixth ray is the ray of devotion and idealism, and contains all the struggles of ideology that result in wars and factionism in the world, whereas the seventh ray is the coming new age and is characterized by order, cooperation, and organization. This moment of transmission and initiation into the esoteric occult tradition was a pivotal point. It raised José's level of consciousness by large increments and prepared him for a number of different levels of empowerments.

After his meeting with Rudhyar, José received many flashes of insight that became the base foundation of his planetary vision. These insights found their way into *The Transformative Vision*.

First, he saw how the geometrical structure of the polar axis and the two hemispheres of the Earth symbolize the polarity of man and the two hemispheres of the brain. Next, he saw the vision of the whole Earth as one interconnected system—a spherical living mandala with intrinsic geometrical structures. He experienced the Earth as a holographic representation of cosmic order, the ultimate manifestation of the cosmic whole, and simultaneously the smallest unit of manifestation in a star system. He understood that all forms of reality in the universe, from the densest to most etheric, are arranged in a sublime, orderly manner.

José concluded that, because the process of modern civilization has stunted people's expressive creativity, human beings—individually and collectively—had to go through a cathartic period, a process of individuation from the profane into a spiritual/artistic rebirth. In *The Transformative Vision*, he wrote:

> In order for us to transcend the combative dualism that is the very essence of our condition, there must be a unitive experience of the world that can be achieved only through a major collective catharsis.

While writing *The Transformative Vision*, José reflected much on his meetings with Rudhyar, and also those with Trungpa and Sun Bear. He empathized with the struggle each of these beings endured while working for the betterment of humanity. Rudhyar struggled to maintain clarity in the hermetic or esoteric tradition that he realized in the lineage of St. Germain. Trungpa struggled through much misunderstanding, being a main forerunner presenting Tibetan Buddhism to the unruly American mind. His struggle was such that he fell into alcoholism and would die in a somewhat tragic way. Sun Bear struggled to make a new path for Native Americans with the formation of the modern day Bear Tribe. José himself would later struggle to assimilate and renew ancient knowledge of the Maya.

From these three men, José learned to honor and appreciate everyone and everything that had gone before him. Through their lives, he realized what a struggle it is to maintain dignity and any kind of truth in this lost world.

Rudhyar's vision about the Earth as an art-whole was a main theme in *The Transformative Vision*. José wrote:

An art-whole is determined by the quality of life-response, and not by a particular aesthetic philosophy. It is no longer of history, for it no longer supports the notion of art as entertainment or of the artist as an isolated genius, the main staples of art-historical art, down to the heyday of popular psychedelic culture with its adulation of rock superstars. Instead, an art-whole is the expressive mode of the creative seed group on its slow, lonely, and often anonymous return to a mythic space where the inner and the outer worlds mirror each other. When expression of any kind proceeds from inner realization, each act bears the imprint of truth; it matters not whether the expression is a work of "art." The path of the seed group is the only path beyond the politics of Apocalypse.

José considered *The Transformative Vision* a seminal text. It introduced many new ideas, including the prophecy of the Thirteen Heavens and Nine Hells as transmitted to him by Tony Shearer. It also introduced the 2012 date as the conclusion of the Mayan 5,125-year Great Cycle.

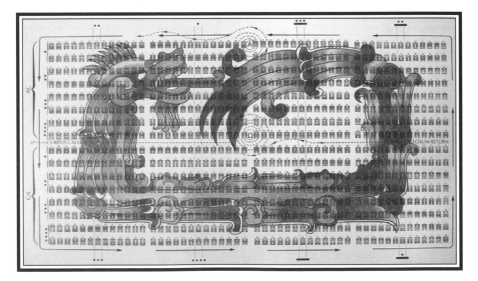

Ororoborus—Feathered Rainbow Serpent. From Earth Ascending: A Treatise on the Law Governing Whole Systems *(originally published by Shambhala Publications in 1984, and republished by Bear and Company in 1996). Reprinted by permission of José Arguelles.*

The Transformative Vision contained so much information that Shambhala Publications scaled it down to one-third of its size, 24 chapters. The book highlights the Kali Yuga, or period of chaos, and says this "Dark Age" was also "foreseen by the ancient Mexicans as the age of the Center ruled by Quetzalcoatl's twin, Tezcatlipoca, the smoking mirror, who symbolized the nocturnal Sun, the earth Sun, which is humanity itself, the matter through which the luminous Sun becomes incarnate."

The Transformative Vision concludes with the vision of the closing of the whole cycle of civilization and history. It describes the period between 1987 and 2012 as the "interchange of tinctures," which occurs when the "ororoborus (serpent) bites its tail, releasing its poison in order to heal itself."

Chapter 27
Meditation in Action

It is said, in the Lankavatara Sutra, that unskilled farmers throw away their rubbish and buy manure from other farmers, but those who are skilled go on collecting their own rubbish, in spite of the bad smell and unclean work, and when it is ready to be used they spread it on their land and out of this they grow their crops. That is the skilled way.

—Chögyam Trungpa Rinpoche,
Meditation in Action

In the fall of 1973, José and Miriam attended the last four weeks of Trungpa's first Vajrayana seminary in Jackson Hole, Wyoming. Trungpa would conduct six more of these Vajrayana seminaries, three-month residential programs introducing a vast body of Buddhist teachings in an atmosphere of intensive meditation practice. It was here that José first took refuge, bodhisattva, and Vajrayana vows with Trungpa, who named him, "Accomplisher of the Ten Bhumis."

José taught one course at San Francisco State University in March 1974, to supplement his income. Finding the university campus sufficiently interesting, he agreed to teach art history full time the following year, after his sabbatical ended.

He was invited to return as a guest speaker for the fourth annual Whole Earth Festival. At the event, he was given an official award from the legislature of the State of California, proclaiming him the "father" of the Whole Earth Festival and commending him for promoting the arts and culture in California.

Upon receiving the award, he told the crowd: "I know that history runs in cycles, but I didn't know the cycles were so brief and that I would be elevated in stature again so quickly after being forced out of this job four years ago."

Pleased that the Whole Earth Festival was now an annual event, José was inspired to continue his own Whole Earth education program, teaching about and studying different cultures, religions, and worldviews of all the peoples of planet Earth.

In 1974, he started his official Vajrayana practices (advanced Tibetan Buddhist practices). These practices, referred to as the "four foundations" or *ngondro*, involved elaborate visualizations, mantras, and use of ritual instruments, a *dorje* and bell. José was required to complete 100,000 prostrations and 100,000 recitations of the Vajrasattva mantra, 100,000 mandala offerings, one million guru yoga recitations, and endless hours of formal meditation practice. Fulfilling these requirements would take him five years.

José with first Tzolkin drawing (behind), 1974. Image courtesy of and copyright the José Arguelles Archive.

In addition to his Vajrayana practices, José continued to study the large Tzolkin graphic he created. He was irresistibly drawn to the vibrational frequency of this mysterious grid; he felt a ceaseless cosmic rhythm, like waves rising and falling with an even periodicity. It was apparent to him that this was far more than just a count of days. He meditated deeply on the different tones and patterns, which opened him in stages, at first unconsciously and then consciously, to different levels of memory, meaning, and multiple purposes. He would wonder and contemplate: Is this the nature of cosmic time? In cosmic time, are these somehow the codes to unlock the keys of life?

He was also immersed in studies of the *I Ching* and eventually discovered Ben Franklin's magic square of eight. He was inspired to plug the *I Ching* codons or hexagrams into those 64 units of the "magic square." This integration of the *I Ching* and the Tzolkin would find its way into his 1984 work, *Earth Ascending*. In 1973, the scientist Schönberger published a book confirming the structural identity of the *I Ching* and DNA and the binary code language.

In many ways, José felt he was finally coming into his own. He was on the right spiritual track, studying Buddhism and doing Buddhist meditation, and also on the right intellectual track, researching and writing *The Transformative Vision*, as well as consistently studying the Tzolkin. He felt he was fulfilling all of the art history visions he'd been developing since his graduate days at the University of Chicago.

Swami Muktananda invited José to darshan at his mansion outside of Oakland. He was told that the Indian guru had heard about him and wanted to meet him. José was taken into Swami Muktananda's bedroom, where the guru, wearing a simple loincloth, was bouncing up and down on a four-poster bed.

"Come," said the Swami. "Sit down on the bed with me." As José went to sit on the bed, Swami Muktanada grabbed his head. "I'm going to give you *shaktipat*," he said. With those words, he brought José's forehead to his own—Bam! Bam! José told him he already had a teacher, Trungpa Rinpoche. "That's okay," the Swami said. "You got shaktipat from me now." José found this response curious and felt slightly uncomfortable. The next day he came down with a high fever.

In the summer of 1974, before starting his full-time teaching position at San Francisco State University, José went to Boulder for the opening of Naropa Institute, where he taught classes on Native American and Tantric art. Founded by Chögyam Trungpa Rinpoche, the university derived its name from Naropa, the 11th-century Indian Buddhist mystic and monk of Nalanda University. Naropa was the second in the lineage of what would later be known as the Kagyu School of Tibetan Buddhism, renowned for bringing together scholarly wisdom with meditative insight. The Kagyu tradition traces back to Milarepa.

The opening of Naropa was a gala event, considered by some as the "Woodstock of education." Trungpa was in high, informal, iconoclast form and attracted all the major poets, artists, and scholars of his generation, including Allen Ginsberg, Ram Dass, Gregory Corso, Diane DePrimo, Gregory Bateson, and many others.

As much as Trungpa was a teacher of the way of "crazy wisdom," he was also a bold, daring artist at heart. José considered his two greatest legacies were his emphasis on mindfulness training and his vision of dharma art. Dharma art is art as everyday life, but an everyday life where the sacred is the normative experience. José understood *sacred* to mean something that evokes a sense of awe that breaks your heart, something that touches and moves you mysteriously and poignantly, even though it may be just an ordinary experience of reality.

In one of his creative, artistic endeavors, Trungpa adapted the Heart Sutra to a type of existential ritual drama. His style of drama was similar to a Japanese drama called "Noh theater," with its slow, ritualistic form. Trungpa asked that José play his new shakahachi flute for a summer performance in Boulder and fall performances in San Francisco.

José's first shakahachi flute was accidentally run over by a car at a gas station on New Year's Day. An American man who later became a successor to Rudhyar had made that flute. José had purchased a new flute, a genuine Japanese shakahachi, in San Francisco. He was happy playing his new instrument along with the ritualistic recitations of the Heart Sutra. The shakahachi was the only music in the performance.

Over the years, José worked closely with Trungpa on many dharma art projects, including flower arranging and brush painting, where he would practice painting circles in one-brush stroke. Through the art of flower arranging, José learned much about participating in the mysteries of creation. He found that, because flowers grow in nature, you can take different flowers and plants, and arrange them in a ceramic container so that they create a composition, which is like a focalized piece of nature. He saw that arranging flowers is participating in creation—that is, by entering the mystery of nature to feel what it's like to place plants and flowers in striking juxtaposition to each other, you create something as bold as any painting or sculpture.

Trungpa emphasized that all activities are a work of art if we are in a state of mindfulness. He also taught that you can view everything as a ceremony or ritual. If you do things in a mindful way, the intrinsic ritual or ceremony of everyday life can reveal itself in ever-higher forms of elegance. This was enormously appealing to José. He loved working on dharma art projects and did so until 1981.

Trungpa taught that dharma art and mindfulness training go hand in hand. The two cannot be separated. He said art is how you organize your life moment to moment in a state of mindfulness. He emphasized that even the smallest activities are not to be taken for granted; every action is significant. Through practice, José applied the awareness of ceremony in his day-to-day activities and slowly learned how to transform his everyday environment.

After the Naropa session, José was at a dharma meeting with the sangha at the Berkeley dharmadatu when it was announced that His Holiness the 16th Karmapa would soon make a visit to the United States. Everyone would have to change their attitude and dress. Formal attire would be the norm: suits and ties for the men and conservative dresses worn with high heels for the women. All dharma practitioners would be required to bow and do prostrations. Everyone who wanted to be in that community was required to follow the new rules. Literally overnight, the Buddhist community went from free-flowing hippie to formal suit and tie. The next day, José went to Brooks Brothers, and bought tweed and pinstriped suits. To him, the change felt comical and unreal, like high theater.

With the Karmapa's visit forthcoming, Trungpa made an immediate decision to choose a dharma heir and so he appointed Thomas Rich to be his Vajra Regent, a traditional position of responsibility for carrying on the teaching legacy left by a teacher. Though José found Tom Rich a friendly and gregarious man, he was surprised at Trungpa's selection. He had first met Tom Rich at the original Whole Earth Festival when he came with his then guru, Swami Satchidananda. In 1973, José and Tom spent an evening together drinking and doing Hare Krishna chants. Now, Tom Rich was known as Vajra Regent Ösel Tendzin, the first Westerner to be acknowledged as a lineage holder in the Kagyü tradition.

When Trungpa first began teaching in the States, he was on his own, especially after he disrobed in 1968. Six years later, he'd built up a big following in an informal hippie style. But now that H.H. Karmapa was coming, Trungpa felt the need to show respect with a costume change. To José, it seemed like Trungpa realized his behavior had been excessive and, now that the boss was coming, he wanted to clean things up to impress. To his credit, Trungpa had thus far conducted the first Vajrayana seminary, opened Naropa Institute, developed a significant following, and appointed a dharma heir. But to really please the boss, he felt he had to change his style of living and his clothes. From that point on, the dharma scene was much more stiff and formal.

The 16th Karmapa had planned a special ceremony passed on from the fifth Karmapa. Dressed in their finest attire, more than 3,000 people gathered at Fort Mason, San Francisco, in October 1974, to witness the first Black Crown ceremony ever performed in America. The air was charged with electricity, and a feeling of high magic was in the air as the Tibetan horns were blown and the sound of ancient chants filled the space. The black hat was placed onto the Karmapa's head, and everyone lined up to receive his blessing.

During the Karmapa's visit, José enjoyed a few audiences with him and found him a simple, straightforward, and compassionate being. He had heard the Karmapa liked to go into pet stores, buy all the birds in the cages, and set them free. José talked about Milarepa with the Karmapa, who encouraged him to walk in Milarepa's footsteps.

In the fall of 1974, José started his full-time job as professor at San Francisco State University. Though well liked and respected by the university faculty, he was reluctant to begin his full-time teaching career due to his increasing distaste for institutions. In the late 1960s and early 1970s, San Francisco State had been a bastion of radicalism, including much violence.

Though confined to an institution, José was grateful to be in the Bay Area and have the freedom to teach whatever classes he wished. He was always trying to figure out ways to get people involved in big artistic projects that would bring out their creativity.

Not long after he began working full-time at the university, he and Miriam used their royalty money from *Mandala* to buy their first house, at 3806 Harrison Street in Oakland. Here, José attempted the role of a full-fledged father and husband. In the backyard, he and Miriam planted a garden, and José bought a playground set with a slide and swings from Sears Roebuck, which he put together for the kids and placed behind the garden. José's favorite times with the children were when he was reading them stories and singing them spontaneous songs.

Josh had finally recovered from his mystery illness. He had developed a strong inclination for art. He and José would sit for long periods and draw dinosaurs; Josh especially loved the Tyrannosaurus rex. After they moved to California, Josh liked watching Japanese cartoons and drawing the monsters, particularly Godzilla and King Kong. José and Miriam enrolled Josh in Aikido lessons, which he loved. José thought Josh must have had strong past life ties to Japan, as his best friend was Japanese, and he showed unusual delight whenever they visited Japantown in San Francisco.

Chapter 28
The Call of the Maya

But as the inner psychic house of history begins to collapse, suddenly appearing through the debris are the glints and glimmers of eternal magic.

—José Arguelles, *Transformative Vision*

In 1974, José experienced his first drugless optical experience in a meditation hall at Berkeley. While meditating, he gazed at the floor and became acutely aware of many wild patterns; he soon realized these patterns were not happening "out there" but inside him. It made no difference whether he opened his eyes or closed them, the patterns remained. He was mystified and at first chalked up the experience to an LSD flashback, but such experiences continued to occur from 1974 to 1979.

By late 1974, he once again felt a deep personal dissatisfaction with his family life. Miriam was independent and busily involved in various women's groups, as well as with taking care of the children while José worked. However, he and Miriam still conducted mandala workshops and were increasingly involved with the Berkeley Dharmadhatu Center. For many members of the Dharmadatu Center, social drinking was a fundamental part of their lifestyle. As a result, José soon found himself falling into old patterns.

In 1975, Trungpa advised José and Miriam to stop all workshops and side projects in order to focus single-pointedly on the Buddhist path. José stopped giving workshops, although he occasionally conducted seminars on *The Transformative Vision*, which was published that same year. Despite its well-documented thesis, *The Transformative Vision* was panned by major art magazines, who thought José had transgressed the boundaries of traditional art history.

Sam Bercholz was disappointed, and, in art history circles, José went from being the successful mandala artist to being perceived as someone who had transgressed the academic norm and, therefore, discredited. One established art historian labeled him "some pied piper from California leading his followers into the sea." Traditional art historians balked the most at his use of non-European criteria to critique European art. José found this judgment blatantly racist.

To counteract his growing personal dissatisfaction, José created the ambitious Shambhala/Tollan Foundation with Bercholz and Fagan. The idea was to make a spiritually based encyclopedia of cosmic knowledge organized in a non-linear structure. José saw Shambhala and Tollan as two fundamental archetypal forces informing the course and process of human civilization, both visibly and invisibly. He recognized that the ancient and future visions of the two needed to merge if the world was to be unified. He knew that the dream he had on the night before he met Trungpa, in which he heard "…when the Eastern Sun meets the Western Sun at the 33rd degree," had something to do with this enjoining of Shambhala and Tollan.

Ultimately, José saw the project as, again, referring back to the vision at Teotihuacán. It was a means of returning the cosmic knowledge that would then be helpful in reorienting the human species to its cosmic nature and divine origin. However, Trungpa Rinpoche thought the Shambhala/Tollan Foundation was too lofty and ambitious and, behind José's back, torpedoed the idea with Bercholz and Fagan, who told José they wanted out. José had always wanted to do something vast, integrative, and whole-systems, but it seemed that the Shambhala-Tollan Foundation might be a bit premature—though the vision never escaped him.

During this time, José's fundamental unhappiness and dissatisfaction with himself became reignited, and having to commute every day to a job at an institution didn't help his frame of mind. It seemed that when he was able to work at home, everything stabilized. Having to take a job in the world and play by someone else's rules had a devastating affect on his psyche, even though he knew he had to go through these steps in order to learn.

Fortunately, he managed to keep himself intellectually challenged by teaching classes on unfamiliar subjects that he had to research. However, he despised being made to attend faculty meetings, in which he felt more and more alienated. He found the level of consciousness with which the faculty approached different issues so conventional and fear-based that the meetings all but extinguished his creative spark. He was too sensitive to deal with it, and his frustration grew. As a result, his drinking increased.

Meanwhile, Miriam had become increasingly involved in women's groups, including the National Organization of Women (NOW), a mainstream politically oriented feminist organization. On New Year's Eve in 1975, Miriam asked José for his help in writing a book on the feminine energy. He agreed and from 1976 to 1977 they worked on what would be called *The Feminine: Spacious as the Sky*. Designwise and artistically, Feminine was envisioned as somewhat of a follow-up to *Mandala*, but the context was far more abstract, with its Buddhist notions and neo-Jungian anthropology.

Even though José and Miriam were writing an intimate book on the feminine principle and male/female energies, their own relationship was suffering. They had been much closer when they created *Mandala*, and it had been an effortless collaboration. Writing *Feminine* was far more of a struggle.

In 1976, José became friends with the dean of the San Francisco Institute of Art, Roy Ascott, who took an immediate liking to him. At the dean's invitation, José became a guest professor at the avant-garde San Francisco Art Institute, teaching graduate seminars in mandala theory and visionary art. He also taught high-level symposiums with notable art critics.

It was here, during a conference on modernist art criticism, that José met radical philosopher Angela Davis. He found her cultured and intelligent, not at all the fiery rebel the media portrayed, although she clearly had passionate convictions. Davis had studied philosophy and aesthetics at Heidelburg University in Germany, and she and José had many discussions about those topics from both Marxist and Tranformationalist points of view, often while driving in her little red sports car.

Because of *Mandala* and *The Transformative Vision*, José was invited to speak at various conferences and art symposiums. He was the only male invited to speak at a feminist art conference in Los Angeles, led by Z. Budapest, the prominent neo-pagan feminist artist. In the audience was 17-year-old Mark Comings, who came to the event with his mother to hear José. Comings would later figure in prominently at various points in José's life.

In 1976, José also began part-time teaching work for the Union Graduate School. Based in Cincinnati, Union was the first and most revolutionary of the University Without Walls external adult graduate degree programs. Students designed their own programs to obtain degrees in their chosen fields.

Outwardly, José was leading a high-end, chic life, teaching advanced symposiums with notable art critics, but on the inside he was going downhill fast. His relationship with Miriam was strained. They never confronted each other or talked honestly about their situation, so their relationship developed many unspoken, unconscious inconsistencies that frustrated them both.

He felt something deep inside calling him—something he couldn't quite reach. That vision had been stoked in the early 1970s when Tony Shearer told him about the prophecy of Quetzalcoatl and the Mayan calendar. He knew the information Tony had shared with him about Votan was crucial to his own destiny and would be the key to what he needed to know. All of his knowledge and studies culminated in the summer of 1976, when he made his first visit to Palenque to visit the tomb of Pacal Votan.

José, Miriam, Josh, and Tara had traveled to Mexico that year for summer vacation, their main stops being Chitchen Itza and Palenque. On the day they were to visit the tomb, it was pouring rain. When José reached the top of the Pyramid, he looked behind him only to see a brilliant rainbow. He made his way down the winding stairs into the crypt. He was awestruck as he gazed at the enormous sarcophagus lid of Pacal Votan: He knew he was in the presence of a genuine mystery.

At this point, he saw himself clearly. He saw himself and all of the current life roles he was playing: husband, father, Buddhist, author, professor, and so on. His soul felt empty, dissatisfied. He was creating many traps for himself: family traps, domestic traps, professional traps, mind traps, ego traps. Between what he currently was and what the tomb represented to him was a painful abyss. This awareness led him to undergo a profound catharsis. From the outside, it looked like a downward spiral, but inside José was burning out lifetimes of karma and illusion, a process that would bottom out when he was 40.

PART V

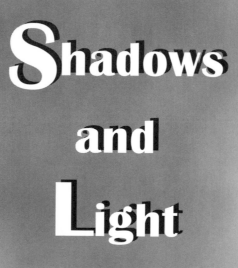

Shadows and Light

Chapter 29
Cycles of Samsara

*Millions go through life very respectably because
they were never put to the test. One who
undertakes spiritual transformation by that very
act rouses and lashes to desperation every
sleeping passion of his animal nature.*

—Madame Blavatsky, "Chelas and
Lay Chelas"

In early 1977, Chögyam Trungpa told José that if he came to live and
study in Boulder he would be "launched in the air and go around
the Earth like a real satellite." That was all José needed to hear.
Both he and Miriam were so immersed in the dharma scene that they
did not hesitate. Vajradhatu in Boulder was the umbrella organization
for many Trungpa centers springing up around the world.

In late spring, Miriam found a house at 430 Gregory Lane on the
southwest edge of central Boulder, right up against Flagstaff Mountain.
By then, José had completed his work at San Francisco State and accepted a full-time job with the Union Graduate School, which required
frequent travel.

In June, José, Miriam, Josh, and Tara loaded their belongings into a
U-Haul truck and drove from Oakland to Boulder, where José saw his
new living quarters for the first time. The house was not particularly
inspiring, but its location was stunning. It had a gorgeous outdoor deck,
Flatiron Elementary School was just a walk down the hill, and there
was little traffic. He was relieved that the children would have a safe
place to play outside.

Tara was immediately enrolled in Buddhist preschool, and Josh entered fourth grade at Flatiron Elementary School. At the time, José was wearing three-piece suits to fit in with Trungpa's community, which had transformed from casual to Wall Street literally overnight. This lifestyle was foreign to José, who felt increasingly alienated from his original self. From the point of view of his earlier beatnik persona, he actually felt like a bourgeois pig.

The redeeming feature of this strange way of life was meditation, and he yearned to have more time to cultivate his inner life. Meditation gave him the opportunity to turn away from his complex external life and inward toward that which he was truly seeking. Though he caught glimpses, it was never enough. He looked forward to weekends when he practiced shamatha (sitting) meditation at the dharma center.

Through meditation, he became increasingly familiar with his mind, though he did not always like what he saw. He had become quite skilled at penetrating into a deeper reality, but he had yet to learn how to untangle himself from third-dimensional illusions. Though he could see how he was perpetuating his own suffering, he could not yet stop these habits. Attempting to release illusions, his mind chased after other illusions to fill the space of illusions he had just released. Therein was his dilemma.

Shortly after moving into their new home, José and Miriam hosted a family reunion. At the reunion, tension arose between José and Miriam and Ivan and Marilla. At this time, José and Miriam were quite successful, materially speaking, as well as avid—if not slightly pompous—Buddhists. Ivan and Marilla, on the other hand, were living a more bohemian lifestyle with Socialist/anarchist leanings. They struggled along in New York with their two children, while Ivan worked as a librarian at New York Public Library. Ivan expressed his distaste for his brother's suburban house, three-piece suits, and newfound Buddhist religion.

At the reunion, an event occurred that would later feel like an omen. Ivan and Marilla's son Max, who was 10 years old at the time, was riding a small bicycle down the driveway. Much too big for the bicycle, Max slipped off and gashed his leg deeply on a piece of concrete protruding from one of the pillars.

Not long after the reunion, in 1978, after a trip to India, Max came down with a high fever, which developed into a grand seizure diagnosed as *herpes encephalitis*. From the seizure, Max suffered severe brain damage. He required around-the-clock care. Not long after, Ivan and Marilla moved to California, finding it the best place to get treatment for Max. Ivan got a job at the University of California, Berkeley, library and Marilla became an activist for brain-damaged children.

Taking care of Max completely changed their lifestyle and greatly limited their mobility. Whereas they had previously been able to travel like carefree gypsies, now their life was restricted to a small radius in the East Bay area of Northern California. Once these difficult circumstances had somewhat normalized, Ivan immersed himself into poetry writing as an all-consuming life passion.

Family reunion, 1977. Image courtesy of and copyright the José Arguelles Archive.

Working for Union Graduate School, José had tremendous creative freedom, but, because he was in the throes of alcoholism, this spelled further difficulties. Being away from home on business for extended periods only exacerbated his feelings of alienation, and he was already frustrated that he could not work in a self-directed manner on the subjects of his passion.

Oftentimes, while flying around the United States to give educational lectures, he drank scotch on the plane and then ate breath mints. Many of his colleagues were drinkers as well, so no one seemed to care that he drank as long as he fulfilled his obligations. However, once he started drinking, it was hard to stop, and soon he entered the dark realm of addiction and utter desperation. The next two years were the test of his soul as he wrestled with his inner demons and the call of his own destiny.

When *The Feminine* was finally published in the autumn of 1977, José was having an affair with a woman from Louisiana. Miriam discovered love letters written to José by the woman and became enraged. He felt remorse for his behavior, but his coping skills were minimal, and the gulf between José and Mirian widened.

In late 1977, José began writing weekly art reviews for the local newspaper, the *Boulder Camera*. He enjoyed the opportunity to write in a popular rather than academic style and studied articles in *People* magazine to learn how to write in a more mainstream fashion. He wrote his weekly art reviews at Tom's Tavern, across the street from the newspaper office. (This job continued through 1984.)

In 1978, Trungpa held the first Kalapa Assembly for the study of Shambhala culture, or enlightened society. Trungpa taught that the premise of Shambhala culture is based on the belief that "there is a natural source of radiance and brilliance in the world, which is the innate wakefulness of human beings." Many people were astonished when, at the end of the first Kalapa Assembly, Trungpa proclaimed (seemingly out of the blue), "What we really have to do is all go do a lhasang (smoke) ceremony around Mt. Sinai in the war zone, then we will pacify the world!"

Trungpa asked José to help with the first annual Midsummer's Festival, a type of festive Shambhala event. He enthusiastically agreed. The Festival was held at different rural settings around Boulder on the Summer Solstice. It turned out beautifully. There were many colorful events and much pageantry under big tents with flying banners and pennants; it was a realization of the vision of Shambhala.

By the late 1970s, José had investigated everything he could find written about the Mayan calendar and prophetic traditions, including a set of prophetic texts, the *Chilam Balam*. These were written in a highly enigmatic language and compiled by a lineage of prophets and seers over a period of centuries following the disappearance of the classic Maya in the ninth century AD.

During 1978–79, he wrote *Flight of the Serpent*, a three-part fictional/autobiographical book. The first part described the original building of Teotihuacán and the creation of the cosmic vision. The second part was based on the life of an actual personality named Netzahuapilli, who was in Mexico just before the Spanish conquest. Netzahuapilli abandoned his kingdom two years before the conquest and, accompanied by a woman named Lady Five Flower, headed northwest, intent on arriving at the land of the Yaquis into North America. The third part of the story was an autobiographical description with the theme of reincarnation, where a man returns to Mexico in search of the mystic root of cosmic civilization. The hero of the story becomes lost as the oil fields catch fire in an apocalyptic inferno.

José could write no further; this was the point his life had come to. He was painfully aware of the need to burn away his earthly personality. He felt misunderstood and misperceived, and suffered an overall disgust with himself for his alcoholism.

In a moment of supreme frustration, he tore up and burned the entire original manuscript, even though he had a contract with Shambhala. It was not enough just to write about a vision; he knew he must *become* it—he would not be satisfied until he became the *living embodiment* of the highest cosmic vision. Somehow, he had to set his life in order and find a way to understand and retrieve the hidden knowledge that constructed the ancient pyramid sites of Mexico.

Chapter 30
Dark Night of the Soul

Not knowing that impermanent things are unreliable,
We still crave and cling to this cycle of existence.
Human life passes in suffering while we yearn for joy.
Bless us that we may cease craving the cycle of existence!

—Padmasambhava

José finished the four foundation practices of Vajrayana Buddhism in early 1979 and then received the *abisheka* initiation into the vajrayogini sadhana practice. As he was performing these intensive practices, it was evident to him that they were releasing karmic poisons in his system, which manifested as uncontrollable patterns of drinking. As painful and self-destructive as it appeared on the surface, in retrospect José saw how these episodes accelerated a state of disillusionment and the rapid wearing out of different karmic streams. Sometimes he felt he was a shamanic medium, absorbing, channeling, and burning out whole histories of karma.

The initiation into the vajrayogini sadhana practice involved attending ceremonies at the New Moon and the Full Moon with other advanced practitioners for the full performance of the *sadhana*, or spiritual practice. This performance sometimes lasted up to five hours and was followed by a feast, which included copious amounts of sake.

By his 40th birthday, José was drinking from morning to night. When the Prophet Muhammad was 40, he began to receive the revelation of the Holy Quran from the angel Gabriel. When José was 40, he was at the peak of his alcoholism, and his marriage of 13 years was about to collapse, along with his entire life as he knew it.

Though he desperately wanted help, he didn't know which direction to turn. At this point, it was evident to all of his friends, including Sam Bercholz, that he was in a bad way, but it seemed nobody could understand why or what to do. He went to see Trungpa and the Vajra Regent Osel Tendzin to get advice. Trungpa's response was: "The only difference between you and me is that you drink in private and I drink in public." The Regent added, "Here is a bottle of sake. Now, go drink it in your living room during daylight hours." José went home and drank the sake in his living room, much to Miriam's disgust.

In June 1979, Miriam called for intervention from the Buddhist Vajra Guards for José's drinking. The guards stayed at home with him for a few days to make sure he had nothing to drink. After he sobered up, José paid another visit to Trungpa to seek advice. Trungpa commented on José's sensitivity and told him it would be a good idea for him to spend as much time as possible lying on the Earth looking at the clouds. José took this advice and found that it not only relaxed his mind, but also aided him in cultivating his visionary powers.

After this episode, José sought help from a Buddhist therapist. In Trungpa's Buddhist community, out-of-control drinking only meant that you weren't meditating right. José saw the Buddhist therapist faithfully and was sober for three months. At the end of three months, the therapist concluded that he was cured and offered him a drink of sake to celebrate. This drink sent José, once again, on a downward spiral.

Stressed to the breaking point, José quit his job at Union Graduate School in the summer of 1979. Soon after, two fellow Buddhists, who happened to be professors at the University of Colorado at Denver, helped him get a job as an art professor. Here, he had great latitude to teach what he wanted, including classes in pre-Colombian art, Far Eastern art, Tantric art, and Islamic art. This new position allowed him freedom to complete his synthesis of ideas about art history in relation to the evolution of human culture and the planet as a whole. This synthesis formed the seed of his book *Earth Ascending*, which would be published a few years later, in 1984.

In late November, he was introduced to another fellow Buddhist, Jay Lippman, who had worked at the Boulder Alcohol Recovery Center. José found Jay the first Buddhist in his community who made sense about alcohol; all the rest denied alcoholism was a problem. Jay was able to acknowledge that, indeed, alcoholism was a disease, and that, if you suspected you might be alcoholic, you probably were. He encouraged José to stay sober and see an alcohol counselor. What impressed José most was when Jay said: "Some great yogis were beggars; some were crippled. So what if you are alcoholic and you can't drink? It doesn't mean you can't be a great yogi." These were the magic words that turned José around. Immediately he stopped drinking—but, as far as his family was concerned, his decision came too late.

Miriam was now spending increasing amounts of time with fellow Buddhist David Garrett. In his sobriety, José was trying desperately to patch things up with Miriam, begging her to accompany him to alcohol education classes. She refused. She had had enough.

In February 1980, José had what he considered "a cosmic moment" with his daughter. While attending a Shambhala Day ceremony, José came down with a fever. As he prepared to return home, 7-year-old Tara approached him and asked if she could go home, too. Returning home with Tara, José felt ill and lay on the couch. Concerned, Tara sat close to him with her hand on his head. In his sleep, he had a dream vision of Charles Henry wearing a violet colored cloak. Charles Henry spread the cloak out, indicating a mystical confirmation to José that he (Henry) was, indeed, a signpost of his destiny.

Not long after this dream, José had another significant dream in which Buckminster Fuller was standing at a podium singing "You are My Sunshine."

The next day, José called his friend Francois DeChanade to see when would be a good time to visit him and retrieve a painting he'd lent him. The painting was a mandala created by Jim Lind, his former student from the University of California at Davis. The name of the painting was "José's Dream." Francois told José he should come get his painting that day, adding, "There is someone here who wants to meet you."

Arriving at Francois's house that evening, José was astonished to see Buckminster Fuller, sitting on a chair in the living room, waiting to meet him. This unexpected meeting, just as he was coming to retrieve the painting "José's Dream" after dreaming about Fuller the night before, instantly rearranged his reality. It had been 10 years since he had correspondence with Fuller.

At the meeting, Fuller confirmed José's white light experience in 1966 at Grant Park in Lake Michigan by informing him that he, too, had a similar experience at the same location in 1927. Fuller talked animatedly about the "mystic temple," assuming everybody knew what he meant. It seemed to José that the mystic temple referred to an invisible kingdom or an etheric structure fulfilling the ideal of humanity's aspirations. Walking home after the meeting, José replayed the unusual synchronicities. The only explanation was that it was all a direct result of the Divine Plan becoming conscious.

After being sober for nearly a year, José realized his efforts at winning Miriam back were getting him nowhere. She was now constantly with David Garrett, so he decided to accept his friend Helen Berliner's proposal to start a consulting firm together. Helen was an upper-class woman from New York with an aspiration to become an art consultant. Helen took José for a visit to the National Center for Atmospheric Research (NCAR), central headquarters for worldwide weather research.

He was impressed with the Center, which looked like a medieval castle set on a high mesa outside of Boulder. He made another visit alone. He picked up a brochure that described, among other things, how the human senses "have been expanded through modern technology to be able to see the weather." Skimming through the brochure, José had a vision of a scroll, but instead of "Planet Weather," the scroll was about the "Planet Art."

At that point, he flashed on Rudhyar and his idea of the "planet art-whole." Never had José felt so strongly the truth of this vision. In a burst of creative fervor, in August 1980, he quickly wrote "Planet Art Report for Desperate Earthlings of the Past," a futuristic visionary essay. The themes in this essay would later cohere to become the Planet Art Network, a new planetary social order based on viewing the planet as a living work of art.

In the opening paragraph, he wrote:

Art is a function of energy. Given the unity of humankind as a single planetary organism, art is the expressive connective tissue binding together the individual organisms through energy transformations focused in the emotional centers of those organisms.... In other words, there can be no proper management of energy at whatever level and for whatever use without bringing into proper deployment the energy system of art. When art dysfunctions all systems ultimately dysfunction.

On Labor Day 1980, Miriam and David Garrett took Josh and Tara on a camping trip. José was devastated. Soon, the tension in his household became unbearable. He cast an *I Ching* oracle and got hexagram 59: Dissolution: "He dissolves his bonds with his group." This clinched it. The next day, he packed a few belongings and moved into a room in Sam Bercholz's house.

During the next six weeks, José fell into a deep depression and experienced his own dark night of the soul. Within the first four weeks at Bercholz's house, José drank every drop of liquor in his cabinet. Bercholz asked him to move out. On top of it, during this time John Lennon was assassinated, which had a deep impact on José. Lennon's genuine passion for peace and conscious music had given José a contemporary personality with which to identify. He'd heard from Bercholz that Lennon and Yoko kept a copy of *Mandala* on their living room table.

Soon after, José moved briefly to the home of his friend Jerry Granelli, a jazz drummer, who was supportive but was battling his own drinking problem. Here José completely bottomed out, forcing Jerry to drive him to the Boulder Alcohol Recovery Center on December 29, 1980. José knew that his time was up. He was completely burned out. All resources had been exhausted.

On New Year's Eve in 1980, José was sitting with a half dozen other alcoholics, eating popcorn and listening to an AM radio station announcing the ball dropping at Times Square. It was bleak, but he knew he had finally come to an end; there was nothing left to do but turn around. Even in his darkest moments, he was always certain of a new beginning. After five painful days sobering up, on January 2, 1981, he was driven to the Rocky Mountain Dharma Center for a 10-day meditation retreat.

Chapter 31
Rocky Mountain Dharma Center

All worldly pursuits have but the one unavoidable
end, which is sorrow: acquisitions end in dispersion;
buildings in destruction; meetings in separation;
births, in death. Knowing this, one should, from the
very first, renounce acquisition and heaping up, and
building, and meeting; and faithful to the commands
of an eminent guru, set about realizing the Truth
(which has no birth or death).

—Milarepa

few months before he left Miriam, José had scheduled a solitary
retreat for himself at Dorje Kunzang, Trungpa's retreat center
in Southern Colorado. However, when he was at the alcohol
recovery center, Trungpa called him on New Year's morning and advised him otherwise.

"You shouldn't be so lonely," Trungpa told him. "You should go
to the Rocky Mountain Dharma Center.... Other people will be
nearby.... Your meditation will go well then."

Late on January 2, 1981, after five days at the Alcohol Recovery
Center, Jerry Granelli drove a shaky but sober José to the Rocky
Mountain Dharma Center for a 10-day retreat. He shared a cabin with
a few other men. Talking was kept to a minimum. Even though he was
in his cabin all day doing vajrayogini sadhana and mindfulness practice, the one time he mingled with other retreatants was when he ate
in the dining hall in the evenings.

Fixed seats were assigned for the evening dinner, and everyone
received a one-bowl meal, served in a silent Zen manner. José was

placed across from 37-year-old Lloydine Burris Mecklenberg, who seemed ordinary enough, with her blue eyes and large-framed glasses. After dinner, she often accompanied him outside to the smoking area off the kitchen, where they'd share a Marlboro cigarette and exchange a few words. Lloydine was very friendly, but José had no eyes for women at this time; he was preoccupied with getting sober and reflecting upon the consequences of his separation from Miriam and his children.

During his 10-day retreat, José's reflections were many, and his life review was thorough. No longer wanting to cut corners and further wander in the cycle of samsara, he was determined to put the dharma teachings into practice. He pondered the sufferings of the cycle of existence and experienced tremendous remorse for his actions as an alcoholic. He experienced a deep revulsion for his previous behavior, seeing how it all but destroyed his family. The emotional pain was excruciating; he felt deeply humbled.

After a week of intense meditation and reflection, he had a great experience of enlightenment regarding the nature of karma and how it is created. In a flash, he realized precisely how different personalities or personas were constructed through the course of his life. When José was 7 (in the Buddhist tradition, this is the age when you become responsible for your own karma), his mother was admitted into a tuberculosis sanitarium, and this was when he asked his father for a lesson in drawing or painting, which initiated the first stage of his artist persona.

At 14, he had a vision on top of the Pyramid of the Sun at Teotihuacán, initiating his life mission. He saw that all along he had wanted to pursue this vision but had never known how to sustain it. He saw that his drinking was largely due to his inability to cope with the contradictions between conventional life and family struggles and the grandiose visions of his destiny.

By age 21, he saw the dissolution of his first-stage persona outwardly symbolized by a severe cut on his hand, causing him to lose partial mobility. At this point, he stopped painting and married Elena in a desperate attempt to stabilize himself. He viewed this as the first-stage "ego death" of his life and the dissolution of his first acquired persona. This set the stage for the next-level persona, the mystic visionary.

Seven years later, at age 28, he painted the *Doors of Perception*—the first manifestation of his visionary personality.

At 35, he viewed the crystallization of the second-stage persona with the writing and completion of *The Transformative Vision*, an encyclopedic effort to write a visionary history where the visionaries were the heroes. Between the ages of 35 and (almost) 42 came the dissolution of the second-stage persona.

These reflections came a few weeks before his 42nd birthday, clearing the way for his third-stage persona to emerge. This persona would focus on embodying the prophecy of Quetzalcoatl and articulating the completion of the cycle of Thirteen Heavens and Nine Hells.

In a flash, José realized that over the prior 42 years he had experienced the dichotomy of his root cosmic consciousness with his worldly role. What exacerbated this cathartic point was the abyss of who he was and who he was supposed to be—the gulf between the knowledge in his head and the knowledge in his heart. This dichotomy became so unbearable that he all but destroyed himself to burn it away.

After this inner realization came a deep self-acceptance and forgiveness. In this way, he experienced his life thus far as a 42-year initiation into the modern world. He understood that everything that had occurred had been part of a grand initiation. He knew his purpose was greater than being an artist or a writer, and he was felt confident that his true mission was about to be disclosed.

Chapter 32
The Winds of Change

*Change does not roll in on the wheels of
inevitability, but comes through
continuous struggle.*

—Martin Luther King Jr.

After returning from the retreat on January 13th, José spent 10 days with Jerry Granelli before renting a room at a nearby boarding house. A few days before his 42nd birthday, José encountered Lloydine at the Vajradhatu Meditation center in Boulder. Dressed up, and wearing a sheepskin jacket and boots, she looked different from the woman who had sat across from him in the meditation hall. He thought, "Wow! Is that the same woman who smoked cigarettes with me?"

On his 42nd birthday, Lloydine met José for lunch at the Kobe-an Japanese Restaurant in Boulder. He felt rapport with Lloydine, a California native and dancer with an interest in the arts and nature. Both had been recently divorced, and they each had two children: a boy and a girl. They connected, but José was still in a vulnerable, emotional condition as he attempted to put his life back together.

After lunch, José took Lloydine to the National Center for Atmospheric Research (NCAR), which he considered a mystical place. In the NCAR parking lot, he was explaining to her his thoughts about human culture as a function of geology—that the Earth is part of the Sun, that the Sun is a galactic being, and that the ancient Maya knew of all of this. While explaining this, José was surprised when Lloydine leaned across the seat and kissed him passionately.

After two weeks, José moved from the boarding house to house-sit at a friend's condominium. On Valentine's Day in 1981, Lloydine arrived at his doorstep with a dozen red azaleas. Although José perceived a karmic bond with Lloydine, he felt things were moving too quickly; he was still feeling raw from his split with Miriam. Lloydine, on the other hand, had already been divorced for a couple of years, though she was still living with her ex-husband and children.

After house-sitting at the condominium, José moved back into his old house on Gregory Lane for a month to look after his children while Miriam was at Trungpa's Shambhala Assembly event in Canada with her new partner, David Garrett. José drove Josh and Tara to Minnesota for spring vacation to visit Enrique and Ethel, who were delighted to see their son and grandchildren.

In late March 1981, José's divorce with Miriam was final. She got the house and custody of the children. José packed his clothes and a few books, and moved into the downbeat Thunderbird apartments overlooking the freeway. At this point, the two most important things in his life were reactivating his creativity and re-establishing a relationship with his children.

In May of that year, José presented the "Planet Art Report for Desperate Earthlings of the Past" at the Contemporary Arts Symposium in Santa Barbara, California. In his newfound freedom, he began to create art for the first time since he had stopped painting mandalas in 1973. Influenced by Trungpa, José tried his hand at creating Sumi style art, Japanese art executed with a big brush and black ink in rapid-fire strokes. He purchased a number of large pieces of glossy silver and gold poster board and created a series of collages with dramatic brush strokes; he called these the *Planet Art Series*. The collages illustrated the secret geological history of the Earth from its origins to the present time—showing the progression through history of the Earth as a work of art.

Tara, José, and Josh, 1980. Image courtesy of and copyright the José Arguelles Archive.

During this time, he also deeply steeped himself in study of the tectonic plates and the formation of the continents. He integrated these studies into the large collages, which interspersed scenes from the geological history and events of the Earth with shocking bouquets of humanly created beauty. These art works were predicated on the "Planet Art Report for Desperate Earthlings of the Past." He saw that the times were going to get worse and what would save it all was a Planet Art Network (PAN). Soon, his tiny apartment was overflowing with his artistic creations. He felt relieved and joyous.

By the summer of 1981, José had started to organize self-help groups for Buddhist alcoholics to help counsel them through their addictions. In the early spring of 1982, with Trungpa's blessings, José's Buddhist alcohol study group received the name *Sarpashyna*, which in Sanskrit means peacock. Trungpa said he chose that name because a peacock consumes its own feces and heals itself. To José, this was part of his karmic payback to the Buddhist community, and he took his role very seriously.

At this time, José applied himself wholeheartedly to the advanced Vajrayana and the Shambhala practices, including the principles of dharma art. In June 1981, Trungpa appointed José as his "shadow warrior," his standby for a series of five lectures on "Dharma Art Seminar." Trungpa told José that he would not show up at one of the five lectures and that José would have to give the lecture. However, Trungpa did not tell José which lecture it would be. It turned out that Trungpa did not show up at the fifth lecture, "On Perception and the Skhandas," which was on the theme of sense perceptions, sensory experience, and artistic organization, a subject Trungpa knew was dear to José's heart.

José felt honored but also acutely aware of the jealousy the appointment caused in others closer to Trungpa and higher up in the community "hierarchy." At Trungpa's request, the "higher-ups" had to allow José a special place in the inner sanctum, where they had to wait on him as if he was the guru. José felt uncomfortable; he knew they did not want to wait on him, and they all seemed a bit resentful.

This same year in September, José traveled with Lloydine to San Francisco to participate in Trungpa's Dharma Art exhibit at Fort Mason. It was here that he met Lloydine's mother, Maya, who would play a significant role in his life.

Chapter 33
Domestic Arts

In Velatropa far away
Though devoid of mind's full sway
In measured form with rhythmic heart
All that's done is done as art!

—José Arguelles, *The Art*
Planet Chronicles

By mid-summer 1981, José's tiny apartment with its living room and adjoining kitchen was crammed full of his art collages. One day, Josh and Tara came over and, after scanning his tiny apartment, Josh said, "Hey, Dad. What's a guy like you doing in a place like this?" Tara added, "Yeah. Why can't you move in with Lloydine? She's got a nicer condo than this."

José took their advice, and the three of them drove to Lloydine's condominium, only to find her suffering from a bad case of bronchitis. José went into her bedroom, where she was lying in bed and good-humoredly said, "The kids say that the time has come and I've got to move in with you. Is it okay?" Lloydine agreed, and in early August (on Hiroshima Day) José moved in with her. The small, two-story condominium had a galley-style kitchen and living room, small decks in the back and front, two bedrooms upstairs, and a little bathroom.

Hiroshima Day had long been important for José. A black anarchist, Geoffrey Stewart, whom José had known in his beatnik days, had introduced him to the notion of dating things after Hiroshima. Geoffrey had used the dating AB (After the Bomb), and José used AH (After Hiroshima). So, on 36 AH, José gave up his short solo stint and he and moved in with Lloydine, though they did not marry until two years later. José braced himself to accept a larger, blended family scene. He realized that he had entered phase two of his domestic cycle, only now the responsibility was doubled, as there would be four children.

José and Lloydine. Image courtesy of and copyright the José Arguelles Archive.

At the time, Lloydine was living with her daughter Heidi, 13, and working a job of selling jewelry and natural cosmetics. At first, Lloydine's son Paul, 14, who lived with his father, was skeptical of his mother's new boyfriend—and he certainly didn't like José's cigarette smoking! On one occasion, José found that Paul had taken his Marlboro cigarettes and broken them all in half. Aside from such initial uncertainties, however, the domestic scene swung into full action, and everyone quickly adjusted to each other and got along well.

By Thanksgiving and on into the wintertime, Josh and Tara regularly visited José and Lloydine, and sometimes Paul came, too. The children liked to camp out together in sleeping bags in the living room, which everyone enjoyed. There was a feeling of a whole new adventure beginning. To the children, José and Lloydine soon became known as "Hoy" and "Lloy."

Josh always surprised José with his sharp and fearless perceptions. On one occasion in the spring of 1982, Josh came over after school and said to José, "You know, I was at school today observing something: Did you know that just about all of the kids come from divorced parents these days? And I found that in every family that gets divorced, there is a winner parent and a loser parent, one who gets the most of it and one who gets the least of it. So my question is, how come you and Lloydine are both loser parents?"

José appreciated his son's savvy insight and knew he was referring to the fact that Miriam and Art had the big houses on the hill, while José and Lloydine—the ones with the blended family—had the tiny condominium. Each month, Lloydine received alimony from her ex-husband Art and gave it to José to pay Miriam her alimony and child support; this left them just enough money to live on. Economically, the first two years were very difficult.

It was a great learning experience for all. José accepted responsibility for the large family—this marked his character in the early 1980s. He was making a conscious effort to "do things right" and be a good husband and father, as he felt that he had somehow failed his first family test.

He learned as much as he could about Paul's and Heidi's interests and social sets and found them an interesting set of contrasts. Wheras Paul was studious, clever, and extroverted, Heidi cared little for formal studies and spent much time alone in her room reading fantasy and science fiction novels. José nicknamed her the "unicorn princess." Heidi was the more rebellious of the two and was proud of the large Rolling Stones banner hung in her bedroom window, facing the condominium parking lot. Though Paul's friends tended to be the more "brainy" types, Paul was also skilled at playing acoustic guitar and gave several solo performances.

During this time, Josh was flowering socially, as was Tara, who often had dramatic episodes involving boys. Josh's friends were fond of José and, for some inexplicable reason, called him "Mr. Fish." Josh often spent hours producing imaginal sports cards of fictitious baseball teams and players while listening to his favorite musicians: Jimi Hendrix, ZZ Top, Judas Priest, and Van Halen.

José also enjoyed Tara's friends, whom he dutifully drove to soccer games every Saturday. Although Josh was keen on becoming an athlete,

Tara was more athletically inclined and later became an award-winning body builder. Though the four children represented a diverse range of characters, José was impressed by the great fondness and tolerance they had for one another.

One day in the summer of 1981, José was having coffee with his friend, John Steinbeck IV (son of the writer and a Vietnam veteran), whom José had met in the late '70s on the Buddhist scene. The two had hit it off immediately. José found John an interesting character with a sarcastic, somewhat cynical sense of humor, coupled with sincere warmth. John had many personal problems, from his stormy relations with his father to constant struggles with drugs and alcohol (he died in 1991 of drug complications), but José felt the sincerity and sensitivity underneath his talkative macho façade. It was easy for John to talk; words flowed effortlessly, yet, although he was brilliant and had dabbled in journalistic writing, he could never seem to find his place in the world.

Often at their coffee meetings, José explained what he was doing in art history. At this particular meeting in the summer of 1981, José was conveying ideas to John about different artistic concepts being generated and popping up in the same places. John replied, "Listen, José—stop all this abstract theorizing. Make it real. All this talk about art and the planet. Why don't you write something fictional, a novel about an art planet?"

Shortly after this conversation, José cleared out the little dining room, which had a sliding glass door leading to a deck, and transformed it into a "scriptorium" with his typewriter and his other sacred objects. Within a few days, José found himself rising every morning at 4 a.m. and slipping downstairs to his scriptorium, where he began the *The Art Planet Chronicles*, a futuristic visionary piece that considers the years between 1987 and 2012 as the time of the Great Dislocation. The plot involves the struggle for supremacy of the world between the artists organized as the Planet Art Network (PAN) and the Syndicate for Material Evolution.

Sitting at an old mechanical typewriter, José began to listen for the voices—voices from another place, from a parallel world. He heard the words *Earth's rings*. Some place inside, José realized that he was getting a King Arthur image. He thought, "Arthur, artheru, Arcturus—oh yes! All of this information is being transmitted from Arcturus!" He felt certain that these voices were from Arcturus, though at that time José didn't know much about the star. He never thought of such things until they occurred. He had written "Planet Art Report for Desperate Earthlings of the Past," and suddenly saw that it was merely an Arcturian channeling. But *The Art Planet Chronicles* marked the first time that José actually experienced clairaudience. He identified the voices as coming from Arcturus. This was a breakthrough. He felt a deep sense of duty to transcribe word for word the entire script recited to him by the Arcturians. In this story also came the code of his mission (108X), the name of this sector of the galaxy (Velatropa), and our Sun's designation, Velatropa 24 (V.24) with Earth coded as V.24.3.

In December 1981, José completed *The Art Planet Chronicles*. On New Year's Eve in 1981, he and Lloydine made a trip to Trinity Site, the place where the first A-bomb was tested. It was also a key transformation place in *The Art Planet Chronicles*, because in the story it is at Trinity Site that radiosonic architecture is first manifested and from there the circumpolar rings are ejected. To José, it was vitally important to get as close to Trinity Site as possible on that New Year's Eve. José and Lloydine drove down and spent the afternoon as close as they could to the site. They spent the night in Truth or Consequences, another site for one of the main scenes of action of *The Art Planet Chronicles*. In this way, José was able to ground the imaginal realm into the third-dimensional realm, which, for him, made *The Art Planet Chronicles* complete. He was now free to embody the vision.

José submitted *The Art Planet Chronicles* to numerous publishing houses only to receive more than one hundred rejection letters. Most of the rejections stated that the theme of the book did not fit into any of their categories and so there would be no way to market it. Other rejection letters said that the manuscript was just "too out of the ordinary," not encompassing or concluding with the high-tech script expected in traditional science fiction. This proved José's point that in the modern world it is unthinkable that true art could be more powerful than mechanistic technology—so unthinkable that, even if it were given a voice, no one would listen.

The rejection of *The Art Planet Chronicles*, which described a world where telepathy is the norm, coincided with the end of José's career as an art historian. No sooner had he been named "Teacher of the Year" than he was denied tenure for no stated reason. Upon hearing the news, he took it as an omen when a limestone low relief carving of Quetzalcoatl mysteriously fell off his wall and shattered. A few days later, Lloydine's younger sister, Lily, died of cancer. José found it interesting that, 12 years earlier, he had been under fire at UC Davis following controversy over the Whole Earth Festival. This event of being honored and fired simultaneously aroused major media controversy both locally and nationally.

With a family to provide for, José knew he had to find a better economic situation for himself, and by 1983 he was re-employed at Union Graduate School with a huge salary increase.

José as professor, 1982. Image courtesy of and copyright the José Arguelles Archive.

Throughout his academic career, José continued to gather information about the nature of world culture and civilization. In some sense, he felt he was synthesizing within himself a compendium of spiritual unification and universal religion. He had to study and teach about all those different world cultures in order to understand them and then envision how unification might be restored at a planetary level.

Despite the rejection of *The Art Planet Chronicles*, José could not get the vision of the Earth's rings out of his mind. He knew that there was an exact science that described the precise sequencing for the triggering of the rings. He thought that, if they could not get the truth of what he was saying through artistic fiction, then he would explain it in scientific non-fiction. Ultimately, *Earth Ascending* came into being as the "sequel" to *The Art Planet Chronicles*.

In the summer of 1982, José, Lloydine, Josh, and Tara made a trip to Minnesota to introduce Lloydine to his parents. On the way, they visited the Black Hills and Mt. Harney, South Dakota, the mountain sacred to Black Elk. Visiting Lakota country was the highlight of the trip for José. He had a deep admiration and respect for Black Elk and held his autobiography, *Black Elk Speaks*, dear to his heart. With Lloydine's sister's recent death and José being fired from his job at UC Denver, the circumstances of this trip were poignant. José particularly identified with Black Elk as another dispossessed visionary and felt deep resonance with his unitive vision of a flowering rainbow tree and the circle of nations.

Soon after returning home, José served as a host at the Naropa Institute tribute, "25 Years on the Road with Jack Kerouac," a beatnik reunion attended by Timothy Leary, Allen Ginsburg, Gregory Corso, Paul Krassner, Ken Kesey, and Abbie Hoffman, among others. Besides spending time with Paul Krassner and listening to a lot of beatnik reminiscing, José took Timothy Leary and his wife out to dinner. José found Leary to be urbane, civilized, gentle, and well-mannered, almost like the Harvard professor he once had been. Leary knew a bit about José's work, and their conversation revolved around how art and culture might evolve in a world increasingly consumed by technology. As the conference concluded, José felt that the event was a tribute to the past, while his destiny called to a far different place—a place somewhere in a future unknown.

Chapter 34
Planet Art Network

> *Art is one—indivisible. Art has its many branches, yet all*
> *are one. Art is the manifestation of the coming synthesis.*
> *Everyone will enjoy true art. The light of art will influence*
> *numerous hearts with a new love. At first, this feeling will*
> *be unconscious, but, after all, it will purify human*
> *consciousness. So bring art to the people where it belongs....*

—Nicholas Roerich

L ate in the fall of 1982, José turned his focus to planetary geomancy while continuing intense studies of the Tzolkin. This work would be synthesized the following year in his breakthrough text, *Earth Ascending.*

What José originally intended as a book about geomancy evolved into a visual demonstration of the one law governing the unity of all creation, and the organic growth of humanity within the biosphere. *Earth Ascending* ultimately reveals that our planet is "not merely a member of a solar field of intelligence, but of a galactic field of intelligence as well."

After much study and contemplation, José discovered the mathematical connection between DNA, Benjamin Franklin's magic square of eight, and Tzolkin. The connection of these three components catalyzed the maps of *Earth Ascending.* José knew these maps as the blueprints of the evolution of cosmic consciousness on Earth. Writing *Earth Ascending* also gave him the opportunity to integrate the information revealed to him by Tony Shearer, as well as demonstrate how the Tzolkin matrix is the basis of a complex phenomenon known as the *psi bank*: the fourth-dimensional telepathic switchboard. The psi bank, he discovered, is the regulating mechanism of Earth's evolution and DNA code, the "thinking band around the planet" that Buckminster Fuller had suggested to him in 1969.

In a document written during this time, "Crystal Earth Geomancy," José synthesized the planetary function of the psi bank:

Earth is a highly evolved system whose evolutionary cycles are timed through operations of a crystal matrix core synchronized with operations of a psi bank, the planet-specific cosmic memory matrix. Geomancy as Earth divination is a radial matrix function. The purpose of geomancy is to activate through clear channels the one universal evolutionary law. Clear channels refer to conduits connecting crystal matrix Earth core functions to the psi bank. Through unimpeded clarity of such functions, Earth becomes the radiant organism to channel directives of the galaxy for the good of the galactic node of which our solar system is the center.

During the process of creating the maps for *Earth Ascending*, José experienced one synchronicity after another; it was like following a bouncing ball. *Earth Ascending* displays in visual and binary mathematical form the nature of the next stage of evolutionary consciousness of the planet, the noosphere. It also includes a holonomic analysis of the present stage of Earth civilization. He wrote:

Essentially the future lies in the radiation of man. This refers first of all to the process by which each individual assumes responsibility for all of his or her actions, and with heightened awareness participates in increasingly integrated group efforts to establish a consciously oriented relationship between biopsychic energy factors and those of the environment. In the most general way this describes the new symbiotic technology, radiosonics, the basis of post-historic synaesthesia.

In the late winter of 1982, José took a break from his writing to conduct a weekend *sarpashyna* seminar at Karmê Chöling in Vermont. Here he met Starsparks (Sparky), a highly affable, intelligent hippie who had sought him out after being inspired by *Mandala* and *The Transformative Vision*. Curious and talkative, Sparky was deeply steeped in Native American tradition and was close with Sun Bear and Dhyani Ywahoo. José felt an immediate connection with Sparky, who would prove to be one of his most loyal supporters and friends until his death in 1999.

In the spring of 1983, José had an opportunity to visit the 13th annual Whole Earth Festival, this time with Lloydine, her mother, Maya, and niece, Yvonne. José was surprised that the festival was still happening, although it seemed quite tame. The vendors and crafts people had signs on their booths saying that they accepted credit cards. Ronald Reagan was president, and ecology, the environment, and the whole Earth were no longer popular topics. Money and power were more fascinating to the new generation. Instead of "hippies" there were "yuppies," and between the two there is no comparison.

In June, José was invited to the First Planetary Congress, a big symposium in Toronto featuring Donald Keys, Barbara Marx Hubbard, and Ram Dass, among others. At this event, José made his first contact with the Nicholas Roerich Peace through Culture group. José found Roerich's idea of Peace through Culture of enormous value and highly compatible with his perceptions of dharma art. The Roerich Peace Pact and Banner of Peace (1935) established the conscious expression of human unification through art as the foundation for global peace. Signifying harmony, nature, and divine spirit, the Banner of Peace was the basis of the Roerich Peace Pact and was intended to be flown over cultural monuments in times of war.

Trungpa used to say, "The artist has tremendous power to change the world." José often pondered the meaning of this perception. To José, the Banner of Peace was a single powerful means for unifying artists on a planetary scale. In 1983, José, with the help of Lloydine, initiated the Planet Art Network (PAN) as a vehicle for promoting "Art as a Foundation for Global Peace," using the Banner of Peace as the official logo.

PAN was envisioned as a global network of artists of every kind who would join forces to create positive planetary transformation. The principle purpose of PAN was the realization of the whole Earth as a work of art. José described the premises of PAN in great detail in the "Crystal Earth Papers."

To José, the creation of PAN was the fruition of a seed planted in him by Dane Rudhyar, who had first articulated to him the principles of the "art-whole" and the "artist as avatar." In an article entitled "Artist as Avatar" (1939), Rudhyar wrote: "In really creative art is revealed that which will ultimately emerge through the evolutionary process as consciousness."

José took these words to heart. In *The Art Planet Chronicles*, the vision of the Planet Art Network was inspired by the victorious band of "telepathic artists who conquered the world by their superior science of harmony." This came about through a skillful understanding of the planet as a resonant field and the consequent triggering of Earth's rings.

For José, the PAN was already inherent in the Whole Earth Festival, which he felt was an example of planet art. The idea of artists around the planet telepathically engaged in transforming the industrial age environment into a massive global-scale artwork was at the root of his vision of the PAN. Through this unprecedented labor, the Earth and its human society could be turned into a cosmic art-whole. With the Planet Art Network and the Banner of Peace, this vision was finally grounded.

From the Peace through Culture group, he and Lloydine began making Banners of Peace and giving workshops entitled "Warriorship without War: Art as a Foundation of Global Peace." Trungpa often emphasized the notion of "Warriorship without War," the artist as a warrior of creative peace. Trungpa strongly encouraged ceremonial theater and, for his teachings, often dressed in a wide range of costumes, including that of a Japanese emperor or a British admiral. Trungpa's example reminded José that it is your life that is actually the creation. These workshops were presented as a preparation for the world-wide event that would occur on August 16–17, 1987: the Harmonic Convergence.

On November 1, 1983, José wrote about the power of art in the article "Art: The Sacred Stream" for the Buddhist community newspaper, the *Vajradhatu Sun*:

A paradigm is not just an idea; it is an elemental realization that passes from the nervous system to the bloodstream and becomes living reality. Not the least of the emerging paradigm is that art is in all of us; that each of us in all actuality is an artist; that art is a verb without whose universal use there will be no peace on earth....
As an action-oriented association of elements voluntarily bound together, the Planet Art Network provides self-transformational means for artists to collaborate on dynamic synthesizing projects of an unprecedented nature and magnitude....

There are moments in the destiny of the human race when, like a magnetic wave sweeping filaments of iron into a singular pattern, a key principle suddenly exerts its power among the people as if by magic and from nowhere. Such a principal is art the sacred stream. Let those who grasp this not hesitate, but like clouds gathered over a parched plain burst forth with the plentitude of vision so needed on this planet today. In this compassionate way, all may drink and nourish themselves again from art, the sacred stream.

Chapter 35
White Wedding

All that we see or seem is but a
dream within a dream.

—Edgar Allan Poe

On September 21, 1983, José, 44, married Lloydine, 40, at the Boulder County Courthouse, witnessed by their four children. This was 22 years after his first marriage to Elena and also was her birthday, though he wasn't aware of it at the time. In late June, Miriam had married David Garrett, and José felt that, if he also married, it would establish an equal stability for the children, and for himself.

José and Lloydine went to the small town of Nederland, Colorado, in the mountains just west of Boulder, where a goldsmith made them two gold rings. Only a few weeks before the wedding, José came down with a fever that lasted an unusually long time. He was in bed virtually every day for 17 consecutive days, and the fever peaked in the afternoons and evenings. However, he was determined to go through with the planned wedding date.

On the afternoon of September 21st, Paul arrived to drive the two to the courthouse. When they got into the car, Paul turned on the ignition and the song "White Wedding," by Billy Idol, blared through the speakers. Arriving at the courthouse, José still had a high fever, which lasted four more days. This was his third wedding, and his thoughts were colored by the timing of the fever. He felt it must have something to do with his deeper destiny or mission; later, he saw the 21-day fever as a form of purification.

Shortly before the wedding, José and Lloydine had purchased a four-story condominium on Spruce Street that resembled a miniature tower. There were now two rooms for the rotating children at the basement level, and on the fourth level was a small but spacious loft that José used as his office and studio. Everybody in the blended family was happy with the larger space. For José, the entire tower-like space was mythical, especially his loft, with its pitched ceiling and a large triangular window that overlooked the flat irons. He called it his "galactic crow's nest."

Left to right: Josh, Heidi, Lloydine, José, Tara, 1984. Image courtesy of and copyright the José Arguelles Archive.

On December 9, 1983, José requested an audience with Trungpa at Kalapa Court. He wanted to present Trungpa with a Banner of Peace and show him the radiosonic watercolor paintings he was working on. About 10 other people were present at the formal meeting, which was held in the *Tenno* (heaven) room. Trungpa was in his characteristic role as sakyong, or Earth holder. A woman who was present interrupted the ceremony to tell Trungpa she wanted to commit suicide. "Well, go ahead," Trungpa replied dispassionately. The woman left. For José, this scenario revealed Trungpa's fearlessness in calling people's bluffs.

When José's turn came, he and Lloydine presented Trungpa with the Banner of Peace and explained the philosophy behind it. Trungpa seemed happy at the gesture and said he was vaguely familiar with George Roerich, Nicholas's son, who was a famous Tibetan translator. The Banner of Peace was placed downstairs at the Vajradhatu center with many other banners and flags. When José showed Trungpa his paintings, someone whispered in Trungpa's ear that José and Lloydine were recently married.

Hearing this, Trungpa ordered that they be given white scarves immediately. Without hesitation, he performed a brief Shambhala-style wedding and had them sing the Shambhala anthem. Lloydine was enthusiastic about singing the anthem, and her voice was strong and loud. The Regent grew stern. "Not so loud!" he told her. Despite this, it was a happy event and seemed a good blessing to receive from the guru.

In his new position at the Union Graduate School, José supervised non-traditional doctorate programs, and was free to investigate art, culture, the psychology and philosophy of all civilizations and eras, as well as become acquainted with many contemporary issues. This was a time of great learning.

PART VI

Opening to the Fourth Dimension

Chapter 36
Face on Mars: Earth Ascending

*This present Earth in its turn appears as
the scene of life; Mars being its last theatre.*

—Sri Aurobindo

On December 1, 1983, José arrived at the Los Angeles home of Marilyn Ferguson. Within a few moments of their first meeting, Ferguson told him, "I have never met anyone who dispensed with small talk as quickly as you." She told him she held *The Transformative Vision* in high regard, "particularly the part about psychedelics and the psychedelic revolution," which she quoted extensively in her book *The Aquarian Conspiracy*.

José showed her his newly finished set of "holonomic maps" intended for *Earth Ascending*, and she asked him to stay the rest of the day to meet researchers from Stanford Research Institute (SRI) who were to visit her later that afternoon. Among them were Paul Shay, of the SRI, and Dick Hoagland, a former science investigator and writer. Hoagland had been with NASA when the *Viking Space Probe* sent back pictures from Mars on July 25, 1976, including the controversial "Face on Mars."

Shay was involved with a group that helped fund Hoagland's research with the NASA photos of the Face on Mars. José had some recollection of the Viking Probe discovering a face on the red planet, so when Hoagland arrived bearing the original photographs he was extremely curious.

The instant he saw the images, he was stunned. Deep recognition resonated through him. A million years of cosmic memory reawakened in a flash. Great streams of memory flowed from the Martian face into his being in what felt like vast spaces and eons of time.

To José, the face verified the certainty of existence on previous worlds, which meant that all of human history had to be re-envisioned. If DNA is truly unitary, he reasoned, and if a form of DNA has been verified on other rocks from Mars, then it proves that life exists in other worlds! In the shock of recognition, he felt great weights of intellectual baggage fall away as he was reminded, once again, of his cosmic essence.

A few days after this Martian recollection, José gave an *Earth Ascending* presentation at the Whole Life Expo in Los Angeles. At this event, he briefly reconnected with Sun Bear and also met Domingo Diaz Porta, head of the large Latin American esoteric fraternity known as the Universal Great White Brotherhood. Diaz Porta was also active in the Indigenous solar community in Mexico. "There is a Mayan who needs to meet you," he told José. That Mayan was Hunbatz Men. José gave Diaz Porta his phone number and soon received several phone calls from Hunbatz Men, whom he would meet in the spring of 1985.

While driving down Wilshire Boulevard the next morning to return his rental car to the Los Angeles airport, José felt something strange occurring and pulled into the nearest parking lot. There, he had a powerful vision of the conclusion of the Prophecy of the Thirteen Heavens and Nine Hells. He pulled out his notebook and fervently drew the vision of many people lying on their backs in a circle with their heads pointing toward the center, where a blazing fire was burning. All of the faces were looking skyward, just like the Face on Mars. Suddenly he heard the words *Earth Surrender Rite*. He knew intuitively that this was how the prophecy of Quetzalcoatl was to be completed. This vision would later be known worldwide as the "Harmonic Convergence."

With this vision, he spontaneously felt the unification of all the different parts of his life: his artistic vision of the whole Earth; the Mayan Prophecy, mathematics, and calendar; his art history experience; his spiritual training; and every other visionary moment he had ever experienced. Everything within him became integrated with this vision.

José returned to Marilyn Ferguson's house once again in March 1984, to view a mysterious stone that she felt he might like to see. When he arrived, Marilyn placed the intriguing 10-inch sculpted stone known as "Jasper" in his hands. The stone was extraordinarily heavy and had been carved to depict a crouching figure seated with its knees drawn up beneath its chin, with one arm over the knees and the other arm cupped behind the ear as if listening.

José sensed that Jasper was an embedded fragment of the planet Maldek (now known as the Asteroid Belt). He intuited that, when the planet exploded, it somehow landed on Earth in the Pacific Ocean off the coast of Malibu, embedded in a fragment of meteoric iron. A scuba diver named Jasper found the unusual stone and took it to various authorities to determine its material composition. All he was told was that it was some kind of fusion of meteoric iron. Jasper had heard about Marilyn Ferguson and brought the stone to her. "I knew immediately that you had to see it," she told José.

Shortly after seeing the mysterious stone, José was at home in his studio office when he received a letter from a friend and medium from New Mexico who referred to Arcturus and Antares and something called the AA Midway Station. He immediately recognized this name. Since he had begun tracking the Arcturian phenomenon in 1981 with the *Art Planet Chronicles*, he had met a number of astronomers and other artists who claimed they were "picking up" Arcturian transmissions. It seemed these transmissions were intended to communicate, through artistic mediums, messages directly pertaining to the salvation and transformation of the Earth through peaceful and artistic means.

José had received much information in his own meditations regarding Antares and Arcturus, which he understood as the two star systems monitoring the Martian experiment. He understood that following the collapse of the Martian experiment, a joint partnership was forged between the advanced intelligences of Arcturus and Antares to maintain surveillance on the Velatropa 24 solar system and particularly on events that would be occurring on Velatropa 24.3 (Earth).

He directly experienced the AA Midway Station as a type of monitoring base mediating between the fourth and fifth dimensions. In the few telepathic visitations that he was allowed there, he observed an equivalent to what we call monitoring screens with simultaneous views of what was happening both on this planet and on other planets or neighboring star systems. He understood that there was a complete record of activities and events related to everything that occurs on Earth. Through the different surveillances (or what we might call remote viewing) conducted by the AA Midway Station, virtually everything that occurs on this planet is known and observed. José understood that the AA Midway group is a part of a larger operation known as the Galactic Federation.

Shortly following the publication of *Earth Ascending*, on June 6, 1984 (the 40th anniversary of D-Day), José coordinated a peace ceremony called World War IV. Flying the Banner of Peace, Lloydine assisted José in a performance of music and dance at the Flagstaff Mountain Amphitheatre.

In fall of 1984, the mayor of Denver, Federico Pena, invited José to give a presentation at the Denver Art Museum on October 9th, the birthday of both Nicholas Roerich and John Lennon. This would be part of a series of lectures by major art critics.

José had been introduced to Mayor Pena two years prior when he was still a member of the state legislature and José was a recently fired art history professor. José's release without justification had created quite a media stir, and Federico Pena, head of the Hispanic-American caucus in the state legislature, was one of his main supporters.

Arriving at the state capital building a few minutes early on that day, José had found the newspapers brandishing a cover story about his forthcoming meeting with Pena, a prominent legislator. At the meeting, Pena expressed to José that he wanted him to fight the university for firing him on what he considered racist grounds. Pena told him that he, along with all the political machinery of the Hispanic-American caucus, would back him legally. After listening to everything Pena had to say, José told him that he could not do it, explaining that, as a Buddhist practitioner, it simply wasn't his way.

Pena looked at José, trying to figure him out, then, after a few moments, declared: "Oh, I get it; you're one of those Carlos Castaneda types of people." Pena seemed happy with his categorization and shook José's hand, saying he was happy to know him. This is why, several years later when he was mayor, Pena saw to it that José was invited to lecture at the Denver Art Museum.

José presented the Banner of Peace to the Office of the Mayor and followed this with a brief lecture on the meaning of the life of Nicholas Roerich as an artist and cultural peace visionary, explaining that the banner signified the values of peace through culture. That portion of the lecture was well received. However, when José switched gears and said that not only was it Nicholas Roerich's birthday but it was also the birthday of another great peace visionary, John Lennon, the mood shifted.

While José was speaking about John Lennon—his life, music, art, and vision—large numbers of the wealthy audience, many wearing furs and diamonds, got up and walked out. José figured they must be a part of the conservative Republican crowd and then remembered what John Lennon had said when the Beatles performed via satellite at Queen Elizabeth's Jubilee Concert in 1967: "Will people in the cheaper seats clap your hands? All the rest of you, if you'll just rattle your jewelry...."

His presentation proved so controversial that, a few days later, several letters to the editor in the *Rocky Mountain News* denounced José Arguelles and voiced hope that the Denver Art Museum would never ask him to speak there again. In their eyes, apparently, John Lennon was not someone worthy of speaking about.

In late autumn, José visited Dane Rudhyar, who was then 88 and living in San Francisco with his wife, Leyla, who was in her late 30s. Caring and sympathetic, José was touched by what great care Leyla took of Rudhyar. The meeting was lively and warm. It was clear to José that Rudhyar was happy with his new wife, who was a bright astrologer in her own right. Rudhyar was delighted to receive a copy of *Earth Ascending* and told José that everything he had envisioned about him was still coming true. It was to be José's last meeting with Rudhyar.

In September 1985, José and Lloydine visited San Francisco for a meeting with T'ai Situ Rinpoche. Leyla tracked them down at their motel room to tell them that Rudhyar had died peacefully the night before. She told José how happy Rudhyar had been with their last visit, and invited him and Lloydine to come view his body. José felt that his encounter with Rudhyar had been a culmination of his deep esoteric studies, which included Rosicrucian studies.

Viewing Rudhyar's body was an amazing experience. The expression on his face looked ecstatic; it was apparent to José that Rudhyar had experienced a conscious and peaceful death. Paying his respects, José was deeply moved by the passing of the man who had given him so much inspiration, guidance, and wisdom.

Chapter 37
Earth Shaman

> *To make the leap, to cross the abyss*
> *From oblivion to wakefulness*
> *Is to merge into Central Channel*
> *Sipapu*
> *To become again*
> *An Earth Shaman conduit*
> *A listening post of the energy bodies*
> *An outlet for the pent-up dreams*
> *Of the Great Ones waiting at last*
> *For the moment of transformative intervention.*
>
> —José Arguelles, *Earth Shaman*

In late summer 1984, when he was 45, José had a near-death experience in Switzerland. After a business trip to Geneva for the Union Graduate School, José traveled to Basel and then Brussels for meetings with Marilyn Ferguson, her husband Ray, Tony Judge, and Sir George Trevelyan, a leader of the English New Age Movement. The five had deep discussions regarding the meaning and nature of the coming new age. José was honored when, a few days later at a public gathering, Sir George Trevalyen read José's poem "Within the Earth We Know There is Another Earth."

Back in Switzerland, on September 6, 1984, just after viewing the Adolf Wolfli collection in Bern and visiting the C.G. Jung Institute in Zurich, José was riding in the back seat of a car with his friend Geraldyne Waxkovsky of Spain. At the wheel was a man named Heinz, whose wife Agnes was in the passenger seat. Heinz and Agnes were employed by the Sphinx Verlag Publishing Company in Basel and interested in publishing José's works.

Resting his eyes while caught in a tunnel during a traffic jam in Zurich, José was seized by a visionary experience that was something like what the *Tibetan Book of the Dead* describes as the after-death experience. He viewed each of his chakras in visionary detail and saw the different karmic patterns of his life that were held in each chakra.

Two hours later, Heinz lost control of the car, and José found himself spinning around at 70 miles per hour as the car plunged off the freeway, rolled over several times, and came to a jarring halt. He thought for sure he was going to die as he spiraled out of his body into a full experience of his destiny. Miraculously, he escaped the crash with nothing more than a crushed aura. Every time José got up or sat down, he could feel his whole aura being crunched like an accordion. The other three suffered severe injuries, particularly Agnes, who was in critical condition but managed to survive.

In late September, José flew to Los Angeles and then to Joan Halifax's Ojai Foundation for the first of a number of visits. The Ojai Foundation thrived in the '80 s as a place for advanced thinkers to meet and share ideas. Native American shaman elders frequented the Center, as well as people like Terence McKenna. It was here that he met Brooke Medicine Eagle and Harley Swiftdeer, both of whose strong Native American teachings had a deep effect on José's envisioning of the Harmonic Convergence.

During the 1980s, José's attention was directed toward shamanism and Native American/Lakota teachings. In Boulder he met Gerald Red Elk, Wallace Black Elk, and Dhyani Ywahoo, Cherokee lineage holder. The latter introduced him to the importance of working with crystals. This was a turning point. The moment he started using crystals, he felt the voice of the Earth begin to come through him. José wrote in the *Earth Crystal Papers*:

> As I worked with and listened to the crystals, I began to learn at another level. Being and knowledge which I had considered to be outside the pale of reason, coming perhaps from outer space, was all resonantly encapsulated in crystal and completely of the Earth.

Shortly after his near-death experience, José wrote *Earth Shaman, the Voyage Beyond History*, a series of cosmic poems and poetic essays in the form of an epic, recounting the history of previous worlds and their replay in the present. While writing *Earth Shaman*, José repeatedly heard the phrase *Harmonic Convergence.* He immediately knew that this was the "Earth Surrender Rite" that he had envisioned on Wilshire Boulevard in 1983, and that it directly correlated with the prophetic dates August 16–17, 1987.

In hindsight, José saw that this near-death experience was an initiation for the role he would play three years later in coordinating a global peace event to conclude the prophecy of Quetzalcoatl. The accident was meant to wake him, clear him out, and direct his attention to preparing this event, which he knew must capture the world's attention. Soon, he began to publicly promote the prophetic dates August 16–17th and the Harmonic Convergence.

On January 24, 1985, his 46th birthday, José experienced the first of his many optical radial tunnel experiences. While in his office at home, talking with his computer repair technician, all of a sudden he remembered that he had had a dream of the exact situation, and he couldn't tell whether he was in a dream or reality. As he was having this experience, someone delivered a package from his friend Dominique in New York City, which turned out to be a powerful crystal that he named Excalibur.

Shortly after receiving "Excalibur," José wrote:

I realize I have shifted to the position of being a channel or more precisely a conduit. As fashionable as channeling has become, I nonetheless hold to this position by virtue of my own surrender to the Earth Force. Not as any fad or passing fancy, but as a real commitment; I have resolved for the rest of my life or until the situation of our world is genuinely transformed, to act and speak on behalf of the Earth. Should anyone question whether I actually believe that I or anyone else has the ability or the right to do this, the answer is unequivocally: YES.

Whether I be deemed mad, a fanatic or a prophet without a pulpit, it is obviously also my conviction that the Earth is now speaking, that it is the Earth's turn, for humans have had their turn. Only by allowing the Earth Her voice, either through us or without us, will a new order based on sanity and respect of everything come about.

…There comes a time when caution and false self-respect must be cast aside. There comes a time when the highest vision must be invoked, the highest dream must be dreamed and shared. This is such a time.

After communication with T'ai Situ Rinpoche regarding *Earth Ascending*, José had a dream on Spring Equinox 1985. In this dream, he encountered Trungpa Rinpoche in an interdimensional tunnel penetrating through the Earth. Trungpa, sitting on a chair wearing his business suit, said, "You will have to do something that will make the rest of the Buddhists think you are not a Buddhist." José asked him what that might be. Trungpa replied, "You have to bring the religion of the Earth back to the people." At that point, José saw a large image of T'ai Situ Rinpoche hovering above Trungpa Rinpoche. He knew the dream was significant.

A few weeks later, Trungpa made a surprise visit to the monthly Buddhist community meeting. At this meeting, José attempted to tell Trungpa his dream. Just as he reached the point in the dream where Trungpa tells him that his mission is to "bring the religion of the Earth back to the people," a student interrupted them to get Trungpa's attention. After the interruption, José continued telling the dream, but before he got to the punchline, Trungpa swiftly grabbed his head and pulled it toward his own, knocking their foreheads together three times in a gesture of *shaktipat*. Through this gesture, José understood that the dream was actually a telepathic transmission.

At the spring equinox 1985, the mayor of Boulder, along with author Antero Ali, joined José, Lloydine, and Barbara Marx Hubbard in an Earth performance event called, "Happy Earth Day Planet Birth." Shortly after, Hunbatz Men arrived at their house to spend a few days. Hunbatz had written a book on the Tzolkin and Mayan astrology, and was a big influence on José at the time, particularly because he was an Indigenous Mayan carrying on the tradition. José felt a deep spiritual connection with Hunbatz and arranged for him to speak at Washington Elementary School in Boulder. As Hunbatz performed a ceremony, he lit a candle; the school officials made him put it out because they were afraid of fire. Hunbatz graciously conceded.

No sooner had Hunbatz left than José joined Terence McKenna at the Ojai Foundation, where he was conducting a seminar on the "mega mushroom experience." José and Terence exchanged views on the *I Ching* and 2012, the date that Terence had arrived at independent of any study of the Mayan calendar and explored in his book *The Invisible Landscape*. José and Terence agreed that, having both arrived at this date through different routes, it must portend a great moment for humanity. Jose would meet up with Terence again in 1995, when he assisted him in delivering a Thirteen Moon Peace Plan to the United Nations on its 50th anniversary.

Shortly after this event, José wrote the following song/poem, titled "Everyone's an Artist":

Everyone's an artist, looking for an outlet
Everyone's a healer, trying to make it whole
Everyone's a lover, looking for a cause
Everyone's a leader, sitting on the goal

The skies are turning crimson, the seas are riding high
The prophecies are comin' round, it's now—it's do or die
The last one who will tell you, is yourself, my gentle friend
The first one who will know, is the first to go beyond the End

Everyone's an artist, looking for an outlet
Everyone's a healer, trying to make it whole

The prophecies have come around, the future couldn't wait
It's up to you to make it true, to break the seal on Heaven's gate
Just past the last horizon, the dragon twists and turns
Genesis he calls it, Mama waiting our return

Everyone's an artist, making real the endless song
Everyone's a healer, knowing light's the right for wrong
Everyone's a lover, making every moment count
Everyone's a leader, drinking from the sacred fount

Yes, everyone's an artist, and the outlet's through your heart
Yes, everyone's a healer, ending war by making art.

In May 1985, José and Lloydine met with JJ Ebaugh at the Antares Room restaurant in a hotel outside the Denver airport. JJ had been Ted Turner's personal pilot and then became his partner, taking an active role in introducing him to new ideas and thoughts. José had first met JJ at one of Marilyn Ferguson's salons in Los Angeles. In her early 30s, energetic, and enthusiastic, JJ was interested in the Banner of Peace and the work José was doing in general.

JJ wanted to do a ritual for Ted Turner based on a commemorative sword that he possessed from the coronation of Elizabeth II. Ted referred to this sword as the "Excalibur." José designed the ritual on the spot. Its purpose was to align Ted's intentions with the highest aspirations of the Earth. JJ made it clear that José was to come alone.

On Summer Solstice 1985, José camped out with Ted, JJ, and a few other invited guests in an isolated outback of Big Sur, California. Looking at the tents and banquet arrangement, José thought the entire bivouac looked like a scene out of Camelot.

The afternoon before Solstice, José and JJ searched for a place to perform the ritual. After finding a suitable location, high on a cliff overlooking the Pacific Ocean, José and JJ laid out crystals on the ground indicating a seal of Solomon and hung the Banner of Peace from a tree. That evening before the ceremony, they had a banquet, and José gave Ted a copy of the ceremony he had designed for the occasion.

"It better not be hokey," Ted told José. José found Ted affable with an almost boyish quality.

José, Ted, and JJ arose at four in the morning on June 22, 1985, for the sunrise ceremony. Catching sight of José's large double-terminated crystal, Ted said to José, "Well, you must be a powerful person." José handed the crystal to Ted, who held it to his heart. The ceremony concluded with Ted's holding up Excalibur to catch the light. As the dawn light glinted off the sword, Ted recited the "Oath of the Law of the Center," promising to "uphold everything born of woman and to do nothing to harm the children."

At the completion of the ceremony, Ted confirmed to José that he was "relieved" that the ceremony "wasn't hokey." Afterward, José and Ted discussed politics and the idea of "mediarchy," rule by media. (Mediarchy is to democracy what democracy is to monarchy. In the Information Age, those who control the media are the real rulers of human thought. This defines the role of mediarchy.)

The following week, JJ called José and said that a brush fire had burned many acres at the site of the ceremony. José took this as a sign of the power of the ceremony.

From 1985 to 1987, José, with Lloydine's help, did much to prepare people for the Harmonic Convergence, including endless promoting of "art as every day life" and "art as an instrument for global change." Much work was done to connect different networks of artists for the purpose of global transformation. During this time, José met Jim Berenholtz, a Los Angeles musician who had the same vision of uniting artistic networks to effect global change. Together, José and Jim generated a list of the main sacred sites in the world; they knew that, if these sites were activated, the Earth could come alive again.

José and Lloydine traveled to New York City to present the Banner of Peace to the Roerich Museum, also entrusting curator Daniel Entin with a second banner to be taken to the Roerich Department of the State Museum of Oriental Arts in Moscow. José had been astounded to learn that neither the New York Roerich Museum nor the one in Moscow had Banners of Peace.

José had kept various types of visionary notebooks throughout the 1970s, but in the '80s he focused primarily on visionary art. Around this time, he also did a series of large watercolors similar to the one on the cover of *Earth Ascending*, followed by another series of watercolors referred to as the radiogenetic series.

In 1985, he began compiling the *Crystal Earth Papers*, which he had begun writing in the summer of 1984 in preparation for Harmonic Convergence. These papers contain the first writings about the prophetic event, much of the material specifically directed at JJ, who would then summarize them for Ted. The introduction to the *Crystal Earth Papers* described the meaning of two prophetic dates (August 16, 1987, and December 21, 2012):

August 16, 1987: Ultimately stemming back to the calendric and astronomical systems of the Maya of ancient Mexico, this date August 16, 1987, marks the end of the ninth of nine 52-year cycles comprising a Hell period that began in 1519 with the landing of Cortez in Mexico. However, the 1519 date was itself a transition between the nine subsequent Hell cycles and a preceding set of thirteen 52-year Heaven cycles.

Thus, the date August 16, 1987 marks the conclusion of an 1144-year cycle initiated in 843 A.D. It is also significant that the date 843 A.D. marks the ebb and disappearance of what is referred to as classic Maya civilization. In this regard, August 16, 1987 is also known as Mayan return, meaning a return of the nature and influence of the kind of consciousness and perspective that dominated classic Mayan civilization. This consciousness and perspective were, needless to say, dominated by a supreme concern for harmony and the synchronization of all levels of reality.

The other date, December 21, 2012 is also Mayan in origin. It marks the conclusion of the 13th baktun of a Great Cycle, which commenced August 6, 3113 B.C (Julian 3114 B.C). Five of these Great Cycles, something less that 5200 years duration, comprise a Platonic Great Year, itself a little less than 26,000 years in length. This later date, December 21, 2012, marks the point of a major synchronization between our star system and at least six others. In actual terms, it marks the moment when our planet is prepared to enter its next evolutionary stage of development.

While August 16, 1987, may mark the end of history, or actually, the reversal of the historical process that was set in motion by August 6, 3113 B.C., December 21, 2012, marks the end of the present stage of evolution and the beginning of the next. A time of a great moment indeed! The 25-year interval between the two dates marks the time during which the obsolescent, polluting and self-destructive tendencies of civilization are abandoned and the apparatus of civilization itself taken down. At the same time it marks a period of ever-increasing harmony in which the frequencies of the Crystal Earth make ever more apparent the wondrous moment of transformation that swiftly approaches.

Chapter 38
The Mayan Factor

Because they (Maya) could accomplish so much with so little,
the Maya have something very important to teach us in our
moment of technological crisis and paradigm shift. Indeed, the
Maya may already possess not only the 'new' paradigm, but also
the scientific knowledge by which that paradigm may be applied.

—José Arguelles, *The Mayan Factor*

Hunab Ku
symbol. From
The Mayan
Factor *(Bear and*
Company, 1996).
Reprinted by
permission by
José Arguelles.

I n December 1985, José and Lloydine traveled to Mexico for a seminar initiating Lloydine's entry into the Union Graduate School to pursue a PhD program in dance therapy movement and Buddhist studies. The seminar was held at Coba, an archaeological site in northern Yucatán. Though most of the Yucatán peninsula accommodated the later Mayan culture, Coba is the single exception. It is the farthest northeastern point of the Classic Mayan culture and flourished in the seventh and eighth centuries, the same time as Palenque.

In Mexico, José discovered a catalytic text, *Mayan Parapsychology* by Domingo Martinez, which said that the Mayans were very "evolved in telepathy," which was a key factor of their existence, and were also "advanced in parapsychological sciences."

José felt this text confirmed what he had written about in *Earth Ascending* regarding the sunspot cycle as the equivalent to 16 Tzolkins or 16×260. With a total duration of 23 years (16×260 days is equivalent to one half of the sunspot cycle or 11.3 years with a total duration of almost 23 years), the sunspot cycles are an intrinsic process of the Sun. In *Earth Ascending*, José illustrates how these sunspot cycles play a key role and are directly connected with the 260-day cycle. A new sunspot cycle was to begin in 1989 and climax in 2012.

José explained sunspot cycles in an interview conducted by Antero Ali:

> The sun is operating through what we might call a galactic program which is generated from the core of the galaxy…what the Mayans called the Hunab Ku. This core emits the master program that is mediated by the different stars to the differing planetary systems. Our sun is then continuously emitting sets of patterns which are simultaneously energy and information. These can be synthesized down to the readings of the binary sunspot cycles…23-year cycles…11.5-year cycles…and these are all accommodated by the Mayan matrix, the 260-unit Tzolkin calendar or mental pattern.

José led a tour in the Yucatán before he and Lloydine returned to Coba just before his 47th birthday. It was here that the energy or perfume of Pacal Votan entered his direct experience, planting within him what would come to be known as *The Mayan Factor*.

After absorbing the book on Mayan parapsychology, José climbed the tallest pyramid of Coba, the Nohoch Mul (large hill), which is some 200 feet high. Upon reaching the top of this magnificent structure, José sat and meditated on the entire sunspot cycle. In his prolonged meditation, he became aware that he was tuning in to the binary sunspot cycles in the same way the Mayans had. As he deepened the meditation, he experienced one binary sunspot cycle that pulses 11.3 years and starts at 30 degrees north and 30 degrees south, both pulsing toward the solar equator.

After 11.3 years, when the two pulses meet, they reverse polarity and the cycle begins again. José saw how the first 11.3-year sunspot cycle is the broadcast and receiving station of Arcturus, and the other 11.3-year sunspot cycle is the broadcast and receiving station of the Pleiades. He perceived how the Mayans had a superior telepathic receptivity that they used to calibrate different synchronizations and calendars.

In a state of concentrated meditation, he had a vision of the 5,125-year Great Cycle as a type of beam emanated through the Sun. The 5,125-year beam is divided into 13 subcycles called baktuns, each a little more than 394 years long. (Presently we are in the final 13th cycle, Baktun 12, which concludes on December 21, 2012). He saw that each baktun was its own evolutionary radio program.

He knew that the purpose of the beam, like the purpose of all galactic beams, is to affect the timing of change. He saw that the effect of this particular beam was to help accelerate human activity around the planet. This acceleration was known as recorded history. He understood that, through telepathic attunement, the Maya were able to calibrate the incidence between solar activity and human activation. This meant they could calibrate human activity and predict its plunge deeper into materialism and further from nature.

José also saw the devastating effects of a civilization acting in disregard of natural order. At the same time, he witnessed from a higher-dimensional standpoint that the solar activation on this planet has never been greater. He understood his mission was to help ensure that, when the planet phases out of this beam in 2012, the humans would have created a unified global civilization living in harmony with nature in preparation for the next evolutionary cycle. From this point on, José experienced a quickening of cosmic energy and information rapidly entering his being.

This experience affirmed for José that Mayan time science had everything to do with understanding the pulsations and frequency of information derived from the solar sunspot cycles. However, he saw the only way this kind of information can be truly known is through *telepathic solar attunement*, attained by stepping out of the technological box and the conditioned thinking of consensual reality.

He felt his cultivation of Mayan studies coming to fruition. Of main importance to him was to finally record all of this information. At the same time, his family responsibilities were growing more complex. Two events had occurred that expanded his blended family duties: In the fall of 1984, Lloydine's niece Yvonne, daughter of Lily, moved in with them to complete her last two years of high school. Virtually an orphan, Yvonne had many needs and an unpredictable personality. The following year, Lloydine's mother, Maya, moved to Boulder into a senior citizen apartment three blocks from their condominium. Maya was encouraging to José, and he took great comfort in chatting with her on her balcony, particularly during the time leading up to the Harmonic Convergence.

During his last two years of high school, Paul became close to José and sought help in his writing, history, and philosophy classes. Paul graduated in 1985. Heidi and Yvonne graduated in 1986, and Josh in 1987. Tara, the youngest, graduated in 1991.

With increased family and career duties, José felt an increasing inner pressure to complete the Prophecy of the Thirteen Heavens and Nine Hells. This would be achieved through a systematic description of the Mayan time knowledge.

Tara and Genji, 1986. Image courtesy of and copyright the José Arguelles Archive.

♊

One evening in late January 1986, not long after returning from Mexico, José walked to the neighborhood store to buy coffee beans and chocolate bars. As he stood in line, he thought it was interesting that both the coffee and the chocolate are made from brown beans, which the Maya knew about. He thought, "Could it be that these two beans, coffee and chocolate, *are* the Mayan factor and that's what accounts for their civilization?" Then he thought, "Hmm... The Mayan factor! Yes, that is the overlooked factor in history. That's the name of the book!"

After receiving the title, José immediately set to work writing *The Mayan Factor: Path Beyond Technology*. After 33 years of study and contemplation, he was now in a position to summarize and synthesize the contribution of the Mayans and Mayan calendar. Every morning he arose early, went to his home office, and worked on the text. It took four months to write the book. He already had graphics for the book, as he had long been keeping visionary notebooks, which he had titled "Pacal Votan and the History of the Earth."

In the Introduction to *The Mayan Factor*, he wrote:

In preparing the presentation of this text, I am guided by two things: the study of a phenomenon that I have come to understand as a galactic master-code and the intuition that a dramatic break with the current scientific paradigm is absolutely necessary if we are going to not only survive but transform in the most positive and benign way possible. Having been so long overlooked, the Mayan Factor must now be examined.

Until then, Mayan mathematics and the Mayan calendar had been his secret life. He'd been nurturing it wherever and whenever he could. At that time he knew he must fulfill himself by writing about his secret life or his internal psycho-telepathic experiences regarding the Galactic Maya and their timing sensibility. José found it exhilarating to write this book, or rather to watch it unfold as he realized a real galactic transmission was occurring." Since his visionary experience in Coba, José became acutely aware that galactic agents, particularly Pacal Votan, were telepathically guiding him.

The Mayan Factor had few predecessors. José felt the text was precisely timed to manifest at the conclusion of the Quetzalcoatl prophecy of the Thirteen Heavens and Nine Hells. This book was the opening to the complete understanding of the prophetic date 2012, the closing of the Mayan Great Cycle. At this point, José understood that humanity, living in ignorance of the laws of nature, would have to make a great shift from destructive material civilization to a civilization based on natural cycles of the order of the universe.

He wrote in the Introduction to *The Mayan Factor*:

It is in the interest of setting the calendar in order—the calendar as the cosmically voyaging Maya knew it—and making clear that we are involved in galactic seasons that this book is presented. Armed and reassured with such knowledge, we might set ourselves aright with the Earth and drop our childish and now very dangerous infatuation with the myth of progress and technological superiority. In this lies the import of *The Mayan Factor: Path Beyond Technology.*

In the four-month process of writing *The Mayan Factor*, José experienced many surprises and discoveries. The last chapter, "The Coming Solar Age," is particularly visionary and outlines a new view of reality envisioned by December 21, 2012. In the last chapter, José wrote:

> Then, as if a switch were being thrown, a great voltage will race through this finally synchronized and integrated circuit called humanity. The Earth itself will be illumined. A current charging both poles will race across the skies, connecting the polar auroras in a single brilliant flash. Like an iridescent rainbow, this circumpolar energy uniting the planetary antipodes will be instantaneously understood as the external projection of the unification of the collective mind of humanity. In that moment of understanding, we shall be collectively projected into an evolutionary domain that is presently unconceivable. And yet, we shall know. Like infants in a vast new playground, we shall retain the highest and most exalted vision.

Chapter 39
Extraterrestrial Text

Telepathy: Transmission projected through
the two Higher Selves (fifth-dimensional)
of two people who are in communication
with each other.

—*Introduction to Cosmic Science*

In the spring of 1986, one of José's students gave him a copy of a mysterious 57-page Spanish text, *Introduccion a la Ciencia Cosmica (Introduction to Cosmic Science)* channeled by Enrique Castillo Rincon, a Colombian engineer and ufologist.

José's student explained that, while living in Ohio in the mid-1970s, he belonged to a UFO society and often attended their meetings. At one meeting, a South American man announced that he had the text of *Introduction to Cosmic Science*, which he claimed was channeled, or received, by extraterrestrial intelligences. José's student had accepted two copies of the text, thinking they would someday be worthwhile.

Later, in the early 1980s, the student told José that he was in South America working with a Peruvian shaman, Eduardo Calderon, to whom he gave one copy of the text. José knew of Calderon because some of his students were studying shamanism with him, but he was surprised to learn that Calderon was the other recipient of the text. José recalled a telepathic communication he had in 1984 with Calderon, which he had even written a poem about. After learning that Calderon was the other receptacle of the mysterious text, José sent him the poem. In 1986, José met Calderon, who confirmed that he had indeed received telepathic communication from José in 1984.

Once he learned that Bear and Company had accepted *The Mayan Factor* for publication, José began reading *Introduction to Cosmic Science*. He was totally blown away. He immediately translated it from Spanish to English. José considered the Cosmic Science text an incredible structure of knowledge with its pithy descriptions of parallel worlds, the origins of spirit, and the formation of planets.

A chapter on the genetic code particularly struck him. He saw that the last 16 codes in the 64-unit template were blank, but written in hand was *super hombre* (superman). He knew that the 16 blanks had everything to do with the next stage of evolution, and he immediately understood how to complete it. Also handwritten on the same page was the only date that appears throughout the entire text: March 7, 1970. This date was significant to José, as it was 10 days prior to the first Whole Earth Festival, March 17–21, 1970. We will now flash ahead several years to 1996 and 1997 in order to illustrate two important synchronicities relating to *Cosmic Science*.

Synchronicity I: From March 17–21, 1996, precisely 26 years after the original Whole Earth Festival, José held the first Planetary Congress of Biospheric Rights in Brasilia, Brazil. Ten days before the congress in Brasilia, on March 7, 1996, UFOs visited the home of Brazilian ufologist José Fraga and left a crop circle on his lawn, which was featured in many Brazilian newspapers. Fraga said he woke up in the middle of the night "to a shaking house." He claimed to have received a telepathic message from the beings in the UFOs who told him the following: "This is about José Arguelles. You have to find him. What he is doing at the Congress is something important for humanity and will last hundreds of years." Finding José, Fraga told him that the "little blue Mayans" had sent him. A few weeks later, José was able to visit the house and see the amazing crop circle: a cross enclosed in a perfect circle.

Synchronicity II: In 1997, José presented the newly finished *20 Tablets of the Law of Time* at an International UFO Contactee Symposium in Costa Rica. This was his first work that incorporated key elements of *Cosmic Science*, namely the genetic code and the activation of 64 DNA. After the presentation, José attended a luncheon party. José was flabbergasted when he learned the host of the luncheon party was none other than Enrique Castillo Rincon! José was stunned by this synchronicity, because, although he had known that Rincon existed, he had no idea where he was and had never considered finding him. He told Rincon how the mysterious text had come to him, and that he had studied and translated it. He showed him how he integrated the *Cosmic Science* into the *20 Tablets of the Law of Time*. Rincon expressed great happiness at seeing that the *Cosmic Science* had gathered such strength in the work he was doing.

José found Rincon serious and dignified, in the style of an old-fashioned Latin American gentleman. Rincon said his contacts with extraterrestrials began in the late 1960s and lasted into the early 1970s. He told José that the *Cosmic Science* text was received from "the UFOs" and "has everything to do with God." Rincon said this message was sent to Earth by extraterrestrial intelligence "because it is the way God the Father is able to bring some kind of intelligence to Earth, and hopefully it will be used right if we follow the teachings of Jesus when he talks about being humble and close to the Earth."

After this meeting, José knew without a doubt that he was being guided by a higher force. Just like the 1980 Buckminster Fuller dream experience, these synchronicities were proofs to him of the divine plan in action. He knew that everything was in perfect order.

Chapter 40
Passages

*The warrior, fundamentally, is someone
who is not afraid of space.*

—Chögyam Trungpa, *Shambhala*

In the spring of 1986, José received the *chakrasamvara* transmission from a visibly ill Trungpa. It was the last transmission he received from his teacher before Trungpa's death the following year.

In the summertime, José and Lloydine attended the annual Midsummer Festival at the Rocky Mountain Dharma Center. In rare attendance was Trungpa's first wife, a Tibetan woman who was the mother of his eldest son, Osel Mukpo. (Osel later became the *sakyong* of the sangha founded by his father.) Trungpa's former wife told everyone, "Don't you see that he is dying?" This comment only highlighted the denial in the Buddhist community regarding Trungpa's alcoholism and related illness.

Nonetheless, the Midsummer Festival was a successful event. José was surprised to hear Brian Eno's "Apollo" playing over the loudspeakers instead of the usual, traditional music. He found "Apollo" an exquisite example of space music, but to hear it played at this Buddhist festival meant change was in the air. Shortly after, Trungpa moved from Boulder to Nova Scotia, based on his desire to establish the center of his organization and teachings in a less-materialistic atmosphere. Over the next few years, hundreds of his students followed in the move, including Miriam and David Garrett.

Later that year, José went on a two-week *chakrasamvara* retreat at Dorje Kyung Dzong, the retreat center he had originally planned to stay in until Trungpa advised him otherwise in 1981. This retreat gave him time to deepen the *chakrasamvara* transmission and meditation practice in preparation for the Harmonic Convergence. The two weeks proved powerful, and he received prolonged telepathic communications from Trungpa.

At one point, he was sitting in deep meditation with his bell and dorje when Trungpa appeared clairvoyantly and told him about the "fall" of Atlantis—the "breaking of the dream." Originally, everyone on Earth was aware of the dreamtime and knew that they were all living the same collective dream. Then something happened. Trungpa explained that, some 13,000 years ago, everyone woke up in a strange new dream where no one remembered the original unified dream. As a result, people thought they were separate from the whole and became increasingly individualized—all because they had lost sight of the original dream. José then had a vision of the 13 original star elders. These star elders continuously transmigrate through different cycles to ensure that the galactic stream of knowledge is transmitted from one cycle to the next. He knew he was one of these 13.

Soon after this retreat, José received a letter from Albert Ruz Buenfil, son of the archaeologist who had discovered the tomb of Pacal Votan. In the letter, Alberto wrote him about his life in the Rainbow Nation as a free radical performance artist. Alberto had a group called the Illuminated Elephants that was based in Huehuecoyotl, Mexico, just outside of Tepoztlan. Huehuecoyotl means "ancient coyote." José immediately felt that Alberto was a kindred spirit and looked forward to meeting with him.

In late 1986, José and Lloydine visited Ted and JJ in Atlanta, where Ted happily showed videos of his Goodwill Games in Moscow. José thought it was a remarkable example of creative citizen diplomacy. Ted then flew José and Lloydine to South Carolina to spend a few days relaxing at his Hope Plantation. José admired Ted's love of nature and deep reverence for the wildlife that still flourished there.

Upon their return home, José intensified the preparation for the Harmonic Convergence. This included many Planet Art Network meetings at his home, in which the group developed strategies to raise awareness for the upcoming global event. A number of social and peace activists, as well as people in metaphysical and other freethinking groups, attended the high-spirited meetings. Healing Our World, the Global Family group headed by Barbara Marx Hubbard and the Culhane sisters, connected in support of the Harmonic Convergence.

On February 2, 1987, José and Lloydine traveled to Palenque with six other people, including Barbara and Gerry Clow of Bear and Co., to ground the vision and to "gather the Galactic Mayan energy" in anticipation of the Harmonic Convergence. A special ceremony was conducted at high noon in the Court of Galactic Messengers, located in the Palace of the Tower of the Winds. During this trip, José felt deeply aligned with the galactic forces; he knew he was entering a new state of being. Twenty days after the ceremony came the first supernova discovered in 400 years: Supernova 1987A.

The new moon a few days later marked the end of the Kalachakra prophecy cycle associated with Padmasambhava. The Kalachakra teachings, or Wheel of Time, describe a series of 16 cycles, each one of 60 years. The first of these cycles began in 1027, exactly 28 years after the departure of Quetzalcoatl, and the 16th of these cycles concluded on February 28, 1987. This 16th cycle was decisive, for it included the end of traditional Tibet and the death of the 16th Karmapa.

On April 4, 1987, José and Lloydine received a phone call from a member of the Buddhist sangha to inform them that Chögyam Trungpa Rinpoche had died earlier that day in Nova Scotia. José was not surprised at the news; though he loved his teacher, he was relieved to know that he was no longer suffering. In the evening, José and Lloydine gathered with other members of the sangha for a special ceremony in the meditation hall. Everyone knew Trungpa had been quite ill for some time, and many of his students had faithfully visited the meditation hall to do longevity prayers on his behalf.

Of all of the people that José had met in his life, no one had a greater influence on him than Chögyam Trungpa. Though he had become an outsider to the Buddhist community, José knew that Trungpa saw in him a much larger vision and mission. He felt Chögyam Trungpa was highly misunderstood by many, even in the Buddhist community. Through this community, José saw how people had certain preconceptions about what it is to be "spiritual" or "enlightened." Gyatrul Rinpoche summed up this situation and the purpose of Trungpa's life in the following way in *Natural Liberation: Padmasambhava's Teachings on the Six Bardos*:

In the history of Tibetan Buddhism in the West, the first person to feed many of the wild stallions of the West was Chögyam Trungpa Rinpoche.... By so doing, he revealed to these people their own nature, and he opened the way for other great lamas—including Gyalwa Karmapa, His Holiness the Dalai Lama, and many other great lamas—to round up these wild stallions here in the West....

To understand the strategy of Chögyam Trungpa Rinpoche, imagine a region in which a peculiar rain has fallen so that whenever people drink any of the water from that rain, they go crazy. Now a king comes who has not drunk the water, and is not crazy, but since everyone else is crazy and he is not, they do not follow him. Because he seems alien, they feel no connection with him. The king then recognizes this, knows he needs to lead these people, and knows he cannot do so as long as he appears to be sane and they are all crazy. Therefore, he drinks the water, appears to be as crazy as they are, and then they follow him. They say, "Oh, he's just like us." That was Chögyam Trungpa Rinpoche's strategy; he appeared to be as crazy as all of us so that he could effectively lead us, and people would think, "Oh, he's one of the guys. He's just like us.

Trungpa's body was taken from Nova Scotia to Karme Choling in Vermont, where it remained traditionally embalmed in butter until the cremation ceremony exactly 52 days later on May 26th. José and Lloydine made their way to Vermont for the elaborate ceremony.

José took it as a positive omen when, on the day before the ceremony, he found two exquisitely carved wooden Guatemalan masks of Quetzalcoatl in an exotic gift shop in Montpelier, Vermont. He purchased one of the masks and offered it as a gift to Dhyani Ywahoo, whom he visited that afternoon.

After giving Dhyani the sacred mask, José suddenly knew he was supposed to have the other mask, so he and Lloydine returned to the gift shop only to find it closed. He knocked on the door. The proprietor answered and allowed them to come in and purchase the mask. The mask felt like an auspicious sign because the upcoming Harmonic Convergence was the conclusion of the prophecy of Quetzalcoatl.

The following day, José and Lloydine attended the day-long cremation ceremony for Chögyam Trungpa Rinpoche. It was a celebratory event attended by more than 3,000 people, many of whom spent much time sitting on the lawn doing sadhana practice. Although there was not a cloud in the sky, brilliant rainbows appeared in every direction.

José knew that, if it had not been for the profound teaching on mind and meditation that he received from Trungpa, he wouldn't have acquired the precise discipline and knowledge of mind to later probe the depths of the time-traveling wisdom of the Galactic Maya.

Chapter 41
Harmonic Convergence

*Harmonic Convergence is a signal from the Earth. It
is calling humans to acknowledge the very, very
precarious state the Earth is in; calling humans to rise
to their highest aspirations.*

—Jose Arguelles, *Los Angeles Times*, 1987

On Good Friday, April 16, 1987—12 days after Trungpa's passing—*The Mayan Factor* was published. This book was the first
of its kind and not only opened the door to a new look at the
Maya, but also to an understanding of time that was anything but chro-
nological. In *The Mayan Factor*, a new dimension of time appeared and
with it a new vision of history.

By the time *The Mayan Factor* was released, José had launched a
word-of-mouth Harmonic Convergence campaign calling for 144,000
"Sun dancers" to gather near sacred sites at dawn on August 16th and
17th to open the doors to the final 26 years of the 5,125-year Mayan
Great Cycle, an era of unprecedented change and preparation for a
new evolutionary cycle on Earth.

The dates of the Harmonic Convergence were based on prophetic
events beginning with Good Friday 1519, when Cortez led the inva-
sion of the Spaniards into Mexico. On the Mexican sacred calendar, it
marked the precise end of a 52-year cycle. Since then, nine 52-year
cycles had elapsed, coming to a close on August 16, 1987. This also
marked the last day of the Nine Hell cycles as prophesied by
Quetzalcoatl. The number nine (1 + 4 + 4) is especially significant
because early Americans believed there were nine levels of the under-
world through which the dead must descend.

José knew that the Harmonic Convergence was an event with meaning extending into other dimensions. What was occurring as a prophetic enactment on the third dimension was something that had been previsioned and foretold in another time, by seers whose sole purpose it is to monitor the karmic unfolding of this planet.

Endless hours were spent faxing and conducting mass mailings to raise awareness about these prophetic dates. The word caught fire and spurred great interest in *The Mayan Factor*. In late May, José was contacted by the *Wall Street Journal*. Hollywood was abuzz with the Harmonic Convergence, he was told, and they wanted to find out what it was about.

On June 22, 1987, José appeared on *Sonja Live* on CNN from Los Angeles. The following day, his portrait appeared on the front page of the *Wall Street Journal* with a breaking story on the Harmonic Convergence and the quote: "Mr. Arguelles says the choice between a new age and all-out destruction is ours, and we had better decide...." The media frenzy was just beginning and, before it was over, every major television network and news magazine would visit, tape, and endlessly interview José in his modest Boulder home.

Early in July, José and Lloydine visited Ted Turner's oceanfront home near Hilton Head, Georgia, to take a break from an intense period of interviews with many large publications including *Time*, *Newsweek*, and *People* magazine, and the *CBS Evening News*. Shirley MacLaine also called him several times to receive information about the deeper meaning of the event.

Upon returning home, José received the following letter from Hunbatz Men:

July 11, 1987

Dear José,

It is a great pleasure to greet you, brother José Arguelles, and to wish you the best in your path of initiation. José, I am sending you my book about the Mayan calendars. I hope you enjoy it. The questions you may have about the information in it I hope can be clarified in the not too distant future.

Solar brother, it is in the interest of the indigenous Mayan tradition that in the next year we will have a meeting about what we know about the dimension of the Mayas....

The solar communication has commenced. For this reason, all the solar human beings will always be in contact.

Sincerely,

Hunbatz Men

Returning home, the media barrage continued. José felt this media frenzy was a display of the mass mind responding with its particular insect-like probes to a phenomenon that, on one hand, was so out of the ordinary, and, on the other, was so hooked into a deep place in the collective unconscious that it couldn't help but be fascinating. At the same time, the fascination was usually short-circuited by the conditioned mind asking the questions. As a result, communicating to the media was often more frustrating than not.

One of the main purposes of the gathering of the 144,000 was to activate the *planetary grid system,* the etheric structure of the Earth or the light body of the Earth. The premise of the planetary grid is based on the position of specific ancient monuments whose location presupposes certain geomagnetic power points. The connection between all of the different power points, whether they are known about or not, constitutes the planetary grid of the Earth.

José knew that, if a large number of people gathered at sacred sites with the right intention to activate the planetary grid, it would be a conscious step in healing the planet. Many people buried crystals at the sacred sites with the intention to activate the planetary healing process. José believed that, with the right intention, crystals could be programmed to communicate and transmit energy to the Earth's interdimensional core.

In the August 11th edition of the *New York Times*, José was quoted in the article "New Era Dawns—or Just a New Day?":

The vibratory infrastructure holding the Earth together is in a condition of intense fever called *resonant dissonance.* Influences such as the arms race and insults to the environment could cause the breakup of the Earth into smaller bodies not unlike the Asteroid Belt.... This can be averted, by harmonic convergence achieved in a synchronized collective of human beings, through which the possibility of a New Heaven and a New Earth is fully present.

Being out of the ordinary frame of everyday consciousness, the Harmonic Convergence was met with skepticism by more conservative factions. José learned that, whenever something that is new and out of the ordinary is presented to the public, it is immediately taken up as an object of ridicule, criticism, and even scorn. Skeptics referred to the Harmonic Convergence as everything from "a crackpot notion" to "New Age fluff."

On August 12, 1987, *USA Today* ran a front-page story titled "Woodstock of the '80s," which quoted one of the skeptics of the Harmonic Convergence as saying the event was just "wishful thinking" and had "no basis in reality": "They are turning their backs on scientific and technological progress to help find the solution to the problems facing the world," said Barry Karr, spokesman for the Committee for the Scientific Investigation of Claims of the Paranormal in Buffalo, New York.

The Harmonic Convergence was even featured as an ongoing spoof in the *Doonesbury* comic strip, which labeled it the "Moronic Divergence," taking the sarcastic slant of those who considered the event New Age "pie in the sky" nonsense. José told the *New York Times* that he was not at all surprised that many academic specialists rejected his ideas. "They (academicians) look at the Mayans in terms of the past," José said, "whereas I consider them in the context of the present."

In a press release for *The Mayan Factor*, José described who the Maya were (are), elucidating the meaning of the Mayans' role in the Harmonic Convergence:

The Maya were planetary navigators and mappers of the larger psychic field of the Earth, the solar system, and the galaxy beyond," he stated, adding that the purpose of the Mayan return is to assist humans in aligning with the cosmic whole. This will lead to "conscious operation within the greater community of galactic intelligence.

Viewing the Harmonic Convergence as the first Mayan return point, José declared that their presence would be perceived in myriad ways, according to an individual being's belief system. But the basic message was simple: Return to the Earth and make peace with Nature! José knew that only by a collective return to Nature could a new galactic culture of peace on Earth emerge.

In an interview with the *Los Angeles Times* on August 12, 1989, José explains the importance of the Harmonic Convergence in highlighting the Earth´s place in the solar and galactic systems.

Earth has a resonant frequency of 7.8 hertz. But it has been increasingly impacted by random, dissonant frequencies—from radio and TV waves, more recently from radioactivity, chemicals, fluorocarbons—to the point where Earth is aphasic with solar and galactic resonance, the effect of what we call the "civilization" we´ve built up is a kind of waxy yellow build-up—but the galactic beam, plus the efforts of Earth Herself will change our frequency. As a living organism, Earth has needs, and a self-healing capacity. With human help, of course.

Although he had no question that extraterrestrial or higher-dimensional intelligence was monitoring the Harmonic Convergence, José was well aware that, from the point of view of consensual reality, the idea of UFOs seemed quite primitive. From the perspective of extraterrestrial intelligence, the purpose of the Harmonic Convergence was to indicate a positive collective sign of higher intelligence radiating from our planet.

To the mainstream mind, the belief in ships or aliens operating with a more sophisticated form of present-day technology was just fantasy. Moreover, José agreed with Carl Jung, who described the UFO phenomena as the result of a symbolic manifestation of the collective unconscious in his book *Flying Saucers: A Modern Myth of Things Seen in the Skies*. But José also perceived that, throughout the galaxy and universe, higher levels of intelligence exist than humans have attained or can conceive of. As he stated in *The Mayan Factor*:

> Opening our long-disregarded sense fields at last for the nourishment of the light body, UFOs will finally be understood as inter-dimensional, Earth-generated, galactically programmed electromagnetic cells available to us for our own educational purposes…. These dimensions or levels of being, now frequented by what we call UFOs, are universally accessible, and hence the meeting grounds of intelligence from different sectors of the galaxy.

On July 26, 1987, José announced the coming of galactic culture to an audience of 1,500 at St. John's College in Santa Fe. The event opened with a spectacular performance by an Aztec dance troupe called Warriors of the Seven Caves, followed by José´s impassioned speech about the upcoming Harmonic Convergence. "Many will gather without any clear idea why," he told the audience. "But *something* is stimulating them—it is as if a signal has gone out, of a particular frequency, regardless of whether or not you comprehend it."

Following this event, interviews and news stories appeared in the *Boston Globe*, *New York Times*, and *Los Angeles Times*. Besieged by the media, José and Lloydine spent the Harmonic Convergence peacefully camped out with family high in the Rockies on their friend's land. Lloydine's son, Paul, kept a fire burning until the dawn, when they would extinguish the old fire and start a new one. Astrologically, seven of the nine planets formed a grand trine on August 16th, meaning they were all in their astrological fire signs and situated within 120 degrees from one another. (A grand trine occurs when three planets in the same element create a triangle with each other. In this case, the element was Fire.)

On the morning of August 16th, José arose and blew the conch 144 times, 36 times to each of the four directions. That afternoon, they drove back down to Boulder to join Barbara Marx Hubbard at KGNU Studio for a live global radio broadcast to all the sacred sites around the planet, including the Great Pyramid, Stonehenge, Mount Shasta, Glastonbury, the Black Hills of South Dakota, the Temples of Delphi in Greece, Woodstock and Central Park (New York), Sedona (Arizona), Mt. Fuji (Japan), Mt. Olympus (Greece), the Ganges River (India), Popocatepel (Mexico), and Mt. Haleakala (Hawaii).

The Harmonic Convergence marked the first time human beings simultaneously coordinated their prayers, meditations, and ceremonies at sacred sites around the planet. This was the first manifestation of a networked thrust toward a unified moment of collective synchronization. Everyone from Shirley MacLaine to Timothy Leary to John Denver celebrated the event. Even Johnny Carson got into the act when, on the evening of August 15th, he said to his television audience: "There is an art historian in Boulder who is having this thing called the Harmonic Convergence.... They called for 144,000 to participate in the event. I hear that there are only 143,500, but there are 500 of us in the audience, so let's all take a moment and OM...." And they did.

The oddest phenomenon that was observed during the Harmonic Convergence was in New Zealand, when a gigantic explosion occurred at about 2 a.m. A huge fireball transformed into an iridescent cloud with a very strong thundering effect. This was observed all over the

North Island of New Zealand and was widely reported in all the major newspapers. Meteorologists said they didn't know what it was, but it appeared that, if the object had hit the Earth, it would have been catastrophic. The reports claimed that it lit up the sky as if the Sun were rising.

Immediately after the event, José and Lloydine met with Ted Turner and JJ at the Denver airport. Ted expressed awe and appreciation of the Harmonic Convergence as a media event, especially because it was done without a professional publicity campaign. A few grassroots networks promoted it, no money had been invested, there was no business plan, and no one choreographed the event.

A few weeks after the Harmonic Convergence, José wrote a letter to the media as a follow up to all who participated in the event. The following is an excerpt:

> The tiny incandescent flame of the new has been kindled. The vision of how peace will be restored to the planet has been manifest. Now begins the hard work. Within two years, the lifeboats of the new must be readied and launched. For the diseased civilization is now out of control, and the earth is thirsty for its sacred warriors to return.

Late in August 1987, *Time* magazine sent a photographer to take pictures of José. At the photographer's request, José posed for pictures playing his shakuhachi bamboo flute while sitting on cliff sides at a picnic in the Rockies outside of Boulder. The photographer asked people at the picnic to gather around him so that it would appear that they were his "followers." Lloydine was unhappy with this photo shoot and gave the photographer a piece of her mind. The pictures never appeared in the magazine.

Shirley MacLaine appeared on the cover of *Time* magazine in 1987 as a face of the new age. She called José several times before the Convergence to check facts to be sure the story was straight. José found her pleasant and engaging on the phone, but he did not hear from her again until years later.

For José, the success of the Harmonic Convergence confirmed all he had previously concluded in his research of the Mayan calendar. Many people thought that it was the beginning of the "new age." Others thought that it helped end the Cold War, and still others thought that it would be the end of the world. But for José, the success of the event showed only the true and serious nature of the prophecy of Quetzalcoatl. It was a signal indicating that only 25 years remained before the end of the Mayan Great Cycle of History on December 21, 2012.

Inevitably, the price of "worldly success" proved overwhelming if not distracting to José, and he found himself the target of many strange projections. Some people perceived him as a "new age guru," while others deemed him a charlatan. Although José had never considered himself particularly "new age," the media labeled him the "high priest of the new age" or a "new age cult hero." He learned firsthand that it is the nature of the media to label and compartmentalize people for its own commercial gain. He also discovered that, if he mentioned UFOs or extraterrestrials in interviews, that topic would become the focus of the entire interview, diverting readers from the actual message he was trying to convey, which was: "The planet is undergoing a major change with very powerful ramifications for the organization of human society and its future!" It seemed that the world was far more fascinated with sensationalism than with the truth.

Being that his goal was to get this message out to as many people as possible, he didn't understand why the publishers of *The Mayan Factor* turned down the opportunity to sell the book to a mass-market publisher immediately after the Harmonic Convergence. Nonetheless, *The Mayan Factor* has been translated and published into several languages and remains in print today.

Following the Harmonic Convergence, world events took an interesting twist. On October 19, 1987, the stock market experienced its biggest collapse in history. About a month later, Russia's Premier, Mikhael Gorbachev, initiated the first break in the Cold War, proposing treaties for the dismantling of nuclear warheads.

José knew these shifts in world affairs were directly related to the impact of the Harmonic Convergence on the collective human psyche and that, at an unconscious level, certain impulses had been triggered that would signal greater acceleration of change. Even *USA Today* queried at the end of its front-page story about the stock market crash: "...and then there was the Harmonic Convergence. Did this have something to do with the crash?"

Chapter 42
Surfers of the Zuvuya

All those synchronicities, déjà vus, and premonitions,
as well as all those dreams—that´s your fourth-
dimensional double doing its number—trying to get
you to pay attention.

—José Arguelles, *Surfers of the Zuvuya*

In the fall of 1987, Josh began college at Colorado State University and, after Miriam and David Garrett moved to Halifax, Tara moved in with José and Lloydine. José looked forward to making up for lost time with his daughter; it had been seven years since he'd lived with her.

Frustrated that *The Mayan Factor* wouldn't be published in the mass-market format, where it would have attracted a wider readership, José felt he had to write something in a more popular style to explain the meaning of the Harmonic Convergence in relation to the Mayan prophecies. Then maybe those who had participated in the global event, but didn't know why, could understand the prophetic meaning.

In September 1987, with Lloydine in Arizona for a weeklong Jin Shin Jitsu training, José wrote the first draft of *Surfers of the Zuvuya* while home alone with Tara. One afternoon, while in a state of hypnogogic reverie, a voice, seemingly out of nowhere, spoke to José. He had developed the facility to "hang out" in the hypnogogic state between waking consciousness and sleep. This required a certain skill of maintaining a lucid, non-conceptual state of mind while entering the vivid, often fast-moving scenery of the multidimensional realms. In this state, José sometimes experienced clairvoyant visions, which in time he identified with travels to the center of the Earth; at other times, he heard voices or words being dictated to him.

So it was that one afternoon, shortly after Lloydine had departed, José heard a voice talking to him. The voice identified itself as Uncle Joe Zuvuya, his dimensional double. He communicated the meaning of *The Mayan Factor* and interdimensional reality in a colloquial language, almost in the voice of Josh and his friends. José was genuinely surprised when he was commanded to listen to Uncle Joe, who informed him in *Surfers of the Zuvuya* that everyone is born with a "dimensional double," also referred to as the soul or higher self:

> The way to understand it is this: the body you look at and see in the mirror is your third-dimensional body.... The dimensional double is in the fourth dimension, the next dimension over. It is there all the time, trying to give your third-dimensional being information that might help it, if the third-dimensional being is ready to hear it. All those synchronicities, déjà vus, and premonitions, as well as all those dreams—that's your fourth-dimensional double doing its number—trying to get you to pay attention.

Uncle Joe told José to consider the fact that maybe he (José) was a "planetary program from the Sun, just a broadcast or a special service announcement meant to be played just for this time period." He explained in detail to José the meaning of the *Zuvuya*.

Zuvuya is the Mayan term for the big memory circuit. It is the memory hotline. It works individually and collectively. Most importantly, it connects equally to the future as well as to the past. Why? Because the Zuvuya is the interdimensional thread. And we are all interdimensional. Harmonic Convergence was and is the interdimensional zap of the Zuvuya riding the consciousness of the human race, giving it the signal that something else is going on. What is going on is the fact that we are not alone. Yes, there is life beyond and within planet Earth—and lots of it.

Completing *Surfers* was but one of many things on José's mind at this time. He knew his life was changing rapidly and that he had to make decisions rather than let the current of events sweep him away. One of these decisions was freeing himself from the obligations and entanglements of the Buddhist community.

On October 27th, José and Lloydine handed in their resignations at the Vajradhatu Buddhist Center, stating that they would no longer be paying dues. José had felt this coming for a long time. The Buddhist community did not support his work, and he felt that remaining in the organization was far too limiting. A planetary healing bodhisattva should be free to operate in the world without any kind of religious jargon. He knew he had to break out of the box.

Later that day, they caught a plane to New Mexico, where they had a successful meeting with Barbara and Gerry Clow of Bear and Company, coming to a higher understanding regarding the publishing of *The Mayan Factor*. At this point, José was scheduled for a three-month book tour and slated for numerous speaking engagements across the United States. Already in a state of exhaustion after the entire hullabaloo over the Harmonic Convergence, José felt he needed to take a retreat in order to regenerate himself. He felt a book tour might not be the best use of his energy.

José and Lloydine returned from Santa Fe late on the night of October 28th. On the morning of October 29, 1987, José woke up at 6:00 a.m. He said he needed to consult the *I Ching* regarding the idea of going on a retreat. He got hexagram 23, "Splitting Apart," changing to hexagram 2, "the Receptive." The answer was obvious: He should stop his activities for a while to renew himself and to find the way to his next stage of development.

José went to get Tara ready for school. She had a new pair of shoes, and it was the first time she'd worn them. At about 6:50 a.m. José noticed she was moving rather slowly.

"C'mon, Tara," José told his daughter. "You had better get going; your bus is going to be here soon." To get to the bus stop, Tara had to walk over the common lawn area of the condominium complex to Pearl Street and then cross to the other side, where she would catch the eastbound bus. José watched her from the window and noticed that she was walking unusually slowly even before she got to Pearl Street. The eastbound bus got to her stop and left without her. José watched her turn around and start to walk back. As it turned out, she walked slowly because her new shoes hurt her feet.

José went upstairs to his room to change out of his kimono into street clothes so that he could take Tara to school. He grabbed, among other things, the sweatshirt that Josh had given him. The sweatshirt was emblazoned with the words and image of Señor Frogs, a popular hangout in Mazatlan, Mexico, where Josh had visited during his last high school spring vacation.

At 7 a.m., José went back downstairs to take Tara to school. As he opened the door, he found a police officer and a woman standing at the doorstep. Before he could say anything, the police officer spoke: "I don't know how else to say this, but at 2:35 this morning, southbound from Fort Collins on I-25 at mile marker 266, your son Josh and his friend Mike Buddington were instantly killed in a head-on collision."

José, Tara, and Lloydine all let out a wail of disbelief and grief. As it turned out, the woman with the police officer was a grief counselor. They had been waiting in the parking lot for the right moment when they knew everyone would be up and around. José recalled that he had awakened suddenly that night and looked at his digital clock, which read 2:35 a.m., exactly. And then he went back to sleep.

Once they gathered themselves together, more or less, Lloydine took Tara to school to let her friends know what had happened and bring them back to the house with her for support. When Lloydine got into the car, she realized that the stereo had been ripped off the night before, leaving only dangling wires where the stereo had once been. Later on that day, José noticed that their two bicycles had also been stolen. He chalked this up to supernatural intervention accommodating Josh's death.

Around 5:00 that evening, José and Lloydine and Carl Springer, who would conduct the funeral ceremony the following day, went to the funeral home to view Josh's un-embalmed body. José expected that, because Josh had been in a car accident, he would see some kind of mangled figure. What he saw was anything but that. Josh was laid out on a table covered in a sheet with his head exposed. José was surprised to see Josh's face completely intact with just a small cut above his left eye. A powerful radiance seemed to emanate from his face; it was palpable upon entering the room. The expression on Josh's face made him look as though he was still present, but just ever so slightly troubled. José kissed him on the forehead and said, "Thank you, Josh." He had last seen his son 12 days earlier, when he had come to Boulder for a visit.

The week before his last visit, on the weekend of October 17th, José received a letter from Josh. Josh wrote: "You know, Dad, I don't have to wait to grow up to be like you. I know I'm already like you." Then he described in his letter how, on Sunday evening, he had received a phone call from his friend, who was at the Denver airport, returning from a visit to his family in San Diego, and realized he had left his car keys in his dorm room. He asked Josh to drive down from Fort Collins to the Denver airport to bring him his keys. Josh agreed to the seven-hour round trip even though it was Sunday night and he had mid-term exams the next morning. He left immediately and managed to make it back to college for breakfast and to do a little studying before his exams.

That was the incident Josh had referred to when he said, "Dad, I don't have to wait to grow up to be like you. I know I'm already like you." José was touched by his son's perception of him and felt that Josh had a certain insight about him that few people had. He had made the remark just a few weeks before his death. In retrospect, José saw that, by that remark, Josh was telling him that he had completed his life and had already accomplished what he needed to accomplish. At the time he received the letter, José didn't realize how prophetically in tone it was with what was about to happen.

José and Josh, 1986. Image courtesy of and copyright the José Arguelles Archive.

After he wrote the letter, Josh called to say that he was coming home for the weekend to attend the Boulder High School homecoming football game. He came down that Friday night and, before leaving for the game, he said, "Dad, make sure you make one of your really good breakfasts in the morning."

The next morning, José prepared breakfast omelets, hash browns, and toast. Josh came upstairs with two girls, one white and one black. They all looked very innocent, and José reasoned that they had all crashed in Josh's old room after a night of partying. José didn't realize that this was the last time he would see Josh.

That afternoon, José took Tara to her weekly modeling school class in Denver. While Tara was at class, José was accustomed to getting a cup of coffee and heading to a nearby park, where he would spend an hour before picking her up. On this occasion, he had brought his Excalibur double-terminated crystal and gazed deeply into it, making drawings of the crystalline worlds he saw. Gazing intently into the crystal, he saw a shape that appeared like a specter or phantom, accompanied by a strange internal sensation. He later recognized this as a prevision of Josh's death.

On Sunday night, October 25th, Josh called José. He had misplaced the car key to his yellow 1978 Honda that he had inherited as a graduation present from Lloydine. Josh asked José if he could send him the spare key. The next morning, José wrapped the key in a piece of cardboard and enclosed a note. The last words in the note were, "Harmonic Convergence is still happening—look out for the UFOs!" José wrote those specific words because he knew that everyone in Josh's dorm room had heard about the Harmonic Convergence and knew he was José's son. Little did he know that these words would be his last communication with his son.

The day before Josh's death, on October 28th, José and Lloydine were in Santa Fe with Jamie Sams, creator of the Medicine Cards. Jamie gave José a recording of an operatic rock artist, Steve Gaines, from Los Angeles. Late in the afternoon on October 28th, their friend D. Treadwell drove them to the airport. On the ride, they listened to Jamie's tape. One song that stood out in the mix was called "Starseed." It proved to be quite prophetic with its lyrics: "Starseed comes thrice splitting the indigo night." On the drive to the airport, they looked into the sky and noticed it was filled with ship clouds, an especially big one hovered over Santa Fe. "That one is called the Excalibur," Treadwell remarked.

José listened to the tape much after Josh's death. He knew Josh was the starseed.

On the other side of the tape was the equally prophetic "The Eagle Will Rise Again," by Alan Parson Project:

> And so, with no warning, no last goodbye
> In the dawn of the morning sky
> The eagle will rise again

As it turned out, on October 29th, Josh was driving his friend Mike Buddington to the nearby town of Greeley for the second time that night, to retrieve keys he had forgotten when they were there earlier. It was after midnight. They were never to return. The family concluded that at 2:35 a.m., the time of the accident, Josh was playing U2's *Joshua Tree* on his stereo, since he had recently given everybody in the family a copy of that tape.

The day after Josh's death, José kept hearing his son say: "Am I doing it now, Dad? Am I doing it now?" José knew when he heard these words that Josh had exceeded himself and was now in a space where he could experience liberation. He had to do it in that way, at that time. José understood that Josh was paving the way for him to learn, in his own way, how to communicate the meaning of the higher dimensions. José knew that Josh was actually communicating that he, too, could now become liberated.

The funeral ceremony came together quickly. Josh's death made front-page news in the Boulder paper on that Thursday afternoon. That night, his body was placed on view in a simple pine coffin in the meditation hall for everyone to see. By evening, Miriam had arrived. Everything was charged with a big adrenaline rush of unreality. No one could believe what had happened. José could not believe Josh was no longer in the world with him. In a daze, they met with the people who would conduct the ceremony and then made all of the arrangements for the cremation. Miriam's mother, Edith, arrived with Miriam's aunt, Ruthie. Edith was a bit confused. She did not quite understand the concept of a Buddhist funeral.

A few hours before the actual ceremony, José, Lloydine, Miriam, Tara, Paul, Heidi, Yvonne, Maya, and Edith all gathered in "A" Suite. The suite, ironically, had been the office of Chögyam Trungpa Rinpoche and was the very room that José and Lloydine had visited just a few days earlier when they formally resigned from the Buddhist community.

By the time of the funeral, late in the afternoon, the meditation hall was jammed beyond maximum capacity, with more than 600 people in attendance. Half of the Boulder High School students were present, even though Josh had graduated the year before. Josh had been a popular student; his friendships ran the gamut of the social spectrum, from artsy types to outcasts to jocks. Tara had a supportive group of friends to help her through the funeral.

The ceremony began with several heartfelt eulogies expressed by friends and family. Carl Springer placed the four Tibetan seed syllables, drawn on paper, over Josh's head, throat, heart, and solar plexus centers: OM AH HUM HRIH. He then burned a picture of Josh and explained the Buddhist concept of the *sukhavati*, the funeral ceremony of letting go of the body, and the meaning of burning the picture. He told everyone that they could now let go of the physical Josh and realize the existence of the pure consciousness Josh.

In the funeral service for Joshua Maitreya Arguelles, a sword, a bottle of beer, a steak, and his favorite shoes were placed in the coffin. The idea was that the items most familiar and/or cherished by the deceased would accompany him on the journey of the dead until he reaches the place of paradise, known as Valhalla in the Germanic tradition or as the Thirteen Heavens in the Mexican tradition. At the end of the ceremony, six of Josh's closest friends loaded the coffin onto their shoulders and carried his body out to be cremated. All of the items placed in the coffin were consumed in the fire as well.

A few days after the funeral, José, Lloydine, Miriam, and Tara were driven to Fort Collins to visit Josh's dorm room and reclaim his possessions. Out of respect, Josh's college roommate had left the room exactly as it was the last night Josh had been there. Several opened books were scattered around the bed and the desk, as well as an unfinished can of beer. José found that one of the books Josh had been reading just before his death was a somewhat arcane text by a 19th-century anarchist Russian philosopher, Plekhanov; it was a study about anarchism in Russia in the 19th century, which was the point at which anarchism began as a social movement. José was impressed by his reading selection. Another book he had been reading was *To Dwell Among Friends*, a sociological study of networking in urban centers. José thought this selection was interesting because Josh was a born networker with a gift for unifying people.

In a period of four weeks, José's life had come to a synchronistic head that indicated radical change in all directions: He was no longer a formal Buddhist; he was no longer a literary personality for someone else's publishing company; and he no longer had a son. Emotionally bankrupt, José took a sabbatical for a few months from the Union Graduate School, and he and Lloydine immediately entered into a 49-day bardo retreat.

During the 49 days, José was in a state of intense grief. In the mornings, he would do meditation practice followed by Shambhala warrior practice, and every other day Lloydine would administer Jin Shin Jitsu to help stabilize his energy. Most of his time, however, was spent in his loft, reflecting on the meaning of life and death, and trying to feel what was coming next.

On a rare outing during this time, José and Lloydine took a brief drive to sit underneath a tree dedicated to Chögyam Trungpa. While José was focusing on the ceramic knot of eternity that sits beside the tree, he heard Josh's voice speaking as from afar: "Where I am, Dad, it's not like you think it is. That's why it's so important that you surrender everything. That way you'll be able to know, and we'll be able to do our job together."

It was the first of many communications from Josh during the 49-day period. José recorded all of his son's messages in his specially designated "Josh Journal." José would often feel Josh's presence strongly in the room with him, primarily at times when he experienced heightened states of grief. There was something about Josh's presence that caused José to glimpse the cosmic joke of the whole drama. Many communications that he had with Josh were in relation to the reality of the fourth dimension and the Mothership that was watching over our planet. During this period, José came to understand, as never before, that there was a Beyond or a Hereafter.

Josh would show him certain realities and say:

This is where you are supposed to go, Dad.
This is what you are supposed to explore.
You are supposed to become a spiritual being.

Josh gave José specific spiritual teachings, which he recorded in his journal:

Don't initiate, be initiated.
Everything takes care of itself.
Don't be foolish enough to believe other people's projections of you.

Josh was clearly pointing the way for José to leave his materialist lifestyle and proceed in a purely spiritual direction. José would soon quit his job at the Union Graduate School in order to pursue the purely spiritual level of the Mayan mathematics: the Galactic Mayan direction.

Exactly four weeks after Josh's death, José got a call from Jamie Sams, who said: "I am hesitant to say this, but I have been channeling, and I seemed to have picked up Josh." Skeptical, José at first brushed off Jamie's admission. But then Jamie gave José a message directly from Josh that proved that he'd indeed been in communication with Jamie. Josh told Jamie, "You can tell my Dad that I used to call Lloydine, _____." José recognized the name, which only family members knew. Stunned, José listened as Jamie went on to tell him that Josh said he was on the Excalibur, one of the Motherships, the head of which was at Mt. Shasta and the tail in Glastonbury.

Thirty-nine days after Josh's death, José made a visit to the meditation hall, where Josh's ashes sat in the center of the altar in a Chinese cloisonné vase with a blue dragon on it, to pay tribute to his son. Around the vase that contained his ashes were several pictures of deceased Buddhist meditation masters, including the 16th Karmapa, Chögyam Trungpa Rinpoche, and Zen master Suzuki Roshi. José was amazed to see that in the middle of all these Tibetan and Buddhist meditation masters was the high school graduation photo of his son, Josh.

At this sight, José received what he felt to be a clear, past-life image of Josh as a Vietnamese Buddhist monk who was killed by American soldiers. His very last thought was to be re-born as an American boy so that he could teach others, through his love, the meaning of death. At this point, José learned never to pass judgment on anyone because you never really know just who it is that you are talking to.

After the 49-day bardo, José slowly began to do some work with a few of his Union Graduate School students. It was all he could do to accomplish the immediate day-to-day tasks at hand, as it was still hard to get Josh out of his mind. He knew Josh's death had happened for a profound reason, and he

Josh's high school graduation, June 1987. Image courtesy of and copyright the José Arguelles Archive.

knew he was being moved into an entirely new phase of existence that had everything to do with the Harmonic Convergence and the Galactic Maya. At the time, he did not quite know where the path would lead. However, he was repeatedly given a clear message instructing him to devote himself to the decoding of the mathematics of the calendar, which had always been at the heart of his work.

The day after the bardo, which was around Christmastime in 1987, José and Lloydine traveled to Nova Scotia to visit Tara, who was living with Miriam in Halifax. It was there that José found the Shield of Arcturus at a Celtic art store in Halifax. José felt that this circular leather shield embossed with brass ornaments was a clear representation of the Mayan star symbol, Lamat, which depicts the four points of a star with four smaller circles around these points. The number of the smaller brass circles indicated numerology related to the Tzolkin: 1 and 13; 64 + 8 + 72 (= 144); + 36 (fourth power of nine, one-quarter of 144). José had always recognized the Lamat symbol as being the sign of the star Arcturus, and so he saw this Celtic shield as the shield of Arcturus, indicating the universality of the Mayan galactic knowledge.

José knew that his 49th birthday would open a whole new phase of life. Up to this point, Lloydine had been relatively active with him, especially in the workshops. But now the interactive level diminished and the relationship began to change in many ways that were unperceivable at the time. This established a kind of co-dependency that would have different ramifications and repercussions as time went on.

Last picture taken of Josh and José, just before Josh's death, 1987. (Note José's shirt: "Where will you be in 2012?") Image courtesy of and copyright the José Arguelles Archive

Josh's death pierced the bubble of domestic happiness and contentment, plunging José into a state of painful catharsis, and from catharsis to inner transformation. It was the beginning of his transition into the full embodiment of the Galactic Mayan messengership.

PART VII

Embodying the New Time

Chapter 43
Riding a New Wave

The entire universe is a great theatre of mirrors, a set of hieroglyphs to decipher; everything is a sign, everything harbors and manifests mystery.

—Alice Bailey, *Esoteric Psychology II*

During the time leading up to his 49th birthday, José was still in a fragile state, dealing with the implications of his son's death. Things that once had seemed important held little value for him. He passed the days tending to the tasks at hand, but nothing more. As he re-evaluated his life, he found the cultivation of his inner spiritual being was all that mattered.

On Easter Sunday in 1988, José placed one-half of his son's ashes in a vase beneath some rocks near Chögyam Trungpa's stupa at the Rocky Mountain Dharma Center in northern Colorado. Josh had died exactly 208 days after Trungpa—sixteen 13-day cycles. This confirmed a synchronistic relation between the deaths of two beings so dear to José.

In the summer of 1988, José and Lloydine returned to Nova Scotia to visit Tara and Miriam and to bury the other half of Josh's ashes at the Gampo Abbey, Cape Breton. Soon after releasing Josh's ashes, José had an inspired dream. In the dream, he walked into a bar where there was raucous music and noisy laughter. He looked around and saw many shamans filling the seats, smoking and drinking strange concoctions. He stepped up to the bar to order a drink.

"No, no, no!" said the shaman behind the bar. "You can't have anything from here."

"Why not?" José asked.

The shaman replied, "Isn't there something you forgot to do? Isn't there something you still need to finish?"

When José woke from the dream, he knew that his next step was to focus all of his energy on completing the decoding of the mathematical system that underlies the Mayan calendar. To do this, he knew he'd have to quit his job and find another way to live. He went to his desk and began constructing an unpublished treatise called"Day by Day the Mayan Way," followed by *Tzolkin: The Book of Destiny*. This was his first attempt to make the mathematical codes and cycles accessible to the people.

In the spring of 1988, he made his first public appearance since Josh's death at the Peace through Education Conference in Arlington, Texas. The Robert Mueller School sponsored the event, which included guests such as Ted Turner, Willis Harmon, Robert Mueller, and Mother Tynetta Muhammad of the Nation of Islam. When José first met Tynetta, he wasn't aware that she was the widow of the Honorable Elijah Muhammad, whom he'd known about from his University of Chicago days.

On their first meeting, José and Tynetta discussed mathematics and *The Mayan Factor*. She told him she'd been in Egypt in August 1987, and that someone had given her a leaflet about the Harmonic Convergence and told her to go to the Great Pyramid to meditate and pray on August 16–17th. She did. Soon after, she discovered *The Mayan Factor* and was impressed by the 0–19 code. In later meetings, Tynetta would introduce José to the Holy Quran and the life of Muhammad.

For his presentation, José spoke about the role of art in transformative education and the transformative principle of peace. It had been a long time since he'd attended such a public event, and he felt an emptiness and strain from the overall situation. He spoke about the Mayan calendar and his notion of the "Campaign for the Earth," a 25-year (1987–2012) program intended to help humanity switch gears from materialism to planetary service.

"We have to form coalitions to clean up the Earth," he told the large crowd. "Only when this is complete can we, as a species, launch into the galactic phase of our evolutionary development."

As it turned out, the spiritual speaker of the conference couldn't attend, so José was appointed as his replacement. He was asked, on very short notice, to lead a prayer or give an invocation. Having no idea what to say, José took his seat at a banquet table next to Ted Turner and sat for a few moments in concentration. Suddenly, words came, and he quickly scribbled them down. No sooner had he written the prayer was he called on stage to recite it:

From the East: House of Light
May wisdom dawn in us
So we may see all things in clarity.

From the North: House of Night
May wisdom ripen in us
So we may know all from within.

From the West: House of Transformation
May wisdom be transformed into right action
So we may do what must be done.

From the South: House of the Eternal Sun
May right action reap the harvest
So we may enjoy the fruits of planetary being.

From Above: House of Heaven
Where star people and ancestors gather
May their blessings come to us now!

From Below: House of Earth
May the heartbeat of her crystal core
Bless us with harmonies to end all war!

From the Center: Galactic Source
Which is everywhere at once
May everything be known
As the light of mutual love!

Ah Yum Hunab Ku Evam Maya E Ma Ho!
Ah Yum Hunab Ku Evam Maya E Ma Ho!
Ah Yum Hunab Ku Evam Maya E Ma Ho!

While reciting the prayer, José noticed Ted counting on his fingers. When he took his seat, Ted said in amazement, "José, I thought there were four directions, but you got seven!" The prayer was known from then on as the "Prayer to the Seven Galactic Directions."

Around this time, Hunbatz Men visited José at his house in Boulder. During the visit, Hunbatz told José that there were two types of Maya: the Indigenous Maya and the Galactic Maya. *The Mayan Factor* and the Harmonic Convergence, he said, represented the "Galactic Maya," whereas he (Hunbatz) represented the Indigenous Maya. Hunbatz wished to honor José as a "Galactic Maya."

Late in 1988, Carl Bendix of Earth Celebrations 2000 (EC2000) contacted José. Bendix had started the organization in 1988 to produce entertainment fundraising events that inspire public action on behalf of the planet. Bendix also worked for Ambrosia Caterers and was the caterer for the 1988 and 1989 Academy Awards ceremonies in Hollywood. Through phone conversations, Bendix told José that his intention was to merge the tradition of the Harmonic Convergence with the 20th anniversary of Earth Day and to set in motion annual Earth celebrations on behalf of planetary transformation.

On December 8, 1988, José and Lloydine flew to Los Angeles for an exploratory meeting with Bendix regarding EC2000. The environmental movement was reunited in Hollywood that night. José was acutely aware that it was the eighth anniversary of John Lennon's death when he arrived at Norman Lear's that evening. Lear was best known as the producer of the 1970s sitcom *All in the Family*. At the meeting, Jeremy Rifkin gave a presentation about global warming and its effects on the environment. Rifkin was head of an environmental advocacy organization formed to insert new, positive messages into mainstream consciousness via popular television. After that evening, Hollywood was a-buzz with "the environment." Even the United Nations Environmental Program opened up an entertainment office in Hollywood at that time.

José and Lloydine spent the night at Bendix's modest but crystal-studded house in Corral Canyon, Malibu. They awoke to the smell of smoke. A major brush and forest fire was occurring in the mountains east of where they were staying. José was reminded of the fire that had destroyed the area where he'd done the ceremony for Ted Turner.

Soon after this meeting, Bendix flew José to California for a second time. This time he offered him a job as President of EC2000. José accepted. Although he was excited at the opportunity to fulfill his whole Earth vision, he was hesitant at taking on such a responsibility; he still had much work to do with the mathematics of the Mayan calendar.

Nonetheless, it was time for a radical change. He gave his 30-day notice to Union Graduate School and, as of January 31, 1989, ended his professional academic career of 23 years. In February 1989, José and Lloydine packed up a few personal items and moved into a small beach house in Malibu with their dog, Genji.

In California, José deepened his mathematical investigations and reduced the Mayan calendar down to its 0–19 code. This was an essential step for what he would soon discover. He shared his mathematic discovery with Ralph Abraham, his former Princeton colleague and mathematician, who came for a visit from Santa Cruz.

One Sunday afternoon when José spoke with his father on the telephone, as was his weekly custom, Enrique was in a contemplative mood. He had just re-read *The Mayan Factor* and, in his broken English, he said, "You know, Yo-sef. I have been thinking, and I want to ask you a question: Did José Arguelles invent *The Mayan Factor*, or did *The Mayan Factor* invent José Arguelles?" José found this a compelling question and led him to further reflect that, somehow or other, the ancient or Galactic Maya had actually created his present life.

Each day, José commuted to the Ambrosia offices on the Pacific Coast Highway. Despite a lot of talk and numerous fundraisers and dinners with people such as William Shatner, nothing was forthcoming. This lasted for three and a half months. With personal funds running low, life at the office soon became draining. So José was not surprised when, upon reporting for duty the morning of February 13, 1989, he found that for no apparent reason all positions had been eliminated.

It soon became apparent to him that at a deeper level this job had been presented to him not because he needed a new "career," but merely to help him transition out of his "normal" suburban lifestyle and release him from the confines of institutional academia. After giving everything up and not having EC2000 pan out, José felt momentarily panicked, having jumped out of the old order and into something with no certainty or security. It was a strengthening test of empowerment. He realized that there is simply no security in the old order. It was up to him to chart his own course. The first step was to clear a space so he could focus wholeheartedly on completing the decoding of the Mayan mathematics.

Temple of Inscriptions. Photo courtesy of Hirohide Yanase.

⁒

In the middle of the short-lived EC2000 experience, José and Lloydine traveled to Palenque with Hunbatz Men, who had requested that José be present for the first ceremonial opening of Palenque in centuries—if not a millennium. It was the first time the Mexican government had officially sanctioned use of an "archeological site" for contemporary ceremony and the first time in perhaps more than 1,200 years that Palenque had been the center of such activity.

About 400 people marched into the entrance of the sacred ruins, led by Aztec dancers in full regalia. Mexican press and television, as well as many tourists, surrounded the site. As coordinator of the ceremony, Hunbatz Men requested that José make a presentation. Standing on a round pedestal in front of the Temple of Inscriptions, which held the tomb of Pacal Votan, José raised his hands in the air, each one holding a crystal, and announced in Spanish the historical significance of the event.

Following his presentation, José led a meditation on the steps of the Temple of Inscriptions. It was during this meditation on March 12, 1989, that he received a clear message from Pacal Votan. After the ceremony, Hunbatz intuitively came running over to him and asked what Pacal Votan told him in his meditation. José told Hunbatz that Pacal Votan said he was "going to return," but in a form that everybody on Earth would understand; he wouldn't rest until everyone had received his spirit and inspiration.

José met Alberto Ruz for the first time at this ceremony. He felt an immediate kinship with Alberto, who was a wild, free spirit, something like a gypsy or pirate, accompanied by a gaily-dressed entourage. The two made an unspoken connection. Immediately, they went to the tomb of Alberto's father, which was across from Temple XIII and the Temple of the Inscriptions. Holding their arms together tightly over the stone that marks his father's grave, Alberto and José acknowledged that a much larger vision and a higher calling had brought them together.

Upon returning to Malibu, José knew something drastic had to change. He knew he had to take action for the next step to appear. With the assistance of Lloydine and his friend Roger Garvin, he arranged the "Campaign for the Earth Conference."

The Campaign for the Earth was a 25-year program (1987–2012) to continue the vision put forth by *The Mayan Factor* up until the closing of the cycle. The intention was to gather spiritually motivated coalitions and create spiritual/ecological programs to regenerate the biosphere of the Earth. The coalitions would also help existing economic structures that were devastating the planet to transition to non-polluting technologies.

A wide range of people answered the call of the Campaign for the Earth. In attendance were Elizabeth Sartouris from Greece, Alberto Ruz Buenfils, Sir Reinhart Ruge of the World Parliament Council in Mexico, David Gershon of the First Earth Run, along with Barbara Marx Hubbard and Marion Culhane of the Global Family.

At the conference, José officially announced his resignation from EC2000 and asked for participants to help organize the Campaign for the Earth. Sasha White of San Francisco volunteered to initiate action of the vision and soon after started her own version of Campaign for the Earth in Boulder, Colorado. Assisting her was Rennie Davis, prominent 1960s radical of the "Chicago Seven."

Also present at the event was José's old friend Howard Roske and Jimmy Nelson, a freewheeling philanthropist from Hawaii. Jimmy, who had been at the Palenque ceremony, was sympathetic to José's cause and donated $100,000 with the suggestion that he move to Hawaii and continue work on behalf of the Earth. José gave $30,000 to Howard Roske and family to continue their "Circle of the Sun" environmental visionary project, and then set his compass for Hawaii.

Chapter 44
Book of Kin

> *Synchronistic events provide an immediate*
> *religious experience as a direct encounter with*
> *the compensatory patterning of events in nature*
> *as a whole, both inwardly and outwardly.*

> —Carl Jung

> *One touch of nature, makes the whole world kin.*

> —William Shakespeare

The first five months in Maui were spent in an idyllic setting "upcountry" on Olinda Road. Here, José was free to focus solely and diligently on decoding. He sought to scientifically isolate the mathematical system from what is called the "Mayan calendar" so he could pinpoint its universal aspects; he knew this held a key to the science of synchronicity.

Through unraveling the mathematical codes of time, José was guided by a process of "telepathically coded messages." He first became aware of this process while writing *Earth Ascending*; the map sequences illustrated in that book came about through following a set of telepathically coded messages. This same process occurred on top of the pyramid at Coba when he received the telepathically coded messages that inspired *The Mayan Factor*. He learned from direct experience that, indeed, the Maya were a telepathic culture; their perceptions, modes of knowing, and communication came from a high degree of telepathic attunement to the cosmos.

José thought that, in order for a telepathic culture of attunement to exist, there must be some type of underlying structure. The underlying structure, he found, was ultimately a system of pure number. The

255

telepathically coded messages are the essence of what he would later call the "synchronic order." (*Syn* means "together," and *chronic* means "time.") From the point of view of the fourth dimension, he discovered, the *synchronic order* represents the "perception of the totality of time at any given moment." Telepathic cultures are dependent upon this method, or synchronic order. This method knows number, the number ratios, the number fractals, and the number relations. In other words, the numbers "talk."

Since the summer of 1988, he had created three versions of the calendar codes, helping him simplify his mathematical understanding. This groundwork showed how the entire system of universal time coordinates, as known by the Maya, were contained in a color-coded template of the Mayan notation system, inclusive of the 20 numbers, 0–19. From this simple code, José understood how the whole calendar could be elaborated in ever more inclusive fractals—a system of units built up from the numbers 4, 5, 13, and 20.

Just before the Harmonic Convergence, José began living various cycles, including a reformulated *Chilam Balam*, where the synchronization date is correlated to July 26th (the rising of Sirius) and the year bearers are *Kan* (Seed), *Muluc* (Moon), *Ix* (Wizard), and *Cauac* (Storm). This would later be known as the *Dreamspell count*. He was aware that the Maya used up to 17 calendars simultaneously at the height of their civilization. From living different cycles himself, José understood that the reason for this had everything to do with synchronicity. He discovered that the experience of synchronicity is actually based on a mathematical order programmed into the universe.

In tracking these cycles, José kept visionary notebooks and coded his daybooks according to the cycles. However, this initial experiment was halted at Josh's death and with the hullabaloo around the Harmonic Convergence.

Settling in Hawaii, José reignited his discipline of living on the natural cycles of time. He found that conscious engagement of these cycles gradually lifted him from the artificial/mechanical plane of existence into a state more tuned to universal or cosmic energies. He found Hawaii the perfect laboratory for this experiment. Here the airwaves were virtually clear, allowing his mind and senses to attune with cosmic rhythms and universal cycles.

Consistent observance of different cycles—13-day cycles, 20-day cycles, and 52-day cycles—caused him to slowly break out of the shell of consensual thought held in place by the Gregorian calendar. He slowly began to realize that a calendar is a programming device; all the values, customs, and norms of a nation, a culture, and a civilization are embedded in the time it keeps. He recognized that the Gregorian calendar, with its uneven units of measure and irregular months, is an unconscious background programming device that operates subliminally and repeats the same programs, whether anyone realizes it or not. In contrast, he found that, by conscious engagement of larger cycles, an increasing quality of recurrence could be experienced. And with every recurrence came a process of "remembering," or "self-remembering." Living this way, he began to reorganize his perceptual experience of reality.

In August 1989, José and Lloydine traveled to Boulder for a family reunion. One week earlier, José had learned that Josh's close friend Dylan had committed suicide. He had just completed his first year of college. Dylan had been deeply disturbed by Josh's death and frequently called José, looking for answers and guidance. José and Lloydine conducted a small funeral service for Dylan in the backyard of a friend's house.

While in Boulder, José was perusing in a comic book shop and discovered *Shadowrun* (1989), a near-future science fiction comic with a Harmonic Convergence/2012 plotline. Tuning into the alternative reality depicted in the comic, José thought some type of role-playing game might make the Galactic Mayan time knowledge more accessible. This inspiration resulted in the "Starcraft Operator's Manual," the predecessor of the *Dreamspell*.

During the autumn of 1989, José delved into the codes and was captured by their mathematical harmonies, which he recorded in the "Green Book." He worked simultaneously on the "Starcraft Operator's Manual," the role-playing script that would serve as a blueprint of the Dreamspell.

No sooner was the "Starcraft Operators Manual" completed in November 1989 than a misunderstanding arose between José and Lloydine and their landlord, regarding Lloydine's daughter, Heidi, coming to live with them. José and Lloydine decided to move out of their house and accept an invitation to stay in Switzerland. Katherine Gunzinger, whom they had met in Hawaii, invited them to her family's home to explore how she could be of further assistance to the vision of the Harmonic Convergence and Mayan Factor.

On the morning of November 15, 1989, just six days after the breaching of the Berlin Wall, José and Lloydine arrived in Dornach, Switzerland, just outside of Basel. A major center of alchemy during the European Renaissance, Basel was also the hometown of Paracelsus, esoteric philosopher Rudolf Steiner, and Albert Hofman, discoverer of LSD.

In Dornach, José arose each morning at 4 a.m. and made his way up the stairs of the cold, dark, Gothic house to make coffee. He brought a cup to Lloydine, who was quite ill with a bronchial ailment. Then, by candlelight, he worked out the formulas for what would be known as the *Book of Kin* while doing his best to treat Lloydine with homeopathic medicines, teas, and steam baths.

Deep mystery enclosed him while he worked during the early mornings in the mystically gloomy, medieval-feeling house, which had been designed in the early part of the 20th century by Rudolf Steiner. José imagined that Steiner himself had spent time in this house, for it was saturated with his energy, which was apparent in the strong sense of geometry, art, color, and structure in the home. He felt it resonated perfectly with the work he was doing.

At the time he hit upon the precise mathematical formula for the *Book of Kin*, José was working with several numerical components simultaneously: the 20 solar seals, the four colors that code them in five sets, the 13 numbers or tones that recur in a sequence of 20, and the 52 units that create the Loom of Maya. All of these components came together as one elegant mathematical construct, composing the essence of the *Book of Kin*—260 coded or galactic meditations bringing the Tzolkin into multidimensional relief.

In *The Mayan Factor*, José described the Tzolkin as a code, like the alphabet, that when a person knows how to write the language, he or she can communicate "at least a suggestion of the knowledge of the wisdom of the universe":

> In the same way (as the alphabet), knowing the code language of the Tzolkin, the Mayan harmonic module, can open up channels of understanding and communication with equal if not greater power than is available to us through the alphabet. For number, no different than symbol, is a condensation of overtones and levels of meaning. And each individual number is a resonant field unto itself....

Through this process, José realized that the mathematics of the Maya were actually the mathematics of the fourth dimension, or the mathematics of time. It became apparent to him that modern science focuses only on the mathematics of space and is therefore an inadequate instrument to measure time; only the mathematics of time can fulfill this goal.

José often felt the presence of Chögyam Trungpa during this process. He was deeply grateful for his teacher, who introduced him to meditation and mind training, essential practices for this intensive work. From years of meditation practice, José had stabilized a high level of concentration and meditative awareness in his day-to-day life. His years of visualization practices made it easier to bring seemingly abstract mathematical codes into manifestation. To him, this work was choiceless; he was a mere instrument of the universal mind, accessed by prolonged, intensive, mental concentration.

To truly universalize the codes, José felt people of the present world would need more concrete clues to assist them through the larger mathematical orders. He spent many hours contemplating each of the colors, the qualities of the symbols, the action and results of the 20 seals and 13 tones, and how to combine them into one integrated circuit. With each facet that was revealed, José could literally feel a change of frequency, a lightness of being. When the codes cohered, he underwent a spontaneous shift of consciousness.

Each of the 20 seals contains an image that combines with one of the 13 numbers, coding each day with a vast amount of information. Being a progression of a mathematical order, the solar seals describe an evolutionary process from matter to consciousness, or from birth to enlightenment, where each stage incorporates the previous stages. Each of the 20 solar seals also corresponds to one of the 10 planets, including Maldek, now known as the Asteroid Belt.

When receiving the codes, it wasn't so much that José was hearing the words as he was feeling the mathematical ordering of the quality of the tones and seals. This followed a precise pattern. The words came from a higher order; he was merely reading the qualities of the mathematical structure as they related to the seals and tones. Once the formula was revealed, he was able to work out and dutifully transcribe the entire *Book of Kin*, with its 260 "code spells." Jose knew the *Book of Kin* was unlike anything that exists on Earth; it was a primary synchronic text, and an utterly new galactic hymnal.

Chapter 45
Discovery of the Law of Time

> Clocks slay time.... Time is dead as long as it is being
> clicked off by little wheels; only when the clock stops does
> time come to life.

—William Faulkner

> The process of mechanization was furthered by an ideology
> that gave absolute precedence and cosmic authority to the
> machine itself.

—Lewis Mumford

> In speaking of evolution, it is necessary to understand from
> the outset that no mechanical evolution is possible. The
> evolution of man is the evolution of his consciousness.

—G.I. Gurdjieff

While in Dornach, José was flipping through the guide map for Geneva, Switzerland, and found what was billed as the Museum of Time. He knew he had to make a visit. Despite Lloydine's persistent illness, they borrowed Katherine Gunzinger's car and drove to Geneva only to find that what was billed as the Museum of Time was actually the International Watch-Making Museum! On December 10th, a cold Sunday morning, after two hours touring the Museum looking at one archaic proto-clock after another, from the cuckoo up to the pendulum and then on down to digital quartz and cesium timepieces, José had a revelation.

"That's it!" he exclaimed to Lloydine. "The world is living in artificial time!" Because she also had been living on the larger cycles, she quickly grasped what he was saying.

Living by the Mayan cycles, José had an experiential and mathematical contrast to evaluate what he experienced in the Museum of Time. His mind raced with realizations. Noting that everything in the museum was according to 12, and everything was related to the clock, he saw immediately that the 12 months and 12 hours were mathematically equivalent. He saw that the 60 minutes and 60 seconds were based on the same mathematical principle: the division of 12. He immediately concluded that the machine frequency was based on the ratio *12:60*.

It all seemed obvious: The 12 and 60 were mathematical constructs of a geometry of space and not of time. In the geometry of space, a two-dimensional circle is divided into 360 degrees. The number 360 is divisible by 12 and by 60, hence the 12:60 timing frequency of artificial time.

He knew that 12 is a static number. It doesn't move or go anywhere. Although it might be good for architecture, it stops time from circulating. He thought if numbers are mental attributes then it is a particular number that keeps people locked in a particular stasis. He realized that 13 is the number that transforms form and circulates time.

José saw in a flash that this 12:60 frequency is the unconscious foundation of the mind that virtually the entire human species operates in, and, if it were not halted, it would lead to the destruction of the world. This frequency is responsible for the acceleration and complexification of form. He saw that living in this frequency can only create a world with more laws, more machines, more wars, more shoes, more cars, more highways, more people, more pollution, and so forth. In other words, this is machine consciousness.

He learned that the mechanical clock was perfected just after the Gregorian calendar reform of 1582. He realized how, after the adoption of this calendar and clock, the human mind accepted these instruments as second nature. He was aware that the Gregorian calendar was a crooked standard of measure based on measurements of space and not time, as summarized in the popular saying:

> Thirty days hath September,
> April, June, and November;
> All the rest have thirty-one,
> Except February, which has twenty-eight
> And twenty-nine each leap year.

In contrast, living by the principles of the 260-day Tzolkin, the rhythms of life were interrelated patterns of 13- and 20-day cycles—hence the *13:20* frequency of natural time. He saw that humans embody this natural frequency in their 20 fingers and toes and 13 main articulations: two ankles, two knees, two hips, two shoulders, two elbows, two wrists, and the neck.

José understood that the Law of Time was a fundamental law, like that of gravity. Just as the law of gravity cannot be seen, neither can the Law of Time, but both are invisible principles fundamental to the universe.

In observing the examples of the evolution of societies and culture, José realized that, from a scientific point of view, what is called "normal society" is actually a consensus reality driven by the combination of two timing standards: the calendar and the clock. Mistaking space for time, this civilization has become fixated with space technologies and exploration, and the biggest complaint is not having enough *time*. By now, virtually the entire civilization is operating under this artificial frequency.

To reverse this error, he knew the calendar must be immediately changed.

From Dornach, José and Lloydine traveled to Spain to visit friends Geraldyne Waxkovsky and Marysol Gonzalez Sterling. Both women were artists and promoted the Planet Art Network as an instrument of positive global change. The four of them journeyed to Mojácar on the Mediterranean coast for the Gregorian New Year's holiday.

The days in Mojácar, a small village of whitewashed houses high atop a precipice, were spent coloring and constructing more of the boards for what would later be known as the Dreamspell. It was now December 31, 1989, and many festivities and revelations in the world were marking the climax of the end of the Cold War and the tearing down of the Berlin Wall. Newspaper articles from major American dailies, including the *Wall Street Journal*, pondered the question: What if the Harmonic Convergence with its promise of peace was true after all?

In light of the recently discovered timing frequencies, José had a new frame of reference to view reality. He saw the Harmonic Convergence as a 13:20 time event, representing a collective conscious break with mechanical civilization, and sending a signal that the artificial order of the 12:60 was in the initial stages of collapse.

Despite the chilly weather, on January 1, 1990, José immersed himself in the Mediterranean Sea 13 times to invoke the cosmic power of 13 for the work that lay ahead. Before returning to Basel, he and Lloydine spent a few days in Zurich, resting at the Hotel Montana. Here, he watched an all-day MTV music marathon displaying the top 100 videos of the 1980s. Watching the evolving styles and sounds of the 1980s, José considered MTV a primitive example of the planetarization of consciousness, a kind of psycho-electronic extension of the human into the psi bank.

Back in Basel, Heinz and Agnes had been given a review copy of the "Starcraft Operator's Manual." Returning the manuscript and graphics to José, Heinz simply asked, "Why should I follow your philosophy?" This was a pivotal point for José, who reflected deeply on these words. He knew that Heinz had a point. He threw the "Starcraft Operator's Manual" in the wastebasket and vowed to redouble his efforts at communicating the purest essence of the Mayan calendar codes in their most universal form.

After two months in Switzerland, José and Lloydine returned to Hawaii, where Heidi found the three of them a house in the Kula section of Maui. The little red house was new and simple, with a drywall structure, a nice deck, and a beautiful view on the slopes of Mt. Haleakala at 211 Mauna Place. The Kula area, set above the industrial sugar cane section of the island, was relatively rustic and remote. At 3,000 feet above sea level, it was cool at night and hot in the day.

Life in Hawaii was externally ideal, although José found there were many distractions. Although he did his best to keep a tight focus, he was often occupied by external affairs. Foremost in his mind, following his mathematical decoding of the 13:20 frequency, was to format the codes in a manner accessible even to children. He knew that the presentation had to be genuinely psychomythic, tapping the interplanetary memory of the planetary human. But, how?

In June 1990, José and Lloydine went swimming late in the morning at Little Beach with their friends Robin and Gary and their dog, Genji. Robin and José swam far out and soon noticed that many people close to shore were moving back on the beach. Before José and Robin knew it, a giant storm had set in, and huge waves were upon them. Gary and Lloydine managed to make it to shore. However, no matter how hard he and Robin tried to swim, they kept being carried out farther by the undertow. Someone on a rubber raft finally rescued Robin, but José was adrift in a turbulent sea.

Again and again, José's body was slammed under the waves and against the ocean floor; after each wave hurled him to the bottom, he swam to the top as quickly as possible, gasping for air until another wave hit, sending him down again. At one point, he was flung against some sharp coral, and when he surfaced he spotted Genji on the beach. By keeping his attention focused on Genji, José could hear the conversations people were having near Genji, as if they were right next to him. Finally, after an arduous process, he was able to make it close to shore, where some people pulled him out. He was convinced that keeping his eye on Genji, which was a way of putting his consciousness out of his body, was what saved him.

Gasping for breath, he lay naked on the glistening white sand. He felt like a 17th-century Spanish sailor after a shipwreck. It took him more than an hour to regain his breath and consciousness. During this time, he noticed a large gash on his right big toe; it kept him off his feet for several days. The experience put him in an otherworldly state of mind.

About a week later, Lloydine went to Boulder to visit her mother, who had recently had a heart attack. A few weeks later, José joined her. Staying at the Foot of the Mountain Motel in Boulder, he had a powerful dream similar to his 1986 visionary experience of the breaking up of Atlantis 13,000 years ago.

In the dream, he saw waves gathering…domes…glaciated hillsides…another world, another time...mastodons...hunters...the world was younger...13,000 years ago...people...then another wave gathered and—Crash!—something calamitous occurred, followed by a great apocalyptic shattering. The original collective dream was broken. What happened? No one could remember. From the midst of the crashing the word *Dreamspell* emerged as an evocation uttered by an ancient voice. Fragmented memories were scattered and deposited in isolated pockets of the collective human mind. They were the seed forms of everything that is now culminating in the state of the present world.

The dream continued into the present time (1990). José was engaged in therapy with people who had been present in the early part of the dream, including Robin and Gary. He was trying to get them to remember what happened 13,000 years ago and also to remember that their current life was merely the continuity of a past life playing out. In the dream, he was saying, "What happened then was the breaking of one Dreamspell and now we are in another Dreamspell." That is exactly how the words came.

José woke up, startled by the intensely visionary dream. He understood the near-death experience on Little Beach with Robin and Gary had been a catalytic trigger. Now he had the piece he was looking for to complete the codes; the Dreamspell had been revealed. He felt like a time traveler after a successful mission of retrieval.

The mathematical codes were the key to entering a new Dreamspell: *The Dreamspell Journey of Timeship Earth, 2013.*

The next few months of 1990 were a miraculous time for José. Suddenly the component parts of the Dreamspell kit manifested themselves; it was like watching coal turn into diamonds. He introduced the timing codes in the form of an interactive "game." This seemed the best option for introducing them in a universal way. The idea was to engage participation so people could begin to experience the galactic cosmic cycles for themselves.

Until then, the five-part Journey Board and *Book of Kin* had been the only pieces in existence. Then came the six moving rings of the galactic compass, which served as a digital mental computer with 18,980 permutations. After much work, he found that the combination of the 365 days of the year combined with the 20 seals and 13 tones made a series of 18,980 permutations, or 52 solar orbits of Earth around the Sun; what is known on Earth as 52 years is equivalent to one solar/ galactic cycle.

The Dreamspell Genesis, the Harmonic Index, the color cube, and the Oracle Board followed the galactic compass. These tools were a bridge to another reality. These parts were revealed in four moons. He knew each part was but a single mathematical integration defining a whole system of knowing.

After receiving another dream message, he asked Lloydine for her support through this elaborate process by serving as a creative sounding board. This was an unprecedented unfoldment, and an all-consuming endeavor. He understood that the universe is created upon a system of exact vibrations, patterns, symbols, and dimensions, all contained in number. The mathematical purity of the codes required precise adherence that could not be subjected to much editing or human opinion.

Shortly after, the Galactic Federation, the community of higher intelligence monitoring Planet Earth, contacted him telepathically. He received two communications: First, he was to live without money—this was the only way to test and show that 13:20 "time is art" is the true frequency of natural time; and second, the Dreamspell was to be a gift, not to be sold. He accepted these communications as a test of faith.

José saw that, in the universal order of nature, it is only humans who have to pay money for things, even for birth and death. He resorted to Jesus' parable of the lilies of the field and understood the profoundly spiritual nature of the Dreamspell and the meaning of the 13:20 frequency in general. In other words, he knew he had to embody the 13:20 frequency to make it real for others.

Last came the Dreamspell script, a translation of the mathematical codes into a type of narrative description of a whole new order of reality. The Dreamspell Genesis came in a single sweep allowing José to view the entire cycle of history all at once. He saw that the purpose of the Dreamspell was, by 2013, to get the human species back to a point where they could actually snap back into the original dream; this was the understanding that humanity was supposed to have received at 3113 BC would be available, once again, after 2012.

The Dreamspell was a new dispensation, a prophecy, and a new scientific system. It was a galactic, multidimensional reflection of the synchronic nature of time—a new perception of reality altogether.

As a new dispensation of time, the Dreamspell is pivoted to a correlate point, July 26, 1987, Kin 34: White Galactic Wizard. This was the day José had announced the coming of galactic culture at St. John's College in Santa Fe.

Both Egyptians and Mayans recognized long ago that July 26th correlates as a starting point of the heliacal rising of the star Sirius. Sirius is a galactic outpost of higher knowledge for this part of the galaxy. Aligning the calendar cycles with this starting point of the great 1,460-year "sothic" cycle of Sirius assured a galactic synchronization for the terrestrial cycles.

On December 21, 1990, the Dreamspell was ready for production. Whereas the Harmonic Convergence had generated interest in the Mayan calendar, the Dreamspell codes revealed the underlying mathematics of the Mayan calendar.

On his 52nd birthday, José received a vision of the imploded cube, the basis of the Cube of the Law. After taking ayahuasca given to him as a gift from a Peruvian medicine man, he entered into a state of synaesthesia and became acutely aware of how his thoughts expressed his sense organs and how sounds left his ears. He realized that all sensory experience was coded inside the human organism in a precisely mathematical way. In this deeply meditative space, he suddenly experienced himself inside a cube. Everything was inside this cube. Nothing else existed.

As he concentrated on the cube, its six walls collapsed and simultaneously became three planes. There was a horizontal plane (later identified as the Plane of Mind); perpendicular to that, left to right, was a second plane (later identified as the Plane of Spirit); and perpendicular to the other two, but running front to back, was a third plane (later identified as the Plane of Will).

To José, this vision revealed a primordial cosmological reality. The next day he made a graphic depiction of his vision of the cube with the three planes inside. After this, he embarked on a series of paintings, including two more *Doors of Perception* entitled "Arcturus Probe" and "Galactic Being."

Operation Desert Storm had just begun. Creating art was the best way he knew to empower himself and not feel victimized by external circumstances. He knew that channeling higher information or energy helped to reform the suffering on this plane by giving it a new vision of a greater reality. For José, incidents like the Desert Storm war were literally psychic rites of passage.

During this time, José was put in contact with Teddy Tsang of Interlink Productions in Hong Kong, who agreed to produce the Dreamspell. Later that year, Kathryn Gunzinger covered production costs for 10,000 Dreamspells. Production commenced with Teddy in the summer of 1991.

Around this time, José got word that Jon Anderson of the musical band Yes was trying to contact him. José knew of Jon's work mostly with Vangelis, a prominent Greek New Age composer, with whom Jon had collaborated on a number of inspired songs. Jon had also written a song especially for the Harmonic Convergence titled "Holy Lamb." José was told that Jon wanted to do a rock opera based on the Dreamspell. Jon told José he had celebrated the Harmonic Convergence at Joshua Tree. José invited Jon to visit him in Maui to explore what he had in mind.

José picked Jon up at the airport and brought him up to their house in Kula. Lloydine had cleared out the simple guest room, which had a foam mattress and a sleeping bag arrangement. Jon took one look at it and told José he would like to get a hotel, as he needed more space. José reasoned that, because he had been the man behind the Harmonic Convergence, Jon probably expected him to have a lavish spread in Maui with a swimming pool and all the amenities.

Slightly amused, José arranged for a hotel room in one of the more remote resort areas of Maui for Jon and then arranged for a cab to pick him up. While waiting for the cab, Jon spoke nervously about a Navajo shaman he knew, emphasizing how simple and ordinarily most shamans lived.

That evening, at Jon's request, José and Lloydine joined him in his hotel room for an elaborate room-service dinner meeting. At this point, Jon's intention seemed vague. He seemed enamored with the word *Dreamspell*, perhaps thinking it would be a great name for a rock opera without inquiring about what actually lay behind it. José did his best to explain what the Dreamspell actually was. Jon responded by asking, "Well, what's in it for the gipper (the common man)?"

Despite a comedy of miscommunications, the meeting ended amicably, and the next morning, after giving Jon a brief tour of parts of the island, José and Lloydine took him to the airport.

That summer, José received a letter from Tony Shearer, who wished to reconcile after his initial skeptical response to *Earth Ascending*. Although he wrote the letter in 1991, Tony had dated it August 17, 1987: Harmonic Convergence. The following is an excerpt from Tony's letter to Jose:

> I owe a billion thanks to Bear and Company for all of their help. And another billion thanks to you. If I say that a great veil of confusion has been lifted from my vision, can you understand and accept me as a friend again? I want to personally give you praise and credit for the fantastic work you have done…. José, I am so steeped in the notion of poetic-myth that I rarely surface to view reality. And when I do it scares the hell out of me. I live on my own little island of dreams and peaceful visions.

On August 16, 1991—the fourth anniversary of the Harmonic Convergence—José and Lloydine, with the help of Chris Whitecloud, convened a small meeting on Maui to inform people of the Dreamspell and the forthcoming Time Shift, a call to a return to the 13:20 timing frequency. In attendance were Sir Reinhart Ruge of the World Parliament Association and Mother Tynetta Muhammad of the Nation of Islam.

Mother Tynetta, originally from Detroit, Michigan, and Reinhart Ruge, originally from Germany, both lived in Mexico, Tynetta in Cuernavaca and Reinhart in Tepotzlan, about 30 miles apart. Although their personalities differed, José found that a common intensity motivated their lives. Reinhart had a great drive to create world peace through a revolutionized sense of human government or human politics, and he believed in universal spirituality as a common ground for all religions. Tynetta was consumed by a seriousness concerning the Quran and the mathematical constituent of the number 19.

After hearing that the Mayans possessed a 0–19 mathematical code, Mother Tynetta told José about the work of Dr. Rashad Khalifa, who discovered the mathematical keys of the Holy Quran with the key number 19. Dr. Khalifa had been killed for his beliefs in 1990. Mother Tynetta told José that she had been in Egypt on August 16, 1987, where someone had given her a leaflet that said to go to the Great Pyramid and meditate for the Harmonic Convergence, and she did. It was during this event that she first heard about José Arguelles and *The Mayan Factor*.

The meeting primarily focused on the situation of time and the calendar. José knew his alliance with these two people was auspicious, but, at the time of the actual meeting, he was very much in a transitional stage—no longer in his academic/professor mode but also not yet fully realized himself as a cosmic messenger.

Chapter 46
Launching the Dreamspell

> *The one essential need of humanity today is the renewal*
> *of the mind as it resonates to the release of a new cosmic*
> *and planetary spirit.*
>
> —Dane Rudhyar
>
> *Mastery of the Dreamspell and the launching of Timeship*
> *Earth, come about through magic flight, time travel.*
>
> —*Dreamspell*

"The Dreamspell comes from the future," José told a diverse group of people at the first official Dreamspell demonstration in Tepotzlan, Mexico, on October 23, 1991. "The Dreamspell count as it is called, is not a count as such, but a systematic frame of references by which the synchronic order of reality—synchronicity—can be known and mapped."

This initial presentation was held on the viewing deck of Sir Reinhart Ruge's rustic estate, 10 miles west of Amatlán, birthplace of Quetzalcoatl. The receptivity to the new information was phenomenal, and José promised a return trip early the following year.

After visiting Huehueycoyotl and Cuernavaca with Reinhart and Mother Tynetta, José and Lloydine made their way to Xochicalco and then Amatlán, as José felt impelled to visit the points where Quetzalcoatl had been. There, Ernesto Aloma, a Cuban-born ex-assistant foreign minister for Daniel Ortega's Sandanista government in Nicaragua, joined them.

A few days later, José and Lloydine were back on the plane to Maui. But first they made a brief stop in San Francisco to meet with Willard Van De Bogart, José's old acquaintance, who agreed to serve as distributor of the Dreamspells in America.

On December 9, 1991, José and Lloydine once again packed their belongings and launched the "Dreamspell planetary pilgrimage" that would take them from Hong Kong to Mexico, Germany, Russia, and Canada.

᠎

Possessing little more than an American Express card, they set out early in 1992 for their first trip to Asia. After a long plane ride, they were greeted by Teddy Tsang, a young, well-mannered Hong Kong entrepreneur, owner of Interlink Productions.

José viewed Hong Kong as a mysterious, modern metropolis with huge skyscrapers tumbling down the hillsides to the bay. The busy waterfront was host to many traditional Chinese and modern boats, and the main part of the city was built on an island that runs steeply into the hills. Founded by the British, Hong Kong was for many years called a "Crown colony," until 1999 when it was given back to China. José was amazed at how densely packed the city was, and, though he considered it a modern marvel, he wondered where it was all going. It seemed the only way it could go was straight up; it already had the tallest shopping malls in the world.

Aware of their Buddhist leanings, Teddy took José and Lloydine to see the "world's biggest Buddha" on Lantau Island and then to a remote shrine, the temple of the Monkey God. This was especially meaningful as the incoming Chinese New Year was the Year of the Monkey.

Meeting with Teddy at his Interlink office, José was able to confirm a strategy for distributing the Dreamspells as well as discuss future production possibilities. José was also introduced to Dale Keller, a prominent architect famous for having built the tallest building in Hong Kong: the Bank of China. He was a follower of Gurumay, the successor to Swami Muktananda. Initially, Keller seemed intrigued by the Dreamspell and arranged for José to give a presentation at a New Age bookstore.

After making their arrangements with Interlink, José and Lloydine headed back to North America, stopping in Boulder to visit Maya and also the Boulder Headquarters of the Campaign for the New Earth. Sasha White and Rennie Davis invited José to their offices to give a presentation on the nature of time and history and the meaning of the upcoming *Time Shift* on July 26, 1992, describing a plan for an orderly transition into Earth-centered consciousness.

Both Sasha and Rennie seemed eager to cooperate in a broader envisioning. Rennie, in particular, was enthusiastic and said he felt it was important to communicate the Time Shift at the upcoming Rio Summit, and invited José and Lloydine to accompany them. Rennie also pledged his commitment to help José attain non-profit status for his Earth projects.

However, none of this was forthcoming. Neither Sasha nor Rennie responded to José's follow-up faxes or mail communiqués. He had put great effort into the Campaign for the Earth and now, for reasons unknown, the core group was no longer communicating. José felt that, if no effort was made to communicate the meaning of the Time Shift at the Rio Conference, then the slide into planetary anarchy would accelerate after July 26, 1992.

Before returning to Mexico on February 1, 1992, José and Lloydine spent a week in Ottawa, Canada, where Tara was attending her first year of college. Tara's college dormitory was reminiscent of the 1960s era, and Tara was in what appeared to be the "Deadhead" dormitory, with constant wafts of marijuana and cigarette smoke. At this point, she was in her high hippie phase, which had replaced her days of high style and fashion in modeling school. Later she would go through a soul-searching anorexic phase, followed by a bodybuilding and Gold's Gym phase. It seemed to José that she was always in search of her identity. José and Lloydine gave a Dreamspell presentation in Tara's dormitory at Carleton College. Tara was happy with the presentation as it seemed to inspire many of her friends.

Returning to Mexico, José found that his perceptions about himself and about reality had altered. His goal was to seed the Dreamspell in the land of the Maya, as well as see to it that a Spanish edition was produced. Everything took on a surreal and mythic quality; he felt he was operating with commands and codes from another time and place. Even though people seemed to think he looked like someone called "José Arguelles," he knew he was really a galactic messenger, scripted and recited from another realm.

As was his duty, he gave many presentations, from Mexico City to Tepotzlan and then to Cuernavaca. There, he was surprised to meet his old friends Marysol and Geraldyne of Spain, who agreed to translate the Spanish edition of the Dreamspell.

Initially, José and Lloydine stayed at the home of Mother Tynetta in Cuernavaca, where she lived with her youngest son, Ahmed. Tynetta told them the story of her husband, the Honorable Elijah Muhammad, and his teacher, the mysterious Fard Muhammad.

Fard Muhammad was from the area of the Caucasus in the mountains of Russia. He came to the United States as a rug salesman. For many years, he studied people and realized that the black people constituted one of the lost tribes. On July 4, 1930, he gave a talk in the city of Detroit. In the audience was Elijah Pool. After the talk, Fard said, "Elijah, you are coming with me."

For three and a half years, Fard Muhammad taught Elijah everything he knew. Early in 1934, Fard Muhammad said: "My mission is complete." He then departed to Mexico, and the last Elijah heard of him was through a letter received from Mexico in the middle of 1934. Elijah Muhammad went on to create the Nation of Islam. Exactly 40 years after Fard went to Mexico, in 1974, Elijah went to Mexico and found a house for his wife, Tynetta, and their four children. Before he departed from this plane, he told his wife that she should study the world's calendars and prophecies, not only those of the black people, but of the brown and red races as well, especially the prophecies of Mexico. Within 20 years, Elijah said, a time would come for a new teaching, and she should look for these signs.

Mother Tynetta insisted that José sit in her husband's chair. As he was sitting there, an overwhelming sensation penetrated José. He felt the presence of both Muhammad and Quetzalcoatl; it felt as though all prophecy was fusing inside of him. This experience prompted him to speak at a courtyard presentation later that day about the mystical fusion of prophecy, where he said that "all prophets and prophecy are one."

A few days later, at Reinhart Ruge's in Tepoztlan, José and Lloydine met with Lourdes Miranda Alvarez and José Garcia, who agreed to fund 10,000 copies of the Spanish edition of the Dreamspell. They lived in Monterrey, where they headed a major Latin American networking organization based on the Harmonic Convergence, called *Accion Guardiana Internacional*.

The next stop was Huehuecoyotl, the far side of the mystic mountains surrounding Tepotzlan, for a few days of rest at an artists' community. Here, José met Domingo Dias Porta, spiritual leader and head of the group called the *Grand Fraternidad Universal* (Universal Great Brotherhood). The organization blended esoteric philosophies with indigenous streams and emphasized maintaining the sacred centers of the Earth throughout the Americas. The group's activities brought them into contact with virtually all of the indigenous peoples of Latin America.

The next stop was Mexico City, where the Dreamspell was introduced to Antonio Velasco Piña, a prominent Mexican author. Highly urbane and sophisticated, Velasco Pina had a literary manner and way of speaking; each of his words was elegantly and carefully chosen. He had gained notoriety for his book *Regina*, depicting the story of a spiritually gifted young Mexican woman who was one of 400 students killed by the Mexican army in the infamous riots of Tlatelolco on October 2, 1968. This book became the center of a rising, indigenous-inspired spiritual movement throughout Mexico, and for this reason, the people involved are known as *concheros*, or blowers of the conch.

Mother Tynetta had arranged for José to present the mathematics of the Dreamspell to Luis Echeverria, the ex-president of Mexico. Echeverria served the standard six-year term (1970–76). At this time, Mexico was a leader of the non-aligned nations of the Third World, along with India and Pakistan. These nations attempted to create a political ideology with a humanistic approach that was neither Capitalist nor Communist, veering away from the Cold War and nuclear weapons. These were the values that ex-president Echeverria adhered to.

To some, Echeverria was considered a charismatic leader who attempted to raise the profile of Mexico in the United Nations and the Third World in general. To others, he was a controversial leader who had played a key political role in 1968 as the Secretary of Interior Affairs during the time of the Tlatelolco student massacre. Because of this, a cloud of suspicion hung over him regarding his role in the governmental ordering of the massacre.

Mother Tynetta suggested Reinhart Ruge accompany José, because he had known Echeverria on and off over the years. Reinhart also invited his gardener, Poncho, and José invited Alberto Ruz as translator. The meeting was scheduled for one hour but ended up lasting four. Alberto was surprised that also present at the meeting (besides a Mexican journalist) was his father's former wife, who said she was there to represent "official" Mayan archaeology.

The air was charged. A feeling of unreality and slight tension pervaded. The meeting room was filled with illuminated reproductions of the mural paintings of Diego Rivera; the entire house looked like a museum of 20th-century Mexican art. In one corner, José glimpsed Rivera's fiery depiction of the prophecy of the return of Quetzalcoatl. He found it amusingly fitting for the present situation and viewed the entire event as a grand psychomythic drama. Cortez was also pictured in paintings of the conquest of Mexico.

These factors created a dynamic backdrop for José's presentation of the Dreamspell. Now the knowledge had returned and was being presented to one of the ex-presidents of Mexico, who was, in some familial way, obliged to have an interest in Mexican history, especially in the pre-Hispanic past.

Echeverria grasped the basic ideas of the Dreamspell and understood it as a mathematical demonstration. He considered the return to 13:20 time as a return to a kind of golden age prophesied by Quetzalcoatl and described by Marxist philosophers as the classless state.

Echeverria was interrupted frequently by telephone calls. Whenever he left the room, the archaeologist's widow and the journalist interrogated Jose, trying to determine his real motives, or disparaging anything but what she considered a truly scientific approach to Mayan studies. This was neither the first nor the last time that José would present the Dreamspell and face opposition.

In the end, Echeverria wanted José to meet with his *cientificios* (scientists) to validate the mathematical and scientific claims concerning the Dreamspell.

Two days later, José, Lloydine, and Alberto Ruz, accompanied by Echeverria's personal secretary, Jorge, visited the offices of IBM Latino America, where José was introduced to Francisco Martinez and several other members of the Department of Educational Research. Within 10 minutes of demonstrating the mathematical codes of the Dreamspell, the computer scientists were overwhelmed. They saw that there was no way to put the mathematical codes into a computer without fully understanding the nature of its cosmological and fractal codes. They recognized that the radial mathematics were so different from the binary, on-off mathematic (the basis of all computer languages), that a fourth-dimensional computer would have to be invented to do the codes justice. José left them with a Dreamspell kit that they passed on to their "games" expert. Before leaving Mexico, José spoke by telephone with one of the scientists, who said that the Dreamspell mathematical codes were of the "highest scientific value with vast cosmological implications."

While staying at a friend's apartment in the Polanco district of central Mexico City, José and Lloydine coordinated Dreamspell affairs. Their American distributor, Willard, had promised to send a carton of *Dreamspells*, but it never arrived. Nor did he keep his promise to send copies of the Dreamspell computer disks to Marysol and Geraldyne in Madrid. Teddy in Hong Kong was also anxious to get clarity on the overall business aspect of Dreamspell distribution. José decided to terminate the remainder of their Mexico visit and fly to Hong Kong. From there, he and Lloydine would somehow have to get to Russia, where they had received official invitations for an April visit.

José's last event in Mexico was a press conference arranged by Alberto Ruz at the once-luxurious, 1920s-style Hotel de la Reforma. Located in the heart of the central district on the great Paseo de la Reforma, this hotel resides in one of the areas that was most severely damaged by the disastrous earthquake on September 19, 1985. José remembered this once-fashionable neighborhood from his early childhood, especially from his first return visit to Mexico in 1953, and again in 1964. In 1992, it seemed like a haunted hotel in a ghost town. One of his long-lost cousins showed up at the press conference with her daughter, who presented him one of her original paper mache sculptures, Mexican folk style. Velasco Pina and many of his group were also present.

In a formal conference room decorated with mirrors and chandeliers, more than 120 people gathered, all sitting in formal rows. José thought such formality strange for the announcement of the discovery of the 13:20 timing frequency with its message "Time is Art."

Following Alberto's introduction, José explained why the discovery of the Law of Time had to be announced first in Mexico and not in Europe. "True science is not exclusive," he told the crowd. "It must leap oceans to start afresh in new continents where ancient wisdom has awaited its time."

Chapter 47
Time Shift

People of the future!
Who are you?
Here am I
All wound and pain.
I will to you the orchard
of my great soul.

—Vladimir Mayakovsky

T raveling the world communicating the Dreamspell codes, José felt as though he had entered a magnetic gate or portal where synchronicity was now the norm. His perceived reality seemed to magically rearrange itself around his growing awareness of a galactically evolved knowledge base. Everything was saturated with meaning. His desire to communicate this knowledge stemmed from a sense of sacred duty that this information should be made universally accessible.

Before departing in March 1992 for their second trip to Hong Kong, José and Lloydine stopped in Boulder for a brief visit with Maya.

On a Saturday evening, they all watched two films: *Excalibur* and *The Day the Earth Stood Still*. Both told a mystical story of redemption and, at the same time, had the element of human failure and human tragedy. José thought they provided a fascinating contrast of mythic elements of different times: One time was a world of horses, castles, knights, wizards, and kings, and the other was a world of technology, modern military, and the fear of outer space. Those two particular films, seen as a double feature, tapped deep archetypal structures in him: a planetary Merlin shutting down the electromagnetic field and opening up a dazzling new reality.

The following day, large clouds blew in while José and Lloydine were walking to the video store to return their rentals. As they walked back toward Maya's apartment, which was situated along Boulder Creek, great peals of thunder burst forth. The temperature rapidly dropped, and by four in the afternoon, it was snowing. By nightfall, the snow was heavy. A full-on blizzard had set in. At midnight, all the power went out. José couldn't help but think of *The Day the Earth Stood Still* and its message of a higher galactic power manifesting through a break in the electromagnetic field of the Earth. He wondered if their early afternoon flight to Hong Kong the following day would be canceled.

By morning, electricity had been restored, and the snow was slowly abating. José turned on the television news and discovered that the Denver airport was closed. It reopened by mid-morning, and their flight to Hong Kong was delayed by only one hour.

Arriving in Hong Kong on March 11th, precisely two months since their last visit, José intended to formalize how to proceed with *Dreamspell* distribution as a planetary operation. Teddy was preparing for production of the Spanish edition. Given the gift nature of Dreamspell, the question of production and distribution costs were paramount in Teddy's mind.

José and Lloydine accepted a dinner invitation with Dale Keller and members of a local metaphysical group. This time the reception was less than cordial. José explained to the small party that *Dreamspell* was a gift. Their hosts seemed offended by the idea of something being given as a gift and told José, "You can't get anything without paying for it." Keller and his group operated with the underlying philosophy that, if you weren't rich, you must be spiritually inadequate. At that stage, José was relying solely on spiritual inspiration as sustenance.

By the end of March, with nothing resolved regarding *Dreamspell* distribution, José and Lloydine headed back to Oahu for a few days, then on to San Francisco to meet with Willard about *Dreamspell* distribution in the United States. José and Lloydine stayed at the Red Victorian Bed and Breakfast on Haight Street, which was filled with older hippies, bikers, and street people, as well as the next generation of flower children. Sitting in Golden Gate Park, José wondered if the new generation would redeem the 1960s by turning the 1990s into a true era of global, spiritual Earth revolution.

The following day was filled with various media engagements, followed by a well-attended evening presentation at the Dakin Center on Sacramento Street. During her career as a dancer, Lloydine had developed a good sense of drama and great stage presence. Throughout the rest of the 1990s, she would co-present the Dreamspell with José.

José and Lloydine arrived in Berlin on April 7, 1992. He had received an invitation in the fall of 1991 from a Russian art group in St. Petersburg, Atrium, to visit Russia via St. Petersburg. However, by December 1991, the Atrium group had obtained a visa to leave Russia and had settled temporarily in Berlin. The Berlin sponsor of the Atrium group, Sergei Rocambole, his partner, Anna Nikolaeva, and their translator, Andrei Vinograd, had allied themselves with a new German organization called Terra Magica Nostra, a publishing house and networking center for activities in Eastern Europe.

Sergei, the "leader" of the group, was an animated man of about 40. José was surprised to find that the Terra Magica group occupied a building that was literally a stone's throw from where the notorious Berlin Wall had once stood. The apartment building was in the Charlottenberg District, a rough neighborhood inhabited by artists and what appeared to be revolutionaries from every ethnic group in Eastern Europe and the Mideast, especially Turkey.

José and Lloydine were immediately immersed in a collective living situation. They spent the first four days of their stay with the Atrium group in a tiny, two-room apartment with Sergei and his wife, Anna, and their two high-spirited children, Donya and Pito. For the most part, José found this collective living situation fascinating. Being part of a lifestyle where people were free and moving in and out of different situations was reminiscent of his beatnik days at the University of Chicago. It could not have been a greater contrast to the situation he had just emerged from in San Francisco. The Russians chain-smoked, drank lots of black tea, and constantly initiated intellectual and philosophical conversations. There was a certain electrical vibrancy to it all, as it had been only a few years since the Berlin wall had come down, and an exciting sense of new possibilities pervaded.

Sergei and Andrei, who were trained in Vajrayana Buddhist practices, related their stories of personal encounters with the KGB and Russian Mafia. Sergei reminded José of the Grand Inquisitor in

Dostoyevsky's *Crime and Punishment*. Sergei took it upon himself to test José to see if he had the nerve to withstand the rigors of their forthcoming Russian visit. Sergei's techniques were similar to that of KGB: mind terrorism and often-blatant fear tactics, administered with utter, if not comical, aggression, like suddenly dropping his false teeth onto his tongue to make a point. It seemed many Russians at the time displayed similar behavior. Having suffered in the hands of the KGB for their freethinking, they in turn had developed the style of their persecutors.

José had scarcely been in Berlin two days when Sergei insisted he take a tab of LSD with him. Many of the Russians were in a highly exploratory phase at the time and were wild about psychedelics, as they had not formerly been available under Communist regime. Knowing that the Russians viewed him as an American artist or literary type, José knew that, by their standards, it was a major test to offer that he take LSD with them.

Taking a dose, José relaxed, intent on enjoying the evening. Staying up until two in the morning with Sergei, who was like a brilliantly mad Russian artist, felt like a strange endurance test. José never lost his presence of mind, even though Sergei continuously tried to intellectually trap or debate him. "You know *The Mayan Factor* was a great book, except for the last chapter," said Sergei, referring to the chapter about a positive future.

Finally, José was tired, had had enough of the social games, and went to bed. A couple of hours later, Sergei came into his room with beer, vodka, and a bag of psilocybin mushrooms. He persistently offered mushrooms and beer to José, who at first declined but then took a few of the mushrooms to appease him. Sergei rambled on for the next four or five hours, trying to find José's weak points. "You know your weakness is that you hide behind your wife because you think she saved you," Sergei told him before offering his own wife to him as a "noble" gesture. José felt this was just a matter of endurance, weathering Sergei's ventings, letting him blow it out and getting out of his way. He chalked the experiences up as his initiation to Russia.

The next day José and Lloydine moved to another flat, where they had more privacy. On the evening of April 12th, they gave a Dreamspell presentation for their German hosts. It was a lively event with much discussion of the Gregorian calendar, the role of the Vatican in the "great historical sabotage of time," and the reason for the repression of the 13th moon. While José was speaking, a rare earthquake occurred in the area of Trier, Germany, causing damage to the ancient Cathedral.

🔆

St. Petersburg is a vast city of millions of people, yet, in 1992, its airport was but a single building. José and Lloydine arrived in Russia with two cartons of *Dreamspell* kits, which raised the eyebrows of the customs police. "Bibles?" they asked suspiciously. When José showed the police his colorful *Dreamspell* demo kit, their faces immediately brightened, and they whisked them through.

Yuri and his girlfriend, Katya, a tall, elegant young woman in blue jeans and a fur-lined jacket, waited for them at the airport. Yuri, a rock musician, was unshaven, had the close-cropped hairstyle, and was dressed in black. In an old Russian car, Yuri drove them wildly down the tramway tracks that run down the center of the St. Petersburg boulevards. As he drove, he chanted in low overtones, chain-smoking cigarettes all the while.

Yuri was their chauffeur and translator, and their hosts were Vladimir and Galina Montlevitch. The Montlevitchs lived with their two teenage daughters in a typical small flat in a smelly government apartment building in the wastelands of north central St. Petersburg. Vladimir, who had also spent time in the Gulag, was now spearheading the revival of the Russian Buddhist movement. This movement, publicly squelched since the 1930s Stalin era, had thrived in prisons through the efforts of a few Buryat Lamas and their followers. The Montlevitchs studies and activities focused around the Buryat Ati tradition, which was similar to Tibetan Vajrayana Buddhism. They had recently hosted Tibetan Lama, Namkhai Norbu.

A whirlwind of activity ensued in St. Petersburg, including an encounter with Constantine (Kika) Ivanenko and the taping of an interview for Russian State television concerning the Dreamspell. José had been in communication with Constantine since 1987, after he organized Harmonic Convergence activities in St. Petersburg. Constantine was well-versed in the teachings of Alice Bailey and held many far-reaching visionary ideas concerning the future of computers and global telepathy.

Accompanied by Yuri, they met Kika at the Black Lake Metro Station. Short and squat, squinting through thick glasses and speaking breathlessly in good English, Kika pointed out that the building next to the Metro Station was now being refurbished, but had once been a casino where the notorious Rasputin had spent time. Kika took them to the northernmost Buddhist temple in the world, which, he said, was his sanctuary. Kika told them this temple had been erected in 1907 and then closed down in the 1930s, only to become a laboratory for biological warfare during the World War II Stalin era. Before they went inside, Kika insisted they do a group meditation on the mystic significance of the building. In the cupola, Kika proudly pointed out the stained glass windows that had been designed by Nicholas Roerich.

After visiting a few more Buddhist sites, José presented Kika with a Dreamspell kit. As he showed him the different parts, Kika shook his head sadly. As a child, he said, he had been a mathematics whiz, and at university he studied mathematical logic and cybernetics. But in the 1970s, the KGB reached him. Using massive doses of LSD as well as psychic torture techniques in a submarine, Kika said, they "destroyed the mathematical part of my brain and thinking processes." Nonetheless, he expressed appreciation for the gift.

The next day a Russian television team, Prognosis, arrived at the Montlevitch's to interview José. The interview was aired on April 26th, the sixth anniversary of the Chernobyl nuclear disaster.

Arriving in Moscow the morning of April 23rd, José was struck by the vast contrast between this city and St. Petersburg. Moscow had a more cluttered, uncared-for quality, but at the same time, a palpable feeling of enormous spirit existed in the people, as comes from weathering great difficulties. Overall, Moscow struck José as the Russian Atlantis. It was constructed in a series of concentric rings and wide boulevards, flanked by brooding Stalin-era high-rises. The chief features were its subway stations and underground train lines. All the art and power of the 20th-century Communist vision was concentrated there: brilliantly decorated people's palaces leading to endless labyrinthine passages full of mosaic, stained glass, and low relief sculpture. He viewed it as an underground artistic wonderland. He found even more fantastic the tumult of life surrounding and rushing in and out of these stations, day and night.

Bronislav Vinogradsky and his wife, Katya, who lived with their three children on the 13th floor of a small flat close to the center of the city, hosted José and Lloydine in Moscow. In his mid-30s, Bronislav was well versed in mathematics, logic, and the history of the I Ching. He quickly grasped the Dreamspell. His English was excellent, and the rapport between them was high. Bronislav had carved a life for himself as an underground bohemian Taoist who managed to escape the Russian bureaucracy. He would later become quite successful for creating a popular tea club, which was frequented by Russian oligarchs, gangsters, artists, and politicians alike.

The afternoon of his arrival on April 23rd, José gave a Dreamspell presentation to a group of graduate students at the Institute for Non-Classical Studies of the Academy of Sciences. He discovered that, in Russia, "non-classical" means "non-mainstream" or "leading edge." That same evening, José and Lloydine met with the Moscow Buddhist Society in a small artists' flat in central Moscow. Many people crowded around a table to hear about galactic time. He told people that the Dreamspell was an invitation to "explore structures of reality and social organization outside from the current paradigms."

He met with mathematicians and logicians who studied *Earth Ascending* as a classic in systems thinking. He met with philosophers and mystics, artists and scientists, and left *Dreamspells* with all. The magazine *Science and Religion* interviewed him. He met with Gnady Elferenco, the head of the Institute for Social Research, who requested *Dreamspells* for his upcoming Russian Leadership conference.

José found the intellectual and spiritual vitality of the Russian people inspiring. He perceived their sharp thinking was a result of the challenges they endured in the Cold War era. During the Communist era, the Russians had to turn inward and excel in their minds, developing intellectual and mystical power because expression was limited. He remembered having dreams as a child that he was in a city on another planet. He somehow felt that both the city in the dream and Moscow were based on a prototype of a previous or alternative underground world on the planet Uranus. And to him, the artistic underground subway stations contained the haunting qualities of Martian or Maldekian Atlantis. He thought, "Am I having a déjà vu of a Martian Atlantis that is working itself out in present time to see if they can create a great civilization and not destroy it?"

The Dreamspell appeared on Russian State television on April 26th, which was both Russian Easter and also the sixth anniversary of the Chernobyl disaster. José felt this was a good omen. He had wanted to travel to Chernobyl for the anniversary, but that was now quite difficult. They were no longer in the USSR, but in Russia, and Chernobyl was in the Ukraine.

The next night, José gave a Dreamspell presentation at the State Museum of Oriental Art. Upon arrival, José and Lloydine were escorted to the Roerich Room, which houses a collection of the memorabilia of Nicholas Roerich. As José entered this quaint chamber, he was thunderstruck. There, high on the wall, facing the entrance to the room, was the Banner of Peace that they had produced in Boulder eight years before! Daniel Entin, curator of the Roerich Museum in New York, had been true to his word in delivering the Banner of Peace to Moscow.

Boarding the Midnight Express, José and Lloydine arrived in St. Petersburg the next morning. The following day, José gave one more formal presentation at the newly formed Free Institute of Science and Philosophy of St. Petersburg. His talk was entitled "The Discovery of the Fourth Dimension and the Coming of Galactic Culture." As it turned out, the seminar conveners were academicians, well known for their studies comparing Carlos Castaneda's Yaqui-inspired ideas with the phenomenology of Hegel. José was amazed at the degree the Russians had taken to Castaneda's ideas.

José and Lloydine reached Berlin on Witches Night, or Walpurgis Nacht, April 30th, and that evening gave a presentation in a beautiful old church in the Charlottenberg District.

The next day was surreal. It was May Day, and the Terra Magica group arranged a rooftop picnic. Just as everyone began to enjoy themselves, the streets below erupted with police sirens, explosions, and shouting. José learned that this was the annual confrontation between the "skinheads," the "anarchists," and the police. At the same time, he listened to radio reports of rioting in the Watts District of Los Angeles.

At the time, José felt he was on an accelerated journey through a time tunnel, crossing various mental and cultural frontiers with scarcely a moment to gain perspective. He never knew exactly what was going to transpire next.

Chapter 48
The Arcturus Probe

Telepathically, of course, we are one, a
single organism spread out over time—
and space.

—José Arguelles, *The*
Arcturus Probe

Upon returning to the United States, a severe case of culture shock set in. After being picked up by an acquaintance at the San Francisco airport, José and Lloydine's first stop was at a fancy strip mall shopping center in Marin County. José got out of the car, looked around, and found that nothing made sense. All the store signs seemed foreign. Exotically named flavors of new, low-cholesterol frozen yogurt brands were just not in his frame of reference. It reminded him of the newspaper editorial he had read in Ottawa entitled "Freedom Is Just Another Word for Too Much to Choose From."

He realized what a vast gulf separated the Bush-era subculture of Marin County from Yeltsin's Russia.

For five months, he had been on a fast-moving wave, successfully seeding Mexico and Russia with the synchronic order as demonstrated through the Dreamspell. A few groups were coming together internationally, but the situation in San Francisco still felt quite unstable. José understood the synchronic order was a new reality that could not be understood unless people were willing to suspend habitual ways of thinking. The Dreamspell was accessible only to those who made themselves, once again, like children.

He saw that, until people became completely disillusioned with the old system, they would consistently resist a new vision and knowledge.

He learned that, more often than not, when people were presented with new knowledge, they resisted it in favor of what they already knew. Many claimed that new information was "beyond" them or that "they cannot learn it," merely because they had not yet cultivated the will to exert in new forms.

Returning to Oahu, José and Lloydine rented a small house in Temple Valley. A visit with Heidi was followed by a visit from Tara, by then 19, and going through a deep stage of soul searching.

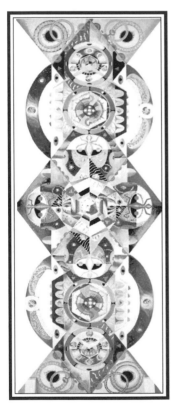

"*Arcturus Probe,*"
painting by José Arguelles.

In the five years since writing *Surfers of the Zuvuya*, José's life had changed dramatically, internally and externally, though he hadn't yet had much time to reflect on how much it had changed. Reluctantly, he settled into another round of family life. With increased domestic duties, it didn't seem introspection would come easily. One night, while watching television with his family, he saw an ad with the message "a mind is a terrible thing to waste." When he heard it, all he could think was: "A planet is a terrible thing to waste." This phrase continued to repeat through his mind.

Upon moving to Temple Valley, José contemplated the Pali, the sheer cliffs of the Koolau Range that fell behind the house, and the Byodo-In Temple, from which Temple Valley derived its name. Right behind the Buddhist temple is a mountain peak that is unnamed on all the maps, known only by its elevation: 2,826 feet. José found this a fascinating number, with its two key numbers of 28 and 26.

Down from the 2,826-foot peak is a triangular rock outcropping that José immediately referred to as the "Arcturus temple," relating it to a similar set of rock outcroppings in the mountains of Tepotzlan outside of Huehuecoyotl. From such contemplation, José sat down at his word processor one Sunday morning in early June and, without a thought, wrote the title, *The Arcturus Probe: Tales and Reports of an Ongoing Investigation*. A powerful feeling came over him, and suddenly he could hear a voice narrating to him from a world 40 light years away: Arcturus, sixth brightest star in the heavens. He wrote:

> For a very long time we have been awaiting the opportunity of sharing this information with you, the information concerning other worlds and what you call travel between worlds. But until you could experience the failures and shortcomings of your nearsighted methods and their diabolically relentless way of drawing you further and further away from your true goals and purposes, there was really nothing we could do. But now you see. A planet is a terrible thing to waste.

Once he heard the voice, José couldn't stop writing until the story was complete. He soon saw that the text that was unraveling was actually a deeper cosmological description of the Dreamspell's background.

The writing of this text took José's mind into ever-deeper levels of time travel, through interplanetary consciousness that he had never systematically explored or accepted before. This opening connected back with the first time he saw the Face on Mars. Since that point, he had found himself capable of being outside his body, perceiving reality in fresh ways, free from conventional human perception.

The Arcturians informed him that the situation playing out on planet Earth is a huge planetary episode resulting from "collective amnesia" and compounded by "karmic debris" that was transferred to this planet from Mars and Maldek. The humans are working through this karma for the last time, as the cycle is soon to close.

The Arcturus Probe describes what happened on Mars in the following way:

> Because of attention to defense and security, neither of the civilizations had paid heed to the deteriorating climate changes on the planet (Mars), and so had not prepared themselves for what was coming. As a result, a fatal double-blow was delivered to the Martian project: a type of atomic war which only hastened the desiccation of the atmosphere and the poisonous thinning-out of the planet's electromagnetic field. Within a very short time, Mars was uninhabitable to its once-proud third-dimensional population. Where the trade and triumph of empire had sent its armies and caravans, empty winds raged and blew chilling blasts of red sand. Everywhere the evil red sand drifted, covering

shattered monuments where no one any longer breathed any kind of air but that which was radioactively poisoned....

The Arcturus Probe was written in an unbidden manner during a five-week span that coincided with Tara's visit; not a word was edited or changed. José dedicated *The Arcturus Probe* to Tara, just as he had dedicated his last published book, *Surfers of the Zuvuya*, to Josh.

After completing *The Arcturus Probe*, José turned his full attention to the Time Shift. He had anticipated an intensification of the galactic beams to occur at this time. Having lived within sight of Haleakala's Science City in Maui, he found it interesting that in 1986 this was the place where the first galactic beams were detected. He felt he had been drawn to this particular place in Kula, Maui, because of the beam information. He described the beam in *Surfers of the Zuvuya*:

> Remember, the purpose of the beam that we are passing through, like the purpose of all galactic beams, is to affect the timing of change. One day there are dinosaurs. The next day they are gone. One day there are woolly mammoths and saber tooth tigers, the next day they are gone. Where do they go? Do they die? Or are they radically transmuted—passed through a time warp that places them into memory capsules in the back of our brains? Will that happen to us, too? What *will* happen to us anyway?

José knew that the Time Shift, like the Harmonic Convergence, was part of an invisible time-release program directed by advanced intelligences. This means it would happen whether anyone noticed it or not. He saw in a vision that, from 1992 until 2012, a momentous wave of natural disasters would be set in motion, and that human society worldwide would experience an even greater acceleration of change. All of this was in accordance with the 2012 prophecy revealed to him at the time of the Harmonic Convergence. In this vision, José saw that only by experiencing such dramatic convulsions of change would humanity finally wake up at the last possible moment and consciously shift gears into a new reality as one collective species.

To prepare for the Time Shift, José wrote numerous papers urging humanity to return to the cycles of nature before it was too late. He realized his position was radical; nonetheless, he knew it had to be voiced. His main premise was that, without the use of the proper timing frequency, humans go out of resonance with nature. When humans go out of resonance with nature, strange mutations and natural catastrophes occur, and in some cases planets might even explode.

Preparing for the Time Shift was no easy task. At that time, a number of people were creating spin-off products and workshops based on the Dreamspell without understanding its true nature. Nonetheless, Time Shift ceremonies were conducted in Mexico, Japan, Germany, Egypt, Spain, England, Russia, and Latin America, as well as in unexpected places such as Arkansas and Virginia.

The starting point of the Time Shift was July 26, 1992. José and Lloydine, accompanied by their friend Patrick Lane, conducted a ceremony to initiate the *Blue Cosmic Storm* year (Kin 39), according to the Dreamspell codes. José foresaw that the year signified endurance of an enormous catalyzation of cosmic energy that would unfold in the cycles of nature conflicting with the dissonance of humans following artificial time. For this reason, the three each took turns ringing a massive temple bell 13 times at the Byodo-In Buddhist Temple. The three of them rang the bell a total of 39 times (13 × 3).

Within a month after the Time Shift, Hurricane Andrew, the worst hurricane in U.S. history up to that point, occurred. It devastated a large portion of Florida and parts of Louisiana. (Exactly 13 years later Hurricane Katrina, the most devastating hurricane in recorded U.S. history, would occur on August 29, 2005. This was followed on December 26, 2005, by the disastrous earthquake and tsunami in southeast Asia and the Indian Ocean, killing more than 200,000.)

Within another month of Hurricane Andrew in 1992, another powerful hurricane hit: Hurricane Iniki, which devastated the isle of Kuaui in Hawaii. Andrew had winds of up to 165 miles per hour, and Iniki had gusts up to 227 miles per hour. Iniki was shortly followed by a third storm that devastated the isle of Guam.

In Madagascar, a single strike of lightning hit the main power center, wiping out the African island's entire electrical grid. In the Philippines, the Pinatubo Volcano was still smoldering. The most powerful earthquake in the history of central Africa occurred south of Somalia, where starvation is endemic. On October 12th (Columbus Day), the most powerful earthquake to hit Egypt devastated the city of Cairo. Daily explosions and disasters affected industrial and urban sites around the planet, releasing unanticipated amounts of toxicity into the atmosphere. Beneath the Russian Earth, the radioactivity continued to click off its deadly trail of cumulative poison.

November 21st began what is known as the 1992 tornado outbreak in the United States, a three-day storm that struck large parts of the

Eastern and Midwestern United States. This was followed, on November 29th, by a series of thunderstorms in Queensland, Australia, spawning two of the most powerful tornadoes ever to hit Australia. This included the Bucca Tornado, one of the most violent tornadoes ever recorded in Australia.

The political climate had also plummeted. Following the collapse of the USSR, just after the fourth anniversary of the Harmonic Convergence, the Group of Seven (the United States, Canada, the UK, Italy, France, Germany, and Japan) consolidated their power. The United Nations, founded as an organization to promote and establish peace, was now controlled by the G-7. The process had been sealed with the alliance against Iraq: Operation Desert Storm. This set the stage for a new phase of covert anti-Islamic foreign policies dominated by "oil politics."

Shortly after the Time Shift, 8,000 *Dreamspells* were given away at a two-day seminar in Monterrey, Mexico, and 1,000 were given away at Mt. Shasta. The Spanish situation proved more challenging, as 2,000 Spanish-edition *Dreamspell* kits remained in Spanish customs for more than two months because, according to the government, Spain had already received its quota of "games" for 1992. Even when it was officially redesignated as a "calendar" instead of a "game," the 2,000 *Dreamspell* kits still had to be shipped back to France and brought into Spain again by truck. To José, this situation only illustrated the complexity of the 12:60 system.

In September 1992, José set to work on a new text to accompany production of the Thirteen Moon calendar, *Thirteen Moons in Motion*. This book explained the workings of the new calendar, the history of the Gregorian calendar, and the nature of calendars in general as devices that shape consciousness. The text begins with a small chapter called "Thinking the Unthinkable" and states:

> Of all the unexamined assumptions and criteria upon which we base and gauge our daily lives as human beings on planet Earth, by far the greatest and most profoundly unquestioned is the instrument and institution known as the Gregorian calendar.

In the process of creating the calendar text, José discovered that this was not the first effort to put forth a perfect, perpetual Thirteen Moon Calendar. In the 19th century, philosopher and creator of the modern study of sociology, August Comte, had also designed a perpetual 13 "month" calendar of 28 days each. The 365th day, which is outside of the count of the days of the week, Comte designated "Year Day." In the *Dreamspell Calendar of the Thirteen Moons*, this 365th day occurs on July 25th and is called the "Day out of Time" or "Green Day." The first day of the year on the Thirteen Moon calendar begins on July 26th, correlating with the heliacal rising of the star Sirius.

Once José completed the text for *Thirteen Moons in Motion*, he knew exactly what had to be done. As he had seen, the error in time is a part of the galactic saga known as the *time wars*. The time wars are what keep people from owning their own time and therefore from knowing their own minds. "Who owns your time, owns your mind," was the phrase José used often to communicate this truth. He saw that the "time war" reaches into all levels of society everywhere on the planet, but its primary everyday tools of control are the Gregorian calendar and the mechanical clock. He reasoned that, if *time* is the fundamental key to any new beginning, the calendar is a practical way for people to begin a new time.

José saw that the Thirteen Moon Dreamspell calendar, as a new dispensation, was ultimately far more than a calendar (as traditionally understood), but a *synchronometer*, a tool for mapping synchronicity or the synchronic order. The synchronic order is a radial order that accommodates and synchronizes all true systems of time and thought, inclusive of the Long Count.

The Quiche or Mayan Long Count is the linear "count of days" that goes from August 13, 3113 BC (Julian Count 3114 BC) to December 21, 2012. There are 1,872,000 days between those two points. That creates a cycle, subdivided into 13 equal parts called baktuns, or into 260 parts called katuns, which are about 20 years each. The last katun began on April 4, 1993, and ends on December 21, 2012.

The *Thirteen Moons in Motion* text was complete, but there was still no calendar template to make it real. The assignment had been given out to various people, but nothing satisfactory surfaced. Then, on October 7th, a Thirteen Moon wall calendar arrived in the mail in perfect form, unsolicited, from a man named Randy Bruner in Covington, Kentucky. Randy's calendar was further proof to José that an American grassroots Dreamspell revolution of time was beginning to form.

Chapter 49
On the Prophecy

> *The old order changeth, yielding place to new.*
>
> —Alfred Tennyson
>
> *Truth has to appear only once in a single mind, for it*
> *to be impossible ever to prevent it from spreading*
> *universally and setting everything ablaze.*
>
> —Pierre Teilhard de Chardin

By autumn 1992, José had written *The Arcturus Probe, Thirteen Moons in Motion*, and the *Treatise on Time from its Own Dimension*. Harper San Francisco rejected them all. Initially, Michael Toms of New Dimensions Radio, a former literary agent for Harper San Francisco, had asked José for all of his new writings so he could submit them. José waited a long time, and then Michael informed him that Harper San Francisco "didn't want to go the direction that Arguelles is going."

José had his own office workspace where he was able to write and, though his time was free, many tensions arose. Paul and his girlfriend, Erica, were staying with him, along with Maya and Heidi.

On November 13, 1992, Shirley MacLaine called him to discuss an astral plane event occurring that day and to consult with him about Earth changes. She had just purchased land in New Mexico and was looking for confirmation that it was the "safest place" for the coming changes. After talking with José for a while, Shirley told him that ever since the Harmonic Convergence, she was making increasing amounts of money. She asked if he knew what that was all about. From the conversation, he knew that a great gulf was opening between his role and perceptions of reality and those of the new age mainstream. He hung up the phone feeling empty.

Later that month, Chris Whitecloud introduced José to his friend David Po. As it turned out, José had met Po (as he was called by friends) in 1984 in Seattle when he was a professor at the Union Graduate School. Po was also a friend of Marilyn Ferguson. A big supporter of the Hawaiian Sovereignty Movement, Po lived in Hawaii with his wife, Atara, and their 4-year-old son, Akua. Po said he had learned about José's work through Whitecloud and would like to support his vision in some way.

Not long before this meeting, José had read an article in the Honolulu newspaper about a man who was descended from the last Hawaiian king, Kamehameha. This man was Bumpy Kanahele. After spending time in jail for his beliefs, Bumpy was spearheading the Hawaiian Sovereignty Movement from a location close to José's residence in Temple Valley. José was struck by Bumpy's plight; the newspaper portrayed him as a type of Hawaiian Martin Luther King, Jr. As it turned out, Po was supporting Bumpy.

Sarcophagus lid of Pacal Votan. Copyright Telektonon, 1993, José Arguelles.

José and Lloydine accepted an offer from Po and Atara to live at their estate in Pualani on Maui, which they were leasing. This was the same property where José and Lloydine had first lived in Hawaii three years prior!

Settled into the North cottage (they had previously resided in the South cottage), José began writing a text called *Pacal Votan's Book of Reality*. This text was triggered by a vision he had had on his previous birthday while in meditation. In the vision, he witnessed Pacal Votan surveying the Earth from another dimension. From this vantage point, José perceived events occurring between 13,000 and 8,000 years prior that illustrated the psychological development of the human species. In anthropological terms, this was the time of the transition between the pure hunting/gathering phase into the early proto-agricultural phase.

At this time, in the North cottage and working on this text, José met Bumpy and, at the request of Po, wrote numerous papers and documents on behalf of the Hawaiian Sovereignty Movement. This immersion provided José with a powerful education in the Indigenous Sovereignty Movement—a necessary ingredient to his mission. Gaining insight into the life of indigenous people proved useful a few years later when he encountered indigenous people around the world in places such as South America and Altai.

He gained valuable insight after numerous discussions with Bumpy and others in the Hawaiian Sovereignty Movement regarding the Gregorian calendar and the Thirteen Moon calendar. The Hawaiians had a lunar calendar, and José explained to them that a lunar calendar is not a solar calendar, as it doesn't account for the orbiting of the Earth around the Sun. He pointed out that the Gregorian calendar is also not a solar calendar, but an error in time, based on measurements of space.

Bumpy listened and then reported the information to the Hawaiian elders, who discussed the matter. "You know," Bumpy told José, "Tutu (elder grandmother) said she remembers when we had 13 moons and 28 days." José found this very interesting. These discussions ignited his understanding of the Thirteen Moon calendar as a vehicle unto itself. He saw that the Thirteen Moon calendar is the form, and that, without this form of order in time, it's not possible to understand all of the Law of Time.

Through talking with the Hawaiian natives, José first understood how accepting the Gregorian calendar had enslaved the people and destroyed their culture more than 100 years previously. It was a typical story: This is what happens when a culture's calendar and culture are taken away, and replaced by the imperialist system of the Gregorian calendar. The result for Hawaiian natives was a slow erasing of ancient cultural programs, and before long many of them were addicted to watching television, and eating Spam and fast food.

Fortunately for the Hawaiians and many other indigenous cultures, José thought, there are grandmothers and grandfathers in the backwoods who stay tuned to Nature and maintain the oral tradition. In contemplating this, José determined that the Thirteen Moon calendar was the simplest form of order for human beings to begin entering into the fourth-dimensional mind.

With inspiration from the Hawaiian Sovereignty Movement, José wrote 13 letters to 13 different leaders and artists informing them of the Thirteen Moon calendar as a rallying point for unification. The premise was as follows:

> Human society is in turmoil. The planetary environment is in a state of continuing deterioration. No existing means, whether through the United Nations, World Court, religious or ideological campaigns, have been found to alleviate the misery and degradation, which multiply daily. Overpopulation, war, starvation and environmental disaster burden the promise of a future for our children. We are in a state of emergency. In this situation, when all remedies have failed, no other solution exists but to voluntarily redirect the course of human affairs. The simplest means for changing this course is adoption of a new calendar, a new standard of common time for all humans.

At that point, life was uncertain. The house in Temple Valley had been suburban and could accommodate the family, which was important to Lloydine. And now there they were in the middle of the Hawaiian Sovereignty Movement. To top it off, another disagreement arose between the same landlord, Will Linneman, and Po, resulting in their eviction from the house. José thought it was all an interesting déjà vu. Here they had been living on this property in the South cottage in 1989, and three moons later—boom! They had to move. Now there he was after just six weeks in the North cottage—and boom! They had to move.

Within days, Po located an opulent, modern estate on the Big Island in the windswept and desolate North point region of Puakea Bay, overlooking the Alenuihaha Channel towards Maui. It was a ghost-like tropical paradise with many lots that hadn't been developed because it was too remote and windy for most people.

By early April, they relocated. There was a big main house and then a beautiful pool house, where José and Lloydine lived. There was no kitchen, so José set up his coffee machine in a small wet bar outside. Though externally ideal, the pool house was not altogether private. Often members of the Hawaiian Sovereignty Movement came for visits and the only place they wanted to be was at the pool. Many of them were quite poor, and when they visited the palatial estate, it was like paradise and they went wild, and had fun on their visits.

Po employed Lloydine as his typist for the Hawaiian Sovereignty Movement. José felt uneasy about the dynamics that developed between Lloydine and Po, as she would often concede to his demands of staying up into the wee hours cranking out documents. Po was the only person who José had ever seen stand up to Lloydine. Po often told her, "Lloydine, watch your mind," and "Lloydine, watch your mouth."

At this point, José became quite removed from the day-to-day happenings of Po and the Sovereignty Movement, though he still wrote occasional papers when requested. José got to a certain point with writing the *Pacal Votan Book of Reality* and then trashed the entire manuscript, realizing it was never meant to be a book, but a living experience.

José and Maya, 1992. Image courtesy of and copyright the José Arguelles Archive.

On May 15, 1993, for Lloydine's 50th birthday, Po flew the entire family out for lavish celebration. Champagne flowed freely and luxurious food of all kinds was served. Po also moved Maya from Boulder to Hawaii and gave her a room in the main house. On a whim, Po bought Maya a VW Cabriolet convertible sports car, even though 80-year-old Maya had not driven in a number of years.

For José, day-to-day life at the Hawaiian pool house was ideal: daily yoga, a simple diet of vegetables and brown rice, and swimming kept him in excellent physical shape. Atara graciously brought him coffee and chocolate-covered coffee beans. Four-year-old Akua loved to visit "Uncle Joe," as he referred to José, and every afternoon he would show up while José was making coffee in his wet bar. Akua patiently waited until Uncle Joe pulled out the chocolate-covered coffee beans. José felt a deep affection for his young friend and always looked forward to their daily visits. Inspired by Akua, José wrote the children's book *The Story of Time: the Story of Turtle and Trees*, and created many full-color graphics.

The story is told through the eyes of "Great Grandmother Galaxy" and concludes with the calling on the spirit counsels of the elders to come down and save the planet so all the children can have a happy celebration at 2012–2013.

꙳

On July 25, 1993, Mother Tynetta Muhammad and her son Ishmael, a minister of the Nation of Islam, paid a visit to José. That day, along with Maya, they all took a ride around the island counterclockwise, discussing prophecy, Islam, and how to connect with the Indigenous Movement.

Back at the estate, Mother Tynetta gave José a book at the request of Dr. Z'ek Balam, a Mayan healer. As she handed him the book, José was struck by the title: *De Tulan El Lejano (From Distant Tollan)*! He thanked Tynetta and asked her to tell Dr. Z'ek that he would read the book with great interest.

The next morning (July 26, 1993; Kin 144), Jose woke up unusually early and picked up the book *De Tulan el Lejano (From Distant Tollan)*. The book claimed to be a translation of a Mayan codex and at first appeared to be a science fiction story by an anonymous author calling himself Chac-Le, "the Ancient One." After reading a few paragraphs, José knew it was much more. He experienced a series of déjà vu when he read the following passage:

My children! I leave this for you, for it might not be completed tomorrow…. As much as I have done, how much could I have done yesterday to improve the life of the humans of this world; and how much have my brothers done, those who, waiting with me, arrived, to occupy with another light the depths of the human being. It has not been in vain. But much is lacking still to get moving, and my legs are sleeping and the message does not arrive, nor have arrived those (from space) who ought to have received our call.

The book described a number of travelers from the star Tau Ceti (Tollan) who were traveling, not in a spaceship, but in a timeship.

José was thunderstruck. Was he reading his own cosmic memory? As the timeship moved through the dimensions into the third dimension, trouble ensued, and it crashed or dissolved. On the ship were many messengers, namely Quetzalcoatl, but also Siddhartha (Buddha), Christ, and Muhammad, as well as Homer.

After reading a few pages, José entered a prolonged visionary state, triggered by the memory of a "shipwreck." Spontaneously, he experienced his physical body transform into the axis of a double-terminated crystal with six transparent facets emanating from the central channel, which was himself. Each facet was a departure point directed by his mind into various "time" tunnels. Each tunnel seemed to contain simultaneous experiences of memories, visions, and dreams.

In one of the time tunnels, he passed up and down the stairs leading to the tomb of Pacal Votan. Weaving in and out of the tomb itself, he found himself at the central control panel of the radial tunnel system. His mind unfolded into multiple split-screen holograms, allowing him the ability to experience simultaneous levels in many spaces at once.

Every tunnel appeared as a moving hologram, in full color. In one tunnel, the experience seemed like a dream that was being remembered. In another tunnel, it felt like a memory that was being recalled, and, in yet another tunnel, it appeared as a déjà vu of an alternative reality. He noticed that some of the tunnels also seemed to be occurring simultaneously on other planets.

In one tunnel he saw Chogyam Trungpa Rinpoche seated on a throne in a Western business suit. "You must bring the religion of the Earth back to the people!" Trungpa told him.

Suddenly, José's attention shifted to yet another tunnel where a song was playing: the "Ballad of Antonio Martinez." He peered into the tunnel only to see Martinez, the sailor, tossed up on a beach—shipwrecked.

Simultaneously, in another tunnel, he spotted a Mayan seer lying in a hammock, repeating an ancient incantation. At the other end of this same tunnel, Alberto Ruz was running his fingers up and down the tile tube that enters the tomb of Pacal Votan. "A psychoduct!" Ruz exclaimed. "That's what it is. It enabled the deceased to talk to the people above!"

Suddenly, José entered yet another tunnel where he saw a young Quetzalcoatl at Xochicalco, being instructed by various elders, among them a Mayan, an Olmec, a Zapotec: "And you must leave the city of Tula foursquare and forsake all its palaces, for you are the Quetzalcoatl.... They have been waiting for you, but elsewhere...."

Splitting into many selves at once, José entered all tunnels simultaneously before dissolving back into one being.

Coming out of his visionary state, José immediately went to his bookshelf, grabbed the Spanish edition of the *Book of Chilam Balam of Chumayel* and spontaneously flipped to page 144—the beginning of the prophecy of the mysterious Antonio Martinez: "And so they read to him the Book of Seven Generations, and it took three months...."

Reaching for his journal, José fervently scribbled down notes as messages and information pored into his being. It seemed as though all the books and everything around him were talking. In an instant, he realized that the entire tomb of Pacal Votan was actually a prophecy in the form of a *terma*, a hidden "text" or treasure, as it is known in Tibetan Buddhist tradition. In this tradition, terma is often hidden beneath rocks or in caverns, and often written in a symbolic script.

From his previous studies, José knew that the Book of Seven Generations, mentioned only twice in the *Chilam Balam*, was the key to the prophecies of Pacal Votan. He knew the seven generations referred to the seven katuns, Long Count 9.13.0.0.0-10.0.0.0. Especially important was the mysterious reference to the Book of Seven Generations mentioned in the prophecy of Antonio Martinez, dated 1692, exactly 1,000 years after the dedication of the tomb of Pacal Votan AD 692.

He also noticed that *From Distant Tollan* was published in 1978 in Havana, Cuba—the same place Antonio Martinez sets sail in the

"Galactic Being," painting by José Arguelles.

prophecy of *Chilam Balam*! After setting sail and then traveling to a strange land, Martinez is shipwrecked.

Many bits of knowledge spontaneously cohered in José's memory and mind. He saw that 144, written in Mayan vigesimal notation, is 7.4 (7 × 20 + 4). He knew that the first verse in the Book of Revelations that mentions the 144,000 is Chapter 7, verse 4: "And I heard the number of them which were sealed: and there were sealed an hundred and forty and four thousand of all the tribes of the children of Israel."

If he had been following the Long Count alone, none of this would have come about. But by following this particular year-bearer count derived from the *Chilam Balam*, which he discovered in Palenque in 1976, the unscrambling could occur. Through this count, he understood Kin 144: the number that unlocked the Book of Revelations and the Prophecy of Pacal Votan, as well as the Book of Seven Generations.

Running down the stairs again, José felt the presence of Earth spirits who identified themselves as *chtonics*. The spirits determinedly called out to him in muffled sounds, though he couldn't make out their words, José knew that the meaning of the tomb of Pacal Votan was in the speaking tube that ran from the tomb up to the floor of the middle chamber containing 140 inscriptions. While contemplating all of these factors, he heard the Earth spirits, once again, whispering to him that they were *chtonics*.

After intense concentration on the voices of the Earth spirits, a word suddenly thundered across his mind: TEL ECH TON ON! TEL ECH TON ON! "Telektonon!" he thought. "That's it! The Telektonon is the name of the Earth Spirit Speaking tube. This is all part of the prophecy of Telektonon!"

Further, he was astonished to discover that the timing frequencies—12:60 and 13:20—that he had discovered in 1989 were also all part of this Telektonon Prophecy. He realized the precision of these two frequencies, when he realized that, between the time of the dedication of the tomb of Pacal Votan in the year AD 692 and the time of its discovery in 1952, there are precisely 1,260 years! He was further astonished to discover that between the time of the dedication date of the tomb in AD 692 and 2012, there are precisely 1,320 years!

Coming down from this experience, José felt like a shipwrecked sailor on a strange planet. He flashed to the boy he was at 904 Seventh Avenue, lying on his bed, looking at his father's painting of the South Pacific Islands, trying to remember what it was that he was supposed to remember! Now he knew. This remembrance changed everything. He was no longer "José Arguelles"; the higher being within, long waiting to emerge, finally had the opportunity to do so.

Afterword

December 21, 2012, marks the conclusion of the Mayan long-count of the 5,125 "Great Cycle of History." This coincides with a galactic alignment in which the sun will align with the center of the Milky Way galaxy, an event that occurs once every 26,000 years. All of José's endeavours have been pivoted around this date, which he views as a galactic shifting of gears, followed by the birth of a new solar age.

In a July 7, 2007 *New York Times* article by Benjamin Anastas about 2012, José said of the anticipated date:

> The resonance between the focused attention of human consciousness in alignment with the galactic center will bring about a radical change of consciousness, the evolutionary shift point....

To bring the reader briefly up to date, José experienced a string of synchronicities following the revelation of the Telektonon prophecy in 1993. This led, the following year, to the creation of the World 13-Moon Calendar Change Peace Movement. Over the next seven years, José took the message of the return to natural time around the planet several times over and made every effort to inform world leaders about the opportunity of calendar change as the basis of unification and world peace. His travels included visits to the Vatican and the United Nations.

This mission took him throughout Latin America, South Africa, Egypt, Russia, India, Hong Kong, Japan, and Europe, and later to Altai

(Siberia), Baghdad, and Istanbul. During this time he convened several congresses, and produced numerous tools and proofs of the mathematics of fourth-dimensional time.

In 2000, José created the Foundation for the Law of Time, a nonprofit educational organization, to further promote the premise of "peace through culture," the law of time, and the synchronic order. Following September 11, 2001, he wrote and published *Time and the Technosphere: The Law of Time in Human Affairs* (Inner Traditions, 2002).

In 2002, José was honored by nine indigenous elders atop the Pyramid of the Sun in Teotihuacán, Mexico, as being the Closer of the Cycle, the one to bring a new knowledge that would complete and regenerate the traditional knowledge. This was the same pyramid where he had received his first vision as boy of 14, 49 years earlier. Shortly after, his relation with Lloydine completed its cycle and the two parted ways.

In pursuing his path over the last decade, especially through his meditations, new psychic dimensions of reality and interplanetary memories opened to José. This caused him to turn his attention toward a renewed study of the biosphere-noosphere transition as the context for the coming of the new time.

For José, the meaning of December 21, 2012, has everything to do with shifting timing frequencies. This transition is anticipated as the transformation of the present material-industrial order of the planet into a full renewal of the human mind, where telepathy is universal. On this theme, in 1997, he wrote the following excerpt in a report for the UR Council for the Theology of Peace, an event he convened in Italy:

> The Earth changes have begun. The Sun is a star. It is undergoing a complete reorientation on its passage to becoming a supernova. The Earth's electromagnetic field is being restructured accordingly…. Not just our solar system, but the entire universe is undergoing a profound cosmic radiation. The Earth's poles are shifting. The seas will be rising very soon. Humans have a role to play. The civilization which they have created and which now encompasses their belief system is crumbling, for it is based on artificial time. A new Earth culture must arise to take its place. To succeed in this transition, the cosmic climax of the biosphere-noosphere transition, the humans must make the decision to change their frequency. The frequency change will allow the

humans to participate in the magnetic stabilization of their planet and to enter a fully fourth-dimensional operating frequency....

To this end, in 2004, José launched, with Stephanie South, the "Noosphere II" scientific research project and organized these activities as the Galactic Research Institute (GRI), 2005. One of the projects of the GRI is the publication of the seven-volume *Cosmic History Chronicles*, of which the first four are now in print. This series is an encyclopaedic effort at reformulating the base and scope of human knowledge according to the higher-dimensional perspective of the law of time.

José will convene the First Noosphere World Congress in July 2009. The theme of the Congress is "Envisioning the Earth as a Work of Art." He is also organizer of the CREST13 project, a network of sustainable communities engaged in a common planetary program of unified telepathic meditations.

2012: Biography of a Time Traveler was originally written as two volumes. The second volume, complete and ready to publish, narrates José's journey up to the present. Readers will find that the second volume goes into greater detail regarding the closing of the cycle and the anticipated dimensional shift.

Bibliography

Arguelles, José. *The Arcturus Probe: Tales and Reports of an Ongoing Investigation*. Sedona, Ariz.: Light Technology Publications, 1996.

——. *The Call of Pacal Votan, Time is the Fourth Dimension*. Forres, Scotland: Altea Publishers, 1996.

——. *Charles Henry and the Formation of a Psychophysical Aesthetic*. Chicago: University of Chicago Press, 1972.

——. "Crystal Earth Papers." Unpublished, 1986.

——. *Earth Ascending: An Illustrated Treatise on the Law Governing Whole Systems, Third Edition*. Santa Fe, N.M.: Bear and Company, 1996.

——. "Earth Shaman: The Voyage Beyond History." Unpublished, 1984.

——. *The Mayan Factor, Path Beyond Technology*. Santa Fe, N.M.: Bear and Company, 1987, 1996.

——. *Surfers of the Zuvuya, Tales of Interdimensional Travel*. Santa Fe, N.M.: Bear and Company, 1988.

——. *Telektonon, Prophecy of Pacal Votan*. Interlink Productions, 1994.

——. *Time and the Technosphere: The Law of Time in Human Affairs*. Rochester, Vt.: Inner Traditions International, 2002.

——. *The Transformative Vision: Reflections on the Nature and History of Human Expression, 2nd Edition*. Fort Yates, N.D.: Muse Publications, 1992.

Arguelles, José, with Lloydine Arguelles. *Dreamspell: The Journey of Timeship Earth 2013*. Hong Kong: Interlink Productions, 1991, 2002.

Arguelles, Jose, and Miriam Arguelles. *The Feminine: Spacious as Sky*. Boulder, Colo.: Shambhala Publications, 1977.

———. *Mandala*. Berkeley, Calif.: Shambhala Publications, 1972.

Bailey, Alice A. *Education in the New Age, 1st Edition*. New York: Lucis Publishing Company, 1954.

———. *Initiation, Human and Solar, 1st Edition*. New York: Lucis Publishing Company, 1922.

"Artist as Psychic: What is Psychic Art?" *Sacramento Bee*, January 24, 1971.

Bernal, Ignacio. *Offical Guide: Teotihuacan*. Mexico City: INAH, 1985.

Blake, William. *Complete Writings*. Ed. Geoffrey Keynes. London: Oxford University Press, 1969.

Blavatsky, Helena Petrovna. *The Secret Doctrine, 2 vols*. Madras, India, and London; Theosophical Publishing House, 1888.

The Book of Chilam Balam of Chumayel. Translated and edited by Ralph Roys. Norman, Okla.: University of Oklahoma Press, 1967.

"Civilization as Psycho-History." *Maincurrents in Modern Thought, Volume 29, Number 2, November–December 1972*.

Coe, Michael D. *The Maya*. New York: Praeger, 1966.

Dass, Baba Hari. *Silence Speaks: From the Chalkboard of Baba Hari Dass, 1st Edition*. Santa Cruz, Calif.: Sri Rama Foundation, 1977.

Dass, Ram. *Be Here Now*. San Cristobal, N.M.: Lama Foundation, 1971, 1978.

De Chardin, Pierre Teilhard. *The Future of Man*. Trans. Norman Denny. New York: Harper and Row, 1964.

———. *The Phenomenon of Man*. Trans. Bernard Wall. New York: Harper and Row, 1959.

Donahue, Deirdre. "New Era for Earth or Just Moonshine?" *USA Today*, August 12, 1987.

"The End of the World (Again)." *Newsweek*, August 17, 1987.

Evans-Wentz, W.Y. *Tibetan Book of the Dead*. London and New York: Oxford University Press, 1927.

———. *The Tibetan Book of the Great Liberation or the Method of Realizing Nirvana through Knowing the Mind*. London: Oxford University, 1968.

———. *Tibet's Great Yogi Milarepa*. New York: Oxford University Press, 1928, 1951, 2000.

Foundatino for the Advancement of Mesoamerican Studies. *www.famsi.org*.

Friedman, Jack. "Hum if you Love the Mayans." *People's Weekly*, August 31, 1987.

Fuller, R. Buckminster. *Operating Manual for Spaceship Earth*. Carbondale, Ill.: Soutehrn Illinois University Press, 1969.

Ginsberg, Allen. *Howl and Other Poems*. San Francisco: City Lights, 1956.

Gyatrul Rinpoche. *Natural Liberation: Padmasambhava's Teachings on the Six Bardos*. Somerville, Mass.: Wisdom Publications, 1997.

Hall, Manley Palmer. *The Secret Teachings of All Ages*. Los Angeles: Philosophical Research Society, 1969.

"Harmonic Convergence, a Braver New World?" *Los Angeles Times*, August 12, 1987.

Huxley, Aldous. *The Doors of Perception and Heaven and Hell*. New York: Harper and Row, 1963; London: Chatto, 1968.

———. *The Perennial Philosophy*. Cleveland, Ohio: Meridian Books, 1962; London: Chatto, 1969.

I Ching or Book of Changes. Translated by Richard Wilhelm and Cary F. Baynes. Princeton, N.J.: Princeton University Press, 1967.

The Journal of Calendar Reform, vols. I and II. New York: The World Calendar Association, 1931, 1932.

Jung, Carl G. *Memories, Dreams and Reflections*. Trans. Richard and Clara Winston. New York: Random House, 1963; London: William Collins Sons, 1967.

———. *Synchronicity, an acausal principle, 2nd Edition*. Princeton, N.J.: Princeton University Press, 1969.

Katchongva, Dan. *From the Beginning of Life to the Day of Purfication*. Translated by Danaqyumptewa. Los Angeles: The Committee for Traditional Indian Land and Life, 1972.

Kerouac, Jack. *On the Road*. New York: Viking Press, 1957.

Khalifa, Rashad. *Quran: The Final Testament*. Fremont, Calif.: Universal Unity, 1992.

Lawrence, D.H. *The Plumed Serpent*. New York: Alfred Knopf, 1926; London: Heinemann, 1955.

Leary, Timothy. *Psychedelic Prayers after the Tao The Ching*. New Hyde Park, N.Y.: University Books, 1968.

Metzner, Ralph, and Richard Alpert. *The Psychedelic Experience*. London: Academy Books, 1971.

McKenna, Dennis J., and Terence K. McKenna. *The Invisible Landscape: Mind, Hallucinogens and the I Ching*. New York: Seabury Press, 1977.

Men Hunbatz. *Tzol Ek':Astrologia Maya*. Mexico City: Ediciones Juarez, 1983.

Morley, Sylvanus Griswold. *The Ancient Maya*. Palo Alto, Calif.: Stanford University Press, 1956.

Neihardt, John G. *Black Elk Speaks*. Lincoln, Neb.: University of Nebraska Press, 1961.

"New Age Harmonies." *Time*, December 7, 1987.

"New Era Dawns—or Just a New Day?" *The New York Times*, August 11, 1987.

Ouspensky, P.D. *Tertium Organum: The Third Canon of Thought, a Key to the Enigmas of the World*. Translated from the Russian by Nicholas Bessaraboff and Claude Bragdon. Rochester, N.Y.: Manas Press, 1920; New York: Knopf, 1922; London: Kegan Paul, Trench, Trubner, 1923, 1934; 3rd American edition, New York: Knopf, 1945.

Popul Vuh: The Sacred Book of the Ancient Quiche Maya. Translated by Delia Goetz and Sylvanus Morley from the *Spanis of Adrian Recinos*. Norman, Okla.: University of Oklahoma Press, 1950.

Rincon, Enrique Castillo. "Introduccion a la Ciencia Cosmica" ("Introduction to Cosmic Science"). Unpublished, 1971. (Translated by Jose Arguelles, 1996.)

Roerich, Nicholas. *Shambhala*. New York: Frederick A. Stokes Company, 1929.

The Roerich Pact and the Banner of Peace. New York: The Roerich Pact and Banner of Peace Committee, 1947.

Roraback, Dick. "Resonating with José Arguelles, a New Age Scholar." *Los Angeles Times*, August 12, 1987.

Rudhyar, Dane. *Art as Release of Power*. Carmel, Calif.: Hamsa Publications, 1929.

———. "Artist as Avatar." *Theosophical Journal*, 1939.

———. *Culture, Crisis and Creativity*. Wheaton, Ill.: The Theosophical Publishing House, 1977.

———. *Occult Preparations for a New Age*. Wheaton, Ill.: The Theosophical Publishing House, 1975.

———. *The Planeterization of Consciousness*. Waasenar, The Netherlands: Servire, 1970.

———. *The Pulse of Life-New Dynamics in Astrology*. Wassenaar, The Netherlands: Servire, 1963.

Ruz, Alberto. *Palenque, Official Guide*. Mexico City: Instituto Nacional de Antropologia e Historia, 1978.

Ruz Buenfil, Alberto. *Rainbow Nation Without Borders: Toward and Ecotopian Millienium*. Santa Fe, N.M.: Bear and Company, 1991.

Sejourne, Laurette. *Burning Water: Thought and Religion in Ancient Mexico*. Boulder, Colo.: Shambhala Publications, 1977.

Shearer, Tony. *Lord of the Dawn, Quetzalcoatl and the Tree of Life*. Healdsburg, Calif: Naturegraph Press, 1971, 1995.

———. *Beneath the Moon and Under the Sun: A Reappraisal of the Sacred Calendar and the Prophecies of Ancient Mexico*. Albuquerque, N.M.: Sun Books, 1975.

Sullivan, Meg. "New Age will Dawn in August, Seers Say, and Malibu is Ready." *Wall Street Journal*, June 23, 1987.

Tillich, Paul. *The Courage to Be*. New Haven, Conn.: Yale University Press, 1952.

Trungpa, Chogyam. *Shambhala: Sacred Path of the Warrior*. Boulder, Colo.: Shambhala Publications, 1984, 1988, 1996, 2007.

———. *Born in Tibet*. Boulder, Colo.: Shambhala Publications, 1985, 2000.

———. *Meditation in Action*. Boulder, Colo.: Shambhala Publications, 1969, 1984, 1991, 1996.

———. "Sadhana of Mahamudra." Unpublished, 1968.

———. *Cutting Through Spiritual Materialism*. Boulder, Colo.: Shambhala Publications, 1973, 1987, 2002.

Van Gogh, Vincent. *Letters of Vincent van Gogh*. Ed. Mark Roskill. New York: Atheneum, 1963; London: William Collins, 1963.

Waters, Frank. *Mexico Mystique: The Coming Sixth World of Consciousness*. Chicago: Swallow Press, 1975.

"Woodstock of the '80s." *USA Today*, August 12, 1987.

Index

About the Author

S TEPHANIE SOUTH is a former journalist and coauthor of the seven-volume series *Cosmic History Chronicles*, of which the first four have been published: *Book of the Throne, Book of the Avatar, Book of the Mystery*, and *Book of the Initiation*. She is currently working on the fifth volume, *Book of the Time-space*. She met Arguelles in 1998 after a series of dreams in which he was demonstrating time travel and telepathy. She is currently working with him on the Noosphere II Project, an investigation into the nature of time, telepathy, and cosmic states of consciousness.